CONFESS AND BE HANGED

CONFESS AND BE HANGED

Scottish Crime and Punishment
Through the Ages

Sheila Livingstone

Birlinn

Published in 2000 by
Birlinn Limited
Unit 8
Canongate Venture
5 New Street
Edinburgh EH8 8BH

ISBN 1 84158 002 3

Typeset by Brinnoven, Livingston

Printed and bound in Great Britain by
Creative Print and Design Wales, Ebbw Vale

CONTENTS

Introduction vii

Adultery, Fornication, Incest and Prostitution 1

Banishment and Deportation 9

Barons' Law 19

Bodysnatching 23

Cattle Lifting – The Borders 40

Cattle Lifting – The Highlands 52

Common Punishments 65

Concealment of Preganancy and Child Murder 75

Covenanters 84

Criminal Justice 90

Highway Robbery 102

Illicit Stills 109

Kidnap 115

Kirk Misconduct 119

Murder 125

Piracy and Privateering 140

Poaching 152

Poison 159

Press Ganged 168

Prison 172

Riots 180

Sabbath Observance 192

Smuggling 195

Treason 202

Witchcraft 206

Glossary 223

INTRODUCTION

Crime is conduct of which the State disapproves or which violates the law, or is behaviour which the State wishes to suppress or prevent. It therefore declares this behaviour to be illegal and deserving of punishment. Unless an activity is condemned by common law or statute as criminal it can be done, however immoral or harmful it may seem to be.

Conduct is also considered to be criminal if deemed objectionable or harmful to the community. Often what is deemed a criminal act by the State is not seen as such by the community. The Highlanders and Borderers saw as heroic behaviour which to others may have appeared to be a hanging offence. Protest and riot is action by the community, but is punishable because it is seen as a threat to those in power.

Smuggling thrived because the people, including ministers of the church, lairds and even lawmen, detested the imposition of taxes. Poaching was seen as a right to nature's bounty and the birds, fish and animals were not considered to be private property. Illicit distilling was using nature's gifts of water and grain. Bodysnatching was the provision of a service to mankind in the eyes of many people. Skirmishes with the forces of the Government led those taking part in the above conduct into committing criminal acts.

Many laws are made for political and economic reasons. If there are too many people too poor to provide for themselves, or too many in prison, they become a burden on the State. If hanging or transportation is more economic then that will be the legal sentence.

It has become obvious through researching the material for this book that many crimes against humanity were committed by those in positions of power and authority. They had little consideration for human life and seem to have enjoyed the feeling of power which torture, maiming and hanging gave them over their fellow man.

There were people who believed that they were acting in good faith when they punished others. They saw the offenders hanging on a gibbet as a warning to others to behave and be good citizens. That those professing to be Christians could encompass torture and burning at the stake might seem contradictory, but they believed

vii

that it was being done to save souls. Everything was for reward in the life hereafter, not on earth. The fact that old women could be punished as witches, and girls forced to suffocate their babies in the name of righteousness, is beyond our twentieth century way of thinking but to them it made sense. Many actions were sins rather than crimes.

Research into criminal activity in Scotland can be a long and arduous process if looking for a specific case or person by name. However, it is greatly helped by the many excellent archives which have been carefully organised by Scottish archivists and librarians throughout the country. Precognitions or statements taken from witnesses, kirk session records, burgh records, treasurers' account books, prison governors' journals, jail books, town council minutes, accounts in local newspapers, comment in national newspapers, and transactions and proceedings of societies are all useful, as are the detailed accounts of trials which were personally attended by William Roughead between 1889 and 1949.

The National Library of Scotland houses many illustrations and photographs, while there are 'black museums' kept by police forces. There are interesting museums of crime open to the public, such as Inveraray Jail where you can take part in the reality of life in a Scottish prison between 1500 and 1700, as well as the 'modern' prison of 1849, visit a courtroom of 1820, view the instruments of torture and see the traditional work of the prisoners being carried out. At Cromarty Courthouse on the Black Isle, the old prison cells can be visited and a reconstruction of a trial from the original court books listened to 'as it happens'. The Old Jail at Stirling has similar reconstructions.

This book is hopefully an enjoyable trail through our quirkish Scottish ways of coping with, and defining, crime. It is selective in its coverage and does not deal with the second half of the twentieth century or juvenile delinquency. We can sleep sound knowing that, whatever we do, we will not end up with our head exhibited on a spike or be tied to a stake and set on fire.

Sheila Livingstone, 1999

ADULTERY, FORNICATION, INCEST AND PROSTITUTION

Adultery and Fornication

The seventh commandment 'Thou shalt not commit adultery' was a money spinner for churches of every denomination. The 'crime' was euphemistically referred to as 'criminalities or irregularities of the affections'. In the middle ages, the bishops of the Roman Catholic Church added to their lands and possessions by imposing a fine and confiscating the goods and land of any man found guilty of adultery, fornication or incest. The Presbyterians saw no reason to discontinue such a lucrative practice and the Episcopalians, up until the eighteenth century, in addition made the offenders stand bare-legged and dressed only in sackcloth, their legs up to the knees in a tub of water, at the door of the church as the congregation were arriving.

Immorality, especially that of a sexual nature, was frowned upon by the Kirk and punished by the State. The elders, who were the ruling members of the Kirk Sessions of the Church of Scotland up until the middle of the nineteenth century, were ruthless when it came to dealing with such cases. They had the power to discipline their members under the court of the General Assembly of the Church. In the eighteenth century, if it was felt that the details were too intimate for the ears of the elders, 'matrons' from the congregation were appointed to make enquiries.

There were few Sundays in few parishes that someone was not paying the penalty for such offences. Fornication was the charge if the couple were unmarried and adultery if one or other was married to someone else. Incest mainly referred to relationships with members of the extended family who were barred as marriage partners by the Bible.

Exceptions

It infuriated many people that, although everyone came under the democratic discipline of the Church, on many occasions the gentry and their families could buy their way out of scandal by contributing money to the church funds. At the very least they were allowed to sit in their own loft, an enclosed box usually on an upper level, to receive a rebuke:

> Now Tam maun face the minister,
> And she maun mount the pillar,
> And that's the way that they maun gae
> For poor folk hae nae siller.
> > Traditional folksong

At Campsie, in July 1704, Janet Paul was cited as being guilty of fornication and she informed the Session that she was pregnant, naming one of the heritors as the father. She was rebuked and sat on the cutty stool on several Sundays. The accused laird was then challenged and faced the congregation in October. After his first appearance he repented and was absolved the following Sunday.

In contrast, all naval and military officers, under a rule of 1708, were ordered to be examples of virtue and were instructed to ensure that every man under their command submitted himself to the discipline of the Church.

Punishment

There was a long list of punishments that Kirk Sessions could choose from for offences of adultery and fornication.

Excommunication

The minister asked each offender in turn if they repented of their sin and, in most cases, the shame of appearing before the whole congregation made them promise to behave in future. This was written in the Kirk Session record as 'penitent and obedient to discipline'. There were others who refused to bow to the authority of the church and many Kirk Session minutes record the verdict 'obstinat' or unrepentant and the offender was sent on to a higher court.

Persistent offenders could also be excommunicated. This was a severe punishment because without a testimonial from the Kirk Session no-one could be employed, get married, have a child baptised or receive a Christian burial. This did not always deter them. John Tulloch, in 1580, told the Session when threatened with losing Kirk membership, 'Little do I care, ye can dae it the morn.' At Aberuthven in 1586 it was reported that fourteen years previously the blacksmith, James McKay, had set up house with his mistress, abandoning his wife and, although excommunicated, continued in his illegal relationship.

In contrast, some men could not face their shame. In Edinburgh in 1574 Robert Drummond cut his throat on being accused:

Robert Drummond, sometimes called Doctor Handie, who had been a great seeker and apprehender of papists, had been punished for adultery by exposure in the church and banishment from the city. Out of favour on account of his services against popery, he was pardoned and brought back; but being again found guilty of the same offence, he was condemned to exposure at the stocks at the Cross of Edinburgh, along with the companion of his crime; after which he was burnt on the cheek. While undergoing this punishment, there being a great [crowd] of people about them and the Doctor Handie being in ane gret furie, said: 'What wonder ye? I sall give you more occasion to wonder.' So, suddenly, he took his awn knife, wha strake himself three or four times fornent the heart, with the whilk he departit.
This done, the magistrates causit harl him in ane cart through the town, the bloody knife borne behind in his hand; and on the morn harlit in the same manner to the gallows on the Burghmuir, where he was buried on the second of April 1574.

Domestic Annals of Scotland, Vol 1, *From the Reformation to the Revolution*, Robert Chambers, 1874

In Forfar, in 1680, Jean Milne, widow of the late provost, petitioned the sitting provost and bailies on behalf of Jean Cuthbert who had borne her a grandchild by her son. He was serving with the Laird of Claverhouse's troops and so could not appear in church to be rebuked. As 'satisfaction' had not been made in the Kirk for their fornication the minister was refusing to baptise the child. The magistrates supported her claim and forced the minister to baptise the child.

In 1693, a cobbler in Edinburgh went raving mad when ordered to provide a sackcloth gown in which he was to be publicly exhibited. George Porteous, in 1736, mortified at being humiliated in public, hanged himself; many others fled the country rather than face public humiliation.

Fines

Fines, known as 'buttock-mail', varied according to the offence and in 1674 were £4 Scots [40p sterling] for the first lapse into fornication, to £8 Scots for further rebukes. For adultery, considered a more heinous crime, the fine was £20 Scots for the first offence and up to £40 Scots thereafter. Those who could not afford to pay could leave items such as spoons or a plaid as their pledge. These punishments were still in use as late as the 1830s in many churches and were only officially revoked after the Disruption in 1843.

Every Sunday, congregations thoroughly enjoyed the spectacle of friends and neighbours being treated roughly and, usually, humiliated. They probably sighed with relief that it was not their turn to be on show. Often, several members were ranted at by the minister as they either stood in a gown of sackcloth on the raised platform called the 'pillar' or seated on a wooden stool called the 'cock' or 'cutty stool'. The details of their offence were announced and the partner named.

Ministers preached sermons warning their congregations about such unworthy behaviour. It was commonly referred to as 'houghmagandy' or 'sculduggery':

> The time of the Peatmosses is now at hand, [when the young people went to the moss or bog land to dig peat] my friens, when the lasses will fling bits o' clods at the lads, my friens, and then they'll seem to rin awa ye see, and the lads they'll follow them; whan heels owre gowdie will they gae [topsy-turvy] as if something had whurled them, my friens; the lads gae out owre them, and sae begins Scullduddderie, my friens, which is the beginning o' a' evil, my friens, and which sends mony a worthy cheil to hell, my friens, there to lie on a bed o' brimstone lowing blue for ever mair. Amen.
>
> *The Scottish Gallovidian Encyclopedia*,
> John Mactaggart, 1824

Hanging

Because the Church and State worked in harmony, adulterers and fornicators were also publicly punished. By an Act of 1563, adultery could lead to hanging for both parties.

John Guthrie, a well-known adulterer, was brought before the Kirk Session of Kirkliston in 1617 and punished in the usual manner. He was later taken before the High Court in Edinburgh and sentenced to be hanged. In 1627, a man and woman were hanged one after another in front of a large crowd on Edinburgh's Castle Hill for a similar offence.

Daniel Nicolson, a solicitor, had carried on an adulterous affair with a widow, Mrs Pringle, for many years. In 1693, his long-suffering wife was framed by them and accused of attempting to murder him. The evidence was a forged receipt supposed to be from Dr Elliot for the purchase of poison. The truth prevailed and

Nicolson was hanged in the Grassmarket in 1694, while the widow was executed 'having her head severed from her body'.

Reoffending

After a couple reoffended the details of the offence were written on a piece of paper which was stuck on the offenders' foreheads as they stood on the public pillory. Their heads were also shaved in public as a warning to others. In Perth, the number of reoffenders was so great in the seventeenth century that the Kirk Session appointed a specific barber to carry out this punishment.

In St Andrews in 1567, even first offenders were thrown into prison as well as having to pay 2/- to the beadle, as the church officer was called. In some areas a first offence was lightly punished, with the couple only being required to sit on the stool of repentance to be lectured by the minister in front of the congregation for six consecutive Sundays. In 1773 this was still the general practice. Robert Fergusson, in his poem 'The Farmer's Ingle' commented:

> And there how Marion, for a bastart son,
> Upo' the cutty-stool was forced to ride,
> The waefu' scald o' our mess john to bide.

At Dundee, in 1559, those repeatedly guilty of fornication had to stand in irons at the market cross for three hours on market day and be ducked in the sea three times. At Glasgow, in 1575, the town officers were paid fivepence for 'dowking' Janet Fawside in the River Clyde. Glasgow Bridge, in 1594, had a special pulley fastened onto it so that fornicators or adulterers could be publicly ducked in the river. Huge crowds gathered to enjoy these spectacles, laughing and cheering at the offenders' misery.

In other towns the couple were taken by the elders to the dirtiest pool that could be found and ducked three times. There would often be a drummer to inform people that such an exciting event was about to take place.

In 1693, reoffending adulterers at Glasgow were first put into prison, then had to stand in the jougs, the dreaded iron collar, where they were whipped before they were banished out of the town in a cart. The children joined in by throwing rotten eggs at them:

> Item to Andrew Davie, lockman, for scurging [whipping] of Katherene Smyt throu the toun for getting a bairn with a soldeour   12/-
> *Dumbarton Common Goods Account, 1657–1658*

Margaret Paterson, described as 'a woman of evil repute', was accused of 'drawing from virtue' two young men named James and

David Kennedy, sons of a late minister. In 1692, she was sentenced at the High Court in Edinburgh to stand for an hour in the jougs on the Castle Hill and then be whipped from there to the Netherbow before being exiled to the plantations of America. The two young Kennedys, rather than stand trial with Margaret Paterson, broke bail and only the plea of extenuating circumstances made by their uncle saw them receive a more lenient sentence.

Those found guilty of pre-marital intercourse at Perth in the sixteenth century were fined £40 Scots or were put in prison on a diet of bread and water for eight days. They were then taken to the marketplace and put in the stocks for two hours. At Dumfries, needles called 'turkas' were used to pierce the heads of adulterers.

In the parish of Balquhidder in the 1820s, the woman was permitted to be rebuked before the Kirk Session and not, as was the fate of her partner in 'crime', before the full congregation. In 1734 in Edinburgh, for acts of adultery, nine young women, 'very naked and meagre beings', were whipped through the city by the hangman before an excited crowd. Drums were beaten and the piper played the tune 'Cuckolds Come Dig'.

Robert Burns, the Ayrshire poet, regularly occupied the stool at Mauchline Kirk. He poked fun at the elders, whose own lives he felt did not live up to their pious ideals, in a satirical poem:

> O Lord! yestreen, Thou kens wi' Meg–
> Thy pardon I sincerely beg,
> O! may't ne'er be a livin' plague
> To my dishonour,
> An' I'll ne'er lift a lawless leg
> Again upon her.
> Besides, I farther mon allow,
> Wi' Leezie's lass three times I trow–
> But Lord, that Friday I was fou,
> Whan I cam near her;
> Or else, Thou kens, Thy servant true
> Wad never steer her.
>
> *Holy Willie's Prayer*, Robert Burns, 1799

Robert Burns, in his poem 'The Holy Fair', a satirical name given to the outdoor celebration of communion, comments on the wild behaviour of the young people:

> How many hearts this day converts
> O' sinners and o' lasses!
> Their hearts o' stane, gin kight, are gane
> As saft as ony flesh is:
> There's some are fou o' love divine;
> There's some are fou o' brandy;

An many jobs that day begin,
May end in 'houghmagandie'
Some ither day.

The Holy Fair, Robert Burns, 1785

Riding the Stang

This was the name given to the punishment where the man was made to perch on a long pole, often a trunk of a tree, which was carried through the town or village while people beat him, threw things at him or made a fool of him. If he was married and was known to have consorted with young women, he was carried by men, but if he was married and was caught with another man's wife, the women carried the pole. If he was unmarried but was caught with a married woman, young men carried the pole.

On occasions a known wife-beater was also treated in this way. In June 1760 at Ayr, Andrew Shennan, a collector for the Customs and Excise, was decoyed from his house and carried on a long pole for some distance. All along the way he was hit with stones and rotten fruit and vegetables and was eventually unceremoniously dumped in a field and left to walk home. Allegedly this was because he was a wife-beater but, in reality, it was probably to warn him not to interfere in some smuggling ploy.

Incest

Most cases of 'incest' arose from a strict interpretation of Biblical law. Relationships regarded as incestuous were reported to the General Assembly of the Church of Scotland and then taken up and tried by the Privy Council.

Nicol Sutherland of Forres was convicted of incest with a woman who had been the lover of his mother's brother and, in 1569, he was hanged. In the parish of Fossoway, in 1583, Robert Millar was reported as open to censure by the Kirk Session after having a child with his wife's niece, but no further punishment is recorded. In 1626, William Hamilton was ordered to be beheaded for committing incestuous adultery when he married the widow of his stepmother's brother, even though she was neither a blood relation nor in-law. John Weir was accused of incest having 'married' the widow of his grand uncle. The case was investigated in April 1628 by the Privy Council, who found him guilty and ordered him to be beheaded at the Cross of Edinburgh. He was imprisoned for twelve months after which he received a special declaration of clemency from King Charles I and was transported abroad for life.

The Maiden, an early form of the guillotine, was a common punishment for several decades. Alexander Blair, a tailor, suffered the Maiden for marrying his first wife's half-brother's daughter in 1630, while Henry Dick, in August 1649, and Donald Brymer, in July 1649, committed similar offences. This was also the fate of Janet Imrie in June 1643 for having incestuous relations with two brothers, while William Lachlane was transported for bigamy in the same year. Alison Beaton was convicted of fornication with her uncle-in-law in 1692, and was whipped, then transported from Leith to the plantations of America.

These 'crimes' took up much of the Kirk Session's time. In addition, the strict ruling that no-one could marry who could not recite the Lord's Prayer and the Catechism often led to people being banned from tying the knot. In contrast, 'handfasting' permitted a couple to live together for a year and a day before either marrying or parting. This was, in effect, a trial marriage and was not outlawed in Scotland until the Marriage (Scotland) Act 1939.

Prostitution

In 1560 the Town Council of Edinburgh ruled that inn-keepers who employed barmaids who offered such a service should be fined £40 Scots.

In 1700 they also proposed that women found guilty of prostitution should be marked in a distinctive way by being branded by a specially designed iron. This was applied to their nose. In the nineteenth century, it was proposed that the women should be encouraged to reform their ways by being placed in a penitentiary such as a Magdalene Asylum.

BANISHMENT AND DEPORTATION

With prisons full and crime rising, the public complained about the cost of keeping 'undesirables'. Banishing offenders from their parish resulted in a host of convicted folk travelling from one part of Scotland to another, still a burden on the parish and liable to commit more criminal acts. There are many reports of trials recommending banishment. This did not mean transportation abroad, but simply forced the person over the boundary and rid their own area of a nuisance. There was usually a rider that if the offender returned then they would be branded with an iron, put in prison or the death penalty would apply:

> Apprehended for stealing shoes in the shoe mercat, banished the Burgh of Lanark, ordered never to be seen again in the Burgh on pain of being whipped, burned and again banished.
> *Records of the Burgh of Lanark, 1744*

A better solution, first mooted by King James VI in 1617, was to send them to the New World, to the plantations of America and the West Indies.

It was 1648 before the transportation of convicted prisoners to the colonies began. The measure was popular because it saved town councils money for their upkeep and provided free convict labour for the development of agriculture, mining and other industries in the New World. It was a convenient way of ridding society of all those labelled as undesirable, including radical thinkers, those who were opponents of the Establishment, people who held religious ideas contrary to the considered norm, and perpetrators of petty and serious crime. It also made profits for the merchants at home and abroad who had a financial interest in the plantations.

The merchants who owned the ships made their profits by selling the convicts to the plantation owners and they virtually became slaves. The Crown benefited, according to the records of the Privy Council, by saving on legal costs and by a security of five-hundred merks paid by the skipper of every transport ship. Certificates of transportation were issued on the safe arrival of the convict; this was signed and sealed then sent back to the Court of

Justiciary in Edinburgh where the owner of the vessel was paid. The merchants took a gamble since a large number died on the journey due to storms, poor feeding and cruelty, so the Crown inevitably made money out of this agreement.

One report of a ship sailing from Leith in 1685 with one hundred Irish beggars aboard states that 'much of the flesh which the captain of the ship had provided for the prisoners began to stink before they sailed out of Leith Roads and in a few days was not eatable'. The sympathy of the writer was not with the prisoners who died but with the grantee who lost the money per head which would have come to him on delivery of the 'cargo' at New Jersey.

Many of those banished had committed simple offences, such as stealing a sheep or an item of clothing, crimes which could result in a sentence of slavery for up to five years, but they were herded 'like sheep at a fair' alongside hardened criminals and murderers.

These convicts were considered bonded labour on arrival and were expected to serve free settlers for a stated time before being given their freedom. This freedom only extended to the new land in which they found themselves. They were not permitted to go elsewhere or to return to Scotland.

Beggars

An Act for the Punishments of 'Randy Beggars, Thiggars and Egyptian Sorners' was passed in 1698 which permitted beggars, vagabonds or vagrants after conviction to be whipped, then burned through the ear-lobe with a needle or a hot iron about one inch in diameter and sent to another county. Magistrates began sentencing those convicted to be transported to the West Indies. Their numbers increased during the 'seven ill years' of 1695–1701. The harvests were ruined by poor weather and food prices rose causing a parallel rise in poverty, begging and thieving.

Andrew Fletcher of Saltoun reckoned that there were 'around 100,000–200,000' vagrants in Scotland; he advocated making them free slave labour and seized on transportation as a means of disposing them. He decided to make an example of the worst element of them, called 'Jockies', and he persuaded the Government to present 300–400 men to the state of Venice to serve in their galleys against the 'common enemies of Christendom' – the Moors. Fifteen hundred Scots soldiers, taken as prisoners at the Battle of Worcester in 1687, were transported to Guinea to work in the gold mines.

Thirty-two women convicted of a variety of crimes at the Magistrates Court in Edinburgh in March 1695, chose banishment without trial to the plantations in America rather than be put in prison. In June of the same year, Janet Cook of Leith also agreed to this punishment and promised never to return under penalty of death. In January 1696, Elizabeth Waterstone was also banished, without trial but with her own consent, to the plantations.

This situation occurred on a number of occasions over a wide period of time. A horse-stealer, Robert Alexander in 1698, and William Baillie, a gipsy, in 1699, received a stay of execution and were put 'under pain of death' should they attempt to return.

> Four boys, notorious thieves, and eight women who were that and worse, were called before the magistrates of Edinburgh, and 'interrogat whether or not they would consent freely to their own banishment furth this kingdom, and go to his majesty's plantations in America...'
> *Domestic Annals of Scotland*, Vol 2, *From the Revolution to the Rebellion*, Robert Chambers, 1874

John Kerr, guilty of theft at Dumfries in 1722, also chose transportation rather than hanging. He was forbidden to return, or he 'wad be hangit'.

> Henderson, a sedan-carrier, and Hamilton, a street-cadie – suspected of being accessory to the murder of an exciseman, having petitioned for banishment before trial, were sent from the jail in Edinburgh to Glasgow, there to wait a vessel for the plantations.
> *Caledonian Mercury*, 20th November, 1732

The American War of Independence in 1776 prevented transportation of convicts to the plantations there and the practice ceased. Jails were becoming overcrowded with those sentenced to be sent away as they had nowhere to go. To relieve the pressure, other places, such as Gibraltar and the coast of Africa, were considered but thought unsatisfactory.

Hulks

By 1796 there were so many prisoners sentenced to be deported that the prisons were overcrowded and, as a stopgap, old warships, known as hulks, were brought into service as prisons. These were based on the River Thames and at Plymouth, Chatham and Portsmouth. The accommodation on the hulks was cramped. The cells were small and had heavy iron doors with tiny gratings in them to admit air. On the bottom deck there were condemned cells which were more like holes, with no light or fresh air. The prisoners were supposed to be washed and clean, and were whipped if not up to standard, but it was difficult to cope in such crowded surroundings with no proper facilities.

Women prisoners awaiting transportation were sometimes sent to Newgate Prison, London, and men and women were kept in Millbank Prison before being transferred. Women from Houses of Correction were shipped to Virginia, for which a fee of £1 per head was given to the merchants. Men were often held at the Calton Jail, Edinburgh, and then taken south to the hulks at London in worn out old ships. One of these, the *Peggy*, sailed from Leith in 1789 for Spithead; a mutiny broke out on board and was quelled by the intervention of two prisoners who were then granted pardons. This ship was confiscated for smuggling in 1792.

Conditions of the Convict Ships

When they were eventually put onto the convict ships, the men were dressed in a blue jacket and waistcoat, duck-trousers, a linen shirt, stockings and a woollen cap. This was all of light material suitable for where they were going, but was very cold while at sea. The women wore a brown serge jacket, a petticoat, a linen shift, cap and neckerchief, worsted stockings and a pair of shoes. They also had a hessian work apron, a black stiff apron and they were given a checked one when they reached the tropics.

There were rules laid down by the authorities as to routines and the care of the prisoners: the prison premises were to be cleaned while the prisoners were on deck; the prisoners were expected to sweep the decks every morning, to scrape and swab them once per week, and to sprinkle them with vinegar; the 'prison' area was to be fumigated every week and the convicts shaved and washed twice per week. These duties were often neglected.

Bedding and hammocks were to be stowed away and they were to receive salt meat, wine and lime juice daily. In reality, the merchants skimped on provisions and instructed the captains to cut corners and, while the chaplains and surgeons tried to stick to the rules, they rarely succeeded.

One chaplain, Reverend Richard Johnson, wrote a letter home in 1790 condemning the treatment and 'lamentable sufferings' on board the convict ships. For days some of the convicts had been chained together, hand and leg. When someone appeared to be dying the others fought over their 'lillipie', a mixture of flour and boiled water. Prisoners often stood up to their waists in water, drank salt water and became delirious. Many corpses were washed up on the shore near Sydney after being thrown overboard at sea.

The men and women, deported for whatever offence, were never allowed to forget that they were criminals. The convicts were confined in the bowels of the ship. They were divided into messes of six men and allowed on deck in rotation for a breath of air. When the ship docked this privilege was withheld and they remained cooped up for the duration of the stay in port, even though the ship's surgeon felt that this led to the spread of disease. At Madeira this meant confinement for nine days, and at Rio de Janeiro for ten. Each ship carried a complement of military guards but the officers were still afraid that attempts to escape might be made.

Many were already in poor health when they arrived from the hulks or prisons; others took sick at sea. Infectious disease spread rapidly. Dysentery, fever, typhus fever and scurvy were rampant and many died either on board or on arrival at their destination. Corpses were wrapped in a sheet and thrown overboard.

In 1814, on a voyage to Port Jackson, Captain Paterson of the *Three Bees* and his surgeon and two mates were so ill that when they drew level with the *Broxbornebury*, an officer was transferred from that ship to take charge. The captain died along with thirty-six convicts, four soldiers and seven crew. Another hazard was pirates. Several ships were attacked and seized, often to the delight of the convicts who often sided with the attackers.

Punishments

Swearing, gambling, singing of immoral songs, fighting or talking out of turn could result in ironing, the name given to the handcuffs and leg irons with which the prisoners were chained to the rails placed throughout the prison area of the ship. An iron ball and chain weighed seventy pounds. For crimes such as theft and insolence, flogging was delivered on a regular basis and the wounds washed with salt.

Other favourite punishments were to place the prisoner in a narrow box on deck, especially in the warmer climes, with only their head free; this acted like a Turkish bath. In the colder areas, if the women bawled, a cistern of cold water was tipped over them to make them keep quiet. Prisoners' backs were scrubbed with a spiky long-handled brush.

Women had their heads shaved, were paraded on deck, and made to dance while a cat-o'-nine-tails was whipped beneath their feet, or they were forced to wear a scold's bridle. If they still showed any spirit, they were branded with an 'M' for malefactor and locked in the coal-hole as a last resort. Many died of jail fever, and the women's ship *Success* was described by contemporary writers as a floating hell filled with corpses, many of which were dumped overboard.

On one of the ships, the *Janus*, carrying 104 women convicts, the women, bribed with a glass of rum, shared the beds of the officers and crew. Many fell pregnant and, on arrival in Sydney on 3rd May, 1820, lodged a complaint for recompense for their treatment. An investigation was set up which agreed that prostitution occurred and that no-one in authority attempted to prevent it. It was recorded as regrettable but no other action was taken.

Gipsies

> In a circuit court at Jedburgh, eight gipsies, six of them women, some of them aged, one of them with a child, had been sentenced to be transported to the plantations, as 'habit and repute gipsies, sorners etc.' They had been brought to Glasgow and lodged in the Tolbooth to await shipment, but no shipowner or shipmaster would take them on the mere prospect of receiving payment from the colonists. Glasgow promptly complained of the burden of supporting criminals with whose delinquencies the city had no concern, and the lords of justiciary, considering that it would cost more to keep the gipsies in prison than to pay for their transport, agreed to expend £13 for their passage to Virginia. The merchants who agreed to accept the freight were James Lees, Charles Crawford and Robert Bontine of Ardoch, and the Border nomads were duly embarked on the good ship *Greenock*.
>
> *Glasgow Burgh Records*, 1st January, 1715

The mother of two gipsies, Charles and James Jamieson, who were executed for holding up the Kinross mail, was tried and sentenced to transportation in 1786 for her part in the robbery.

Jacobite Prisoners

Another class of prisoner was transported to London aboard prison ships after the 1745 Rebellion. One hundred and twenty-five

Jacobite supporters taken prisoner at Culloden were badly treated on the long journey south on board ships such as *James* and *May* of Fife. Eyewitness accounts exist to show the deprivation which they suffered after eight weeks when they were transferred to a larger ship, *Liberty and Property*.

> There were thirty-two prisoners more put aboard the said *Liberty and Property*, which makes one hundred and fifty-seven and before we came ashore there was only life in forty-nine... They would take us from the hold in a rope, and hoist us up to the yard-arm, and then let us fall into the sea, in order for ducking of us; and tying to the mast and whipping us if we did anything however innocent that offended them; this was done to us when we was not able to stand.
>
> Will Jack, Tilbury Fort, 1747

The Covenanters, sentenced to transportation in their hundreds during the 'Killing Times' in the seventeenth century, are discussed under a separate heading (pp. 84–89).

New South Wales

At last a suitable place was identified to receive convicts. New South Wales was being opened up and the Government of Australia needed labour. The first fleet set sail on 13th May, 1787 from Portsmouth and arrived at Sydney on 18th January, 1788.

A new Act, replacing the one of 1597, was passed by Parliament in 1787 governing transportation in England and Wales. It omitted to name Scotland, making the sentence illegal there. However, this did not stop judges declaring this sentence and they were never challenged.

Amongst the first 788 convicts there were a few Scots drawn from the hulks. Although all records mention Botany Bay as the settlement in relation to transportation to Australia, it was discovered that Botany Bay offered little shelter, was swampy land and that there was a lack of fresh water.

> Rosehill, 11th November, 1791.
> As to Botany Bay it is given up as they can make no good of it, the ground is so bad...We have four different settlements – viz; Sydney Cove, Rosehill and two others not yet named . . . The only thing we have to drink is sweet tea, that grows in the woods – Rum is 24/- per gallon and porter 1/3d per bottle but very scarce.
>
> Letter to the *Sunday London Gazette*, 15th July, 1792

In reality it was Sydney Cove, Port Jackson, where the penal colony was built in 1788 and this area eventually developed into New South Wales. Australia remained a transportation destination for many years. As late as 11th August, 1843, thirty-one female convicts were embarked at Granton Pier on board the steamer *Leith*, to be transferred at Woolich to the convict ship, *Woodbridge*, destined for Australia. Between 1787 and 1868, 7600 Scots were transported to Australia.

Thomas Muir

Thomas Muir was an advocate who was tried in 1792 for sedition because he believed in parliamentary reform and led the 'Friends of the People' movement. His friends insisted that Lord Braxfield and the High Court of Justiciary no longer had the right to transport him for fourteen years, as such legislation only applied south of the border but, despite their claim, Muir was imprisoned at Edinburgh. When the authorities heard rumours of an attempt to spring him from jail, they hastily removed him to London. He was housed at Newgate Prison and then a prison hulk on the River Thames.

> Last Saturday we were put aboard the *Stanislaus* hulk; after being treated with every kindness and attention by Captain Ogilvie, we were put in irons, and slept in a room with about 100 cut-throats and thieves. Our company, however, was a mutual solace to one another; but last Saturday we were deprived of this by his [Thomas Muir's] removal to the *Prudentia* hulk, two miles higher up, by order of the Under-Secretary of State. His heroic spirit rises under every difficulty.
>   Letter from T. Fyshe Palmer, 2nd December, 1793

Thomas Muir set sail for Australia on 2nd May, 1794. After surviving the voyage he arrived at the Sydney Colony on 26th October. He lived with a Mr and Mrs Boston along with Thomas Palmer, who records in a letter dated 13th June 1795 that they are all well. After sixteen months Muir escaped and found a ship bound for America, but he ended up in Cadiz as the Spaniards believed him to be a spy. He died in Paris in 1799 aged thirty-three.

Petty Thieves

For stealing three cows and a horse, two men from Inverness were deported in 1815. For housebreaking, two boys had their sentence reduced fron death to transportation in 1823. Another horse stealer, despite being severely ill, was carted in irons from Dornoch to Aberdeen.

Jamie Raeburn, a Glaswegian, fell in with bad company and was arrested and sentenced to transportation to Botany Bay in the 1830s. A popular street ballad 'Jamie Raeburn's Farewell' was sold as a penny-sheet and told of his plight:

My name is Jamie Raeburn, in Glasgow I was born,
My place and habitation I'm forced to leave with scorn;
From my place and habitation I now must gang awa',
Far frae the bonnie hills of Caledonia.

Vagabond Songs and Ballads, edited by Robert Ford, 1899

In 1840, New South Wales stopped receiving convicts, and when John Cameron, who was a depute postmaster in Argyll, was charged with defrauding the public of £197.10/-, Lord Cockburn sentenced him at Inveraray to fourteen years' transportation in April 1947. He was taken to Millbank Prison in London, then on to Portland Prison, where he was put to stone breaking. In 1850 he was sent to Tasmania; forty-three other convicts followed in December 1851. They were transferred from Perth Prison to the hulk the *Stirling Castle* at Portsmouth to await transportation. This was an irony, for many of them would already associate the name with Duke Street Prison, Glasgow, called 'The Stirling Castle' after its governor, John Stirling. It was possible to spend up to eighteen months in solitary confinement at Perth before being sent south. The practice of using convict labour survived in Tasmania until 1868.

Man-Stealing

The Privy Council Records for the late seventeenth and early eighteenth centuries show that it was a common practice for owners of plantations to commission ships to sail to Leith with the sole purpose of finding men and women whom they could transport to work as slaves on the plantations.

This practice was considered an offence and the charge was man-stealing. In 1668, attempts were made to ensure that anyone on board such a ship at Leith was either sentenced to banishment by the courts or had agreed to go voluntarily. Some Highlanders, who could not afford to pay their passage, sold themselves to the captain, who in turn sold them on as labourers to the plantation owners.

Another group who supplied the representatives of the owners with men and women were the barons. Although technically no longer legally permitted to do so, they still exercised their rights to hereditary jurisdiction. It suited the barons to sell as slaves those who offended them, rather than keep them in their pit, and the barons sometimes made money out of it. A bond of a thousand merks was given to the merchant on return of a certificate of transportation for each convict delivered. Other merchants also made money from this trade and even bought and sold children.

> Captain William Hutchison of Maryland, in 1704, petitioned the Privy Council for permission to transport six young pickpockets, and twenty-two degraded women, then in the correction house of Edinburgh, who had all, 'of their own choice and consent' agreed to go along with him.
> *Domestic Annals of Scotland*, Vol 2, *From the Revolution to the Rebellion 1745*, Robert Chambers, 1874

The Privy Council agreed so long as he paid for their keep until they left Scotland. They also allowed an Edinburgh merchant, John Russell, to take twenty prisoners, mainly women, to sell in America.

False accusations of theft led about one hundred people, men, women and children, aboard the *William* when it arrived in Skye, Harris and Uist in September 1739. A plot to dispose of them at a profit was hatched by the owners of Uist and Harris who were selling the 'criminals' into slavery in Pennsylvania. They managed to escape at Donaghdee in Ireland where they had been taken ashore and alerted the authorities to their plight.

The offence was still rife when, in 1740, Peter Williamson, an eleven-year-old Aberdeen schoolboy, was seized by merchants. Along with other boys he was imprisoned in a barn until sufficient numbers were gathered before embarking for America and slavery. They were bound to serve for five to seven years. Peter Williamson was sold for £16. When he returned home in 1758 and told his tale he was pilloried. The pages were publicly torn out of his book and burned by the hangman. He was fined 10/- and banished from the city.

Some families were so poor after the famine of 1740 that they offered their children, and received only 1/- or 1/6d for them. This trade was carried on by so-called respectable members of the Merchant Company of Aberdeen, some of whom were magistrates.

The authorities were fearful of seditious gatherings and often they over-reacted. Six baker's boys who were singing and noisily enjoying themselves on the streets of Edinburgh in 1795 were arrested by the Town Council and transported without charge, trial or conviction.

BARONS' LAW

I know of some [gallows hills] where the surrounding ground is full of the remains of poor wretches who died by the barons' law.

Scotch Legal Antiquities, Cosmo Innes, 1853

The hanging tree, the beheading pit and the dungeon were familiar sights to those who lived under the 'protection' of the barons or nobles. In the middle ages the barons, many of whom also owned estates in England where the feudal system was endemic, were all-powerful and were exempt from acting under the law of the land. Instead they claimed the right of hereditary jurisdiction – *fossa* and *furca*. This allowed the barons to have their own pit, prison or gallows, and to be answerable to no-one in the punishment of their vassals – anyone who paid tithes to them – including putting vassals to death. This right was granted by the king in return for the promise that the baron and his henchmen – the lesser barons – would provide men for military service should the need arise.

Courts of Regality were held either directly under the baron himself or by his baron-bailie. These baron-bailies feathered their own nests and were often granted 'duties' as a perk. This meant a share of the goods of those convicted and hanged, and of the fines collected. It also included the horse or cow as a heriot or death tax from the widow. If she had no animal then the 'uppermost cloth' – her warmest blanket – was taken instead.

If found guilty, the accused was often punished immediately, including being strung up on the gallows tree. In cases that went to trial, if the jury of fifteen gave a verdict opposed to the wishes of the baron, its members could be tried before another jury made up of twenty-five landed proprietors and each member imprisoned for one year plus forfeiture of their personal effects. This ensured that any jury consisted of 'yes' men.

Fines imposed by the judge went into his own pocket to defray baronial costs. He could hang a man on a trumped-up offence and confiscate his land. The barons could also declare someone insane and seize their possessions. At Lossiemouth, a man could be drowned in the Order Pot for stealing a sheep supposedly belonging to his lordship.

Under the right of *jus primae noctis* – law of the first night – the baron could demand that he deflowered the bride of any vassal on her wedding night. To avoid this some brides did not tie the knot until they were several months pregnant and some barons relinquished this right if a large enough marriage tax was paid.

In 1331, Thomas Randolph, Earl of Moray, beheaded fifty 'delinquents' because they rebelled against him and he had their heads placed on spikes around his castle walls as a warning to others.

In the fifteenth century, a spectator sport at Borthwick Castle was to tie a prisoner's hands behind his back and force him to jump the twelve-foot gap between the towers. If he succeeded he went free.

At Finhaven in 1452, under the barons' law, Earl 'Beardie', the Earl of Crawford, hanged one of his ghillies, Jock Barefoot, because he had cut himself a walking stick from a branch of the Covin Tree. This tree was believed to have grown from a chestnut thrown down by a Roman soldier. For a previous misdemeanour, Jock's tongue had been cut out, rendering him unable to protest. His ghost is still supposed to haunt the area:

> Oak, ash, and elm tree,
> The laird may hang for a' the three;
> But for saugh and bitterweed,
> The laird may flyte, but mak naething be 't.
> Traditional

The barons were described in *The Complaynt of Scotland*, published in 1549, as 'violent usurpers'. Many records of this period have been lost but in those which exist, few describe kind, beneficent barons. Most seemed to be selfish, greedy and inhuman. They used torture and every method in their power to evict the original owners of land on trumped-up charges.

Gilbert, Earl of Cassilis, described as 'a werry greidy manne', was given the post of Commendator of Crossagruel Abbey after the Reformation by the last abbot, his uncle, Quentin Kennedy. The earl was angry because King James V, in whose gift this Crown position was, rescinded the appointment and replaced him with Allan Stewart, a relative of the Lord of Balgany. In 1565, the earl had Stewart seized and carried to the black vault at Dunure Castle. There he was stripped, covered in oil, bound to a spit and roasted in front of a great fire. In agony, he was forced to sign a paper renouncing the abbey lands.

A week later the fire was relit and he was asked to sign a confirmation document, which he refused to do. He was severely burned and, although he survived, never walked again. He complained to the Privy Council but under the rights of hereditary jurisdiction they could not interfere and his lands were not returned to him but remained with the Earl of Cassilis, who escaped with a fine of £2000 Scots [£200 sterling].

Barons usually had places for imprisoning their vassals. These were often damp, dirty holes dug in the ground, usually deep and with smooth sides to make it difficult for the prisoner to escape. Others used the dungeons beneath their towers or castles for this purpose.

Sir Alexander Jardine imprisoned Porteous, a miller on his estate, in his dungeon in 1605 then rode off to Edinburgh taking the key with him and telling no-one. The man, clapped in irons, had no food and starved to death. His spirit was said to haunt the place for decades and was eventually exorcised by means of a Bible.

Occasionally the vassals attempted to revolt. In the thirteenth century King Alexander II had 400 peasants gelded for an uprising against their bishop in protest at having to pay tithes – a tenth of everything they owned – to the Church. In 1672, Edward Smith was fined at Corsehill for attacking the baron's officer with a stick, and John Lachlane had to pay a fine of £20 Scots and sit in the stocks for the same offence.

In 1692 a young boy, for stealing a part of a plough, was sentenced by the baron-bailie of Grant of Rothiemurcis to stand absolutely still for an hour after having a nail hammered through the lobe of his ear. The only way he was to be allowed to be set free was if he tore his ear away from the nail. In other cases the ear was cut off as a punishment. Three men were charged with stealing a horse in the same year and were taken to the baron's pit before being hanged on the gallow tree at Ballintore.

The barons were often arrogant, causing vassals to be put to death simply to emphasise that they had total power over their life or death.

> Lindsay of Dunrode, in 1693, moved about among his miserable tenants attended by twelve soldiers mounted on milk-white horses. When playing on the ice he ordered a hole to be made in it, and one of his vassals, who had inadvertently disobliged him in some trifling circumstance, immediately to be drowned.
>
> *History of Rutherglen and East Kilbride*, W. Ure, 1874

At Abernethy two brothers were hanged on one tree by the baron-bailie, then taken down and set on fire by the roadside, while another two thieves had their heads removed, par-boiled and set on spikes for everyone to see.

After the Reformation, the barons became heritors of their parish church and strictly upheld church discipline. Many of them used their courts to reinforce it. At Stitchill, in 1696, delinquents who broke the Church's law were also sentenced by the Baron's Court to be chained in the stocks or placed in the jougs 'during the laird's pleasure'.

For the slightest offence, or imagined misdemeanour, punishments, including torture, which was legal in Scotland until 1709, were used. Men were hung up by the thumbs, hung by the feet in a room filled with nauseous smoke and had knotted strings tied around their head. Women had red-hot tongs placed between their shoulders and under their armpits until the tongs went cold, fingers were deliberately broken, faces branded and backs lashed with the whip. The barons had epileptics gelded and lepers buried alive.

Women were usually drowned if found guilty of theft. Near Gordonstoun, a woman accused of taking two webs of cloth and £30 Scots from a chest was drowned in Loch Spynie and cursed the baron as she went under.

That the power of the baron was sacrosanct is illustrated in an apocryphal story that at Ballindalloch a man condemned to die was put into the pit to await execution. When the baron's men came for him he drew his sword and threatened to kill anyone who climbed down into the pit. His wife was sent for and instructed him to 'Come up quietly and be hangit, Donal', and dinna anger the laird'.

A pit at Finlanrig Castle, Killin, was known as 'The beheading pit of Black Duncan of the cowl'. It had a block into which chains were sunk which was used to secure the victim before the hangman swung his axe. The body presumably fell into the pit.

When hereditary jurisdictions were abolished in 1748 by an Act of Parliament, as a means of lessening the power of the Highland clans after the Jacobite Rebellion, the barons protested and demanded compensation for their loss of revenue. They then proceeded to comply with the administration of justice in the rural districts, which was transferred to the sheriffs and justices of the peace, by using their influence with the judiciary to ensure that many of those appointed to these new posts were themselves or their baron-bailies.

They continued to blackmail juries and adapt the legislature to suit their needs and transported men and women, whom they considered to be their property, to the plantations of America and the West Indies, often at a profit, even after it became illegal for them to do so.

BODYSNATCHING

Bodysnatching – the practice of digging up the corpse of the newly buried – grew out of need and greed. Anatomists needed to learn about the organs of the human body in order to carry out treatment and surgery, and students desperate for corpses to experiment upon took to robbing graveyards. Through time, as the demand continued, some men discovered that they could make money from the supply of bodies to the anatomists and the occupation of bodysnatcher or 'susie-lifter' came into being. They were also known as resurrectionists.

The Scots had a superstitious reverence for the dead. This was borne out in the customs which were attached to death and in the belief that the powers of evil would be unleashed if these were not adhered to. They also believed that the body would be resurrected in Heaven and worried that dissection would prevent this happening. This led to revulsion at the idea that the corpses of their relations could not rest safely in their graves for fear of violation.

On 9th March, 1742, the body of Alexander Baxter was buried in the West Kirkyard, Edinburgh. It was later discovered in the dispensary of a surgeon, Martin Eccles. The people seized the Portsburgh drum and beat it through the Cowgate. The contents of his shop were demolished and the windows of his and neighbouring surgeons' premises were smashed by the angry mob. He and his apprentices were summonsed to the High Court but the charge was dropped for lack of proof as to who had 'lifted' the corpse. In the same month a house was burned down by a mob at Inveresk because its owner was identified as lifting bodies.

A riot took place in Glasgow in March 1749 when a mob, suspicious that students had rifled bodies from the graveyards in and around the city, especially at Gorbals, demolished the windows of the University in High Street, injuring several people. The riot was only quelled by the arrival of the militia. In 1830, a mob stormed Dr Andrew Moir's Anatomy Theatre, known locally in Aberdeen as 'the burkin' hoose', when the limbless body of a man was found dug up by a dog. A crowd of over 2000 paraded through the streets, smashed the windows and burned the theatre down. Dr Moir escaped through St Nicholas Churchyard.

Those who carried out this 'crime', whether for use or gain, were not breaking any known law by removing corpses from their graves but they were upsetting families and incurring public outrage. By the 1800s, magistrates began to bring charges of committing a felony, the punishment being six months' imprisonment for a first offence and two years for a second. However, identifying the culprits and catching them red-handed was not always easy.

A professor of anatomy at Aberdeen in 1815 was reportedly seen carrying corpses in his coach on his way to classes. Two of his students were arrested and tried, the charge being *crimen violati sepulcri* – violating graves. The sentence was imprisonment and a fine of £100.

Throughout Scotland the number of graves robbed increased until in the early part of the nineteenth century, when public outrage led to the people suppressing their superstitious fears of visiting graveyards at night and organised the watching of them. In churchyards these watches consisted of elders of the Kirk and of householders, as well as the relations of the corpse. Every householder was expected to take their turn and if they could not do so had to pay for a substitute.

Three men were on duty each night and watch houses were built. These had a fireplace to keep the watchers warm. In many parishes the watchers were armed with rifles, and shots were often exchanged between lifters and watchers, resulting in wounds on both sides. It was a rule that no strong drink was to be taken while on watch to ensure that the men were alert, but this was often ignored. The grave-robbers used this fact, and the watchers' sense of eeriness and fear, to their advantage.

Iron covers called mort safes, which were shaped like a coffin, became popular and were placed over the grave for up to six weeks, and those families who could afford it had an iron cage, often ornamental, built over their lair. This additional vigilance forced the bodysnatchers to move into the country graveyards. Nowhere close to a canal or road was safe.

In 1824, the Bridgeton Grave Protection Society was formed in Glasgow and a song was composed to be sung at a fund raising venture held there. The title is 'Ye Who Mourn Your Dear Departed' and the second verse is:

Midnight prowlers bent on robbing,
Shall no more your dead molest;
Now, 'the wicked cease from troubling',
Now,'the weary are at rest'.
Soundly sleeps your sire or mother,
Faithful husband, virtuous wife,

Son or daughter, sister, brother,
Safe from the dissector's knife.

Alexander Rodger, 1824

Sometimes young men managed to make the task of watching enjoyable and have a bit of fun. They were known to make a meal by rifling nearby potato pits and hen houses and to have a whip round to buy a drop of whisky and ale to accompany the feast. Young women, on occasion, kept them company in the evening.

Sometimes the meetings were not unlike a Hogmanay nicht,
a bottling or Paddy McDade's wake.

Maryhill from 1750 to 1894, Alexander Thomson, 1895

Charlie was a gipsy hanged at Perth in 1830 for horse-stealing. His associates in the band all kissed his corpse when it was released from the gallows. They then held a lyke-wake after which Ann Brown, one of his wives, who herself had served fourteen years transportation – seven in prison at Aberdeen, seven in the Sydney Colony – and a cousin put his body into a pit of hot lime so that it would be unfit to be taken by the bodysnatchers.

After the trial in 1828 of William Burke and William Hare, who grew greedy and when bodies were scarce started to provide them by luring victims to their homes and murdering them, demands grew for consideration of legally obtaining subjects for anatomical research. It was, however, a copycat of their crime by Bishop, Williams and May in London in 1831 which spurred on the authorities. The trio drugged their victims with opium and drowned them by forcing their heads into water. Bishop and Williams were executed after trial at the Old Bailey, but May was sentenced to transportation for life. These men created in England the same revulsion as Burke and Hare had in Scotland and the government decided to act.

From 1829 to 1832, Parliament concentrated on passing an Anatomy Act. In 1833 an Act was passed which granted a certificate to practise anatomy to licentiates of the Royal College of Physicians and Surgeons, professors of anatomy and students attending a school of anatomy. The executor for the deceased could, unless aware of express objection by the corpse in its life-time, permit anatomical examination to be carried out forty-eight hours after death. A valid death certificate had to be produced before this could take place, and arrangements had to be made for the body to be removed and buried in consecrated ground. Three inspectors were appointed to ensure that these clauses were carried out fairly.

Tight regulations were put in place. Bodies had to be identified and a record of dissections kept. The old Act, which stipulated that the bodies of those hanged could automatically be dissected, was revoked. The instruction had to be included in the sentence. There was still a shortage of subjects for dissection in Scotland; the Presbyterian ethos balked at the idea and it took a long time for the public to accept that the corpses of their relations could help further the cause of medicine.

A twist to the lifting of bodies occurred in 1881 when the corpse of Alexander William Lindsay, 25th Earl of Crawford was stolen from its grave at Dunecht. A rat catcher by the name of Soutar demanded a ransom of £6000 for its return. However, the Act did seem to bring about a decline in bodysnatching and fewer graveyards required constant watches, mort safe manufacture declined, and the crime passed into history and legend.

Anatomists

How Early Medical Students Were Trained

Up until 1722 barbers and surgeons were united. Two organisations existed in Scotland to train them: the College of Surgeons and Barbers in Edinburgh whose rules in 1505 included that an apprentice must have a knowledge of anatomy, veins and bleeding, and the Faculty of Physicians and Surgeons of Glasgow, formed in 1599.

Apprentices to the trade of surgery paid £50 sterling to be instructed in the art. They trained for three years with a 'qualified' practitioner and also sat an exam at which they dissected a prescribed part of a body – usually of a condemned man, after he had been hanged – bled a patient, gave a clyster [enema], spread a plaster and prepared a potion. The degrees were issued after this simple training and young men could call themselves chirurgeon-apothecaries after working for three years with a qualified practitioner.

One of the earliest references to the dissection of a corpse in order to study its anatomy appeared in Edinburgh in 1505. The body of one condemned man per year was released for this purpose. By 1645, it was the practice in the dissecting room that a corpse was divided into ten parts and distributed between ten practitioners of the Incorporation of Surgeons and Barbers of Edinburgh, who then demonstrated a variety of procedures to instruct their apprentices.

Teachers of Anatomy

There were many teachers of anatomy who ran private schools where they demonstrated the procedures of surgery. Dr Archibald

Pitcairn, who had distinguished himself as a professor of medicine
at the University of Leyden, Holland, had come to live in Edinburgh
where he was anxious to carry on the advances which he was making
there. The Town Council of Edinburgh was petitioned in 1694 by
his friend, Dr Alexander Monteath, to permit the bodies of
abandoned babies, known as foundlings, who died after birth and
the bodies of those who died in the Paul's Wark – the House of
Correction – to be given for the study of anatomy.

> Bodies of foundlings who dye betwixt the tyme that they are
> weaned and their being put to schools and trades, all the dead
> bodies of such as are styflit [suffocated] at the birth . . . and
> have none to owne them, likewise the bodies of such as are
> put to death by sentence of the magistrates and have none to
> owne them and suicides.
> *Social Life in the Eighteenth Century*, H. G. Graham, 1899

The permission was given, but certain stipulations were put upon
it. The bodies, after use, must be buried in College Kirk cemetery,
the intestines within forty-eight hours and the remainder of the
corpse within ten days, and then only during the winter months
and at Dr Pitcairn's own expense. He was given a dissecting room
by the Town Council and a grant towards equipping it and he
promised to have a proper theatre ready to use before the
Michaelmas term, which started in November, 1697.

In 1696, William Gordon, Professor of Medicine and Anatomy
at the University of Aberdeen, who had only had the carcasses of
beasts upon which to experiment until then, requested that the Privy
Council instruct the Sheriffs and Magistrates of Aberdeen to allow
him to have the bodies of criminals or of any poor people who
might have died friendless in one of the hospitals, in order that he
might better instruct his students. He was permitted two criminals
and the bodies of poor people who had died in the poorhouse who
had 'no friends to take exception'.

In 1704 a public dissector in anatomy was appointed in
Edinburgh at a salary of £15 per year. He gave public
demonstrations of dissection for apprentices, but few bothered to
attend as they were not obliged to do so. In 1720, Alexander Munro,
at the age of twenty-two, was made Professor of Anatomy at the
Surgeons' Hall, Edinburgh, and was appointed to the University
of Edinburgh in 1726.

In 1722 in Glasgow and 1727 in Edinburgh, the barbers were
disunited from those who now called themselves doctors. As the
numbers studying to become doctors grew, so did the need for a
greater number of corpses, and the medical schools were desperate

for more and more dead bodies for dissection. The anatomists rarely asked questions about the source of such corpses as came their way.

In 1792, John Burns studied anatomy at Edinburgh before being appointed, at the age of twenty-two, to the Royal Infirmary of Glasgow. In 1797, he rented rooms in Virginia Street for teaching anatomy. He was the first person unconnected with any public medical institution to teach anatomy privately in the city. He became involved in robbing graves and was forced by the magistrates to stop teaching. In 1799, however, he became Professor of Anatomy at Anderson's University and taught in rooms in College Street. His brother Alan also studied anatomy and became a member of the Royal College of Surgeons in London.

In Edinburgh it became known that Dr Knox, who ran a private school of anatomy so popular that in 1828 he had 504 students, would pay from £8 to £14 per body and up to £20 for fresh corpses. He had to repeat each lecture three times per morning. After 2 p.m. he spent his time in the dissecting rooms with his assistants, Ferguson, Jones and Goodsir who later became famous surgeons. Dr Knox was also involved with Burke and Hare (see pp. 33–36).

Lifting

Surgeons and students often solved the problem of the lack of corpses for themselves and there is a catalogue of cases about their exploits in and around graveyards. The general public were horrified at the idea of the corpses of their relatives and friends ending up on the dissecting table and several riots broke out after word of such 'liftings' spread.

Four gipsies named Shaw, a father and three sons, were interred in Greyfriars Churchyard, Edinburgh, in February 1678. They were not coffined but placed in a hole in the ground with their clothes on. The next morning it was discovered that the body of the youngest, the last buried, had disappeared.

> Some thought he being the last thrown over the ladder, and first cut downe, and in full vigor, and no great heap of earth, and lying uppermost, and not so ready to smother, the fermentation of the blood, and heat of the bodies under him, might cause him rebound and throw off the earth and recover ere morning, and steal away . . . more probably . . . his body [was] stolen away by some chirurgeon, or his servant, to make ane anatomicale dissection on; which was criminal to take at their owne hand.
> The History of Burke and Hare, George MacGregor, 1884

In 1711, the College of Surgeons drew up a minute stating that 'of late there has been a violation of sepulchres in the Greyfriars Churchyard by some who most unchristianly has been stealing, or at least attempting to carry away, the bodies out of their graves'. A ninety-line Broadside ballad appeared on the streets of Edinburgh after this news became known.

> . . . These monsters of mankind, who made the graves,
> To the chirurgeons became hyred slaves;
> They raised the dead again out of the dust,
> And sold them, to satisfy their lust.
> As I'm informed, the chirurgeons did give
> Forty shillings for each one they receive;
> And they their flesh and bones assunder part
> Which wounds their living friends unto the heart . . .
>   Ballad, May 1711

The College of Surgeons, in 1721, then included in the indenture of apprentice surgeons a clause forbidding them to violate graves, but this seems to have gone unheeded. A further scandal came to light in 1722 when a delivery took place of bags of linen and cotton rags off an Irish vessel at the Broomielaw. They were destined for a warehouse in Jamaica Street, Glasgow and had been sent by Irish medical students to their colleagues there. The owner, not realising what the consignment was, balked at the cost and refused to take delivery and the carter took them back to the quay where they were stored in a shed until it was decided what to do with them. They began to give off an atrocious smell and a police officer was called to open them. Inside, the dead and putrefying bodies of men, women and children were disclosed. The Sheriff and magistrates had the bodies interred at Anderston and it was believed that these bodies were worth ten to twenty guineas (£10.50 to £20 sterling) each to the anatomists. Warning notices now appeared in every churchyard and cemetery and strict searches were made of cargoes arriving at the Broomielaw.

A similar case ocurred at Leith, as late as 1826, when eleven pickled corpses, six male and five female, arrived from Liverpool bound for Ironson, an Edinburgh merchant. The police discovered a further twenty-two corpses, pickled in barrels, stored in the cellar of an innocent clergyman who had rented out his premises to a James Donaldson. This latter gentleman received a sentence of one year in a house of correction and was fined £50.

Also in 1826, the Leeds – Newcastle coach carried a box for a Mr Simpson which was jolted onto Edinburgh's cobbled streets and a corpse fell out. The students found out where burials were to take place and, no matter whether the graveyard was in town or country, they would make an attempt to filch the body from its coffin.

At Limekilns and Rosyth, the students would arrive by boat to desecrate the burial grounds, but the people's anger was roused and they lay in wait for them. Some students, disturbed by the watch before they could bag their prey, fled. One of them refused to let go and hauled the body of a woman clad in her shroud onto his shoulders. As they ran to their boat she began to slip and her legs kicked his as he ran. He thought that she had come back to life and threw her over a wall in panic before escaping.

In university cities, graveyards were plundered by the students, and freshly interred bodies were removed under cover of darkness to the nearest laboratory. They usually re-filled the grave with earth so that no evidence of any disturbance was obvious. After having successfully carried out a raid they would visit a tavern or a tripe house to enjoy themselves. Having been undetected for some time they became careless.

Two burials were to take place in Glasgow on 13th December, 1813, one at the Ramshorn Churchyard, the other at the High Churchyard. The students successfully removed one body from the former cemetery and two from the latter and were in high spirits.

A police officer in his sentry box nearby grew suspicious and, waving his wooden rickety, or rattle, gave chase. Mr Lang, the beadle of the Ramshorn Church, also became suspicious and was more vigilant. He managed to follow the students one night almost to the dissecting room and raised the alarm, but nothing was found. However, his accusations caused a sensation and many mourners became anxious as to the safety of their dear departed.

In 1813, Dr Granville Sharp Patterson, teacher of anatomy at the medical school in Glasgow, hired a room in College Street and issued twenty to thirty of his students with a key. When news of a death reached them, they would meet and draw lots to determine who would attempt to 'lift' the body, release it from its coffin and smuggle it into the hired premises. They called themselves 'The Patent-Leather Club' (other people would have called them resurrectionists), and promised that they would not reveal the secrets they learned from their studies within its walls.

In their favour, they were genuinely interested in the reasons why the corpse had died and were anxious to discover the nature of the ailment or disease and work out methods of curing this, should it occur in others.

Later in the same year a Mrs McAlister, the wife of a haberdasher in Glasgow, died suddenly and was buried in the Ramshorn

Churchyard. Her relatives, worried about the possibility of her grave being robbed, returned that night to the churchyard to find that her body had disappeared. They rushed to the home of the Professor of Anatomy and smashed his windows. The police were ordered by the magistrates of Glasgow to search for her body and were issued with a warrant to search every anatomy room in the city.

Two friends who could recognise her (one of whom was her dentist, James Alexander), accompanied the officers of police. They arrived at the hired rooms of Granville Sharp Patterson and friends in College Street. The main entrance was up a narrow stair. Set into the floor was a trap door which gave access to a chamber beneath. The party was politely received and given every co-operation to search cupboards but found nothing untoward.

On the floor within the rooms there was a tub filled with water. The dentist decided to return to examine this tub which had caught his eye. He insisted that it be emptied. At the bottom of the tub there was a jawbone. He identified the teeth as belonging to Mrs McAlister, and there was also a female finger. A military guard had to be called out to march the culprits to the Tolbooth as the crowd, now gathered outside in College Street, was growing nasty and calling for blood.

When the basement was examined, several dead bodies and parts of bodies were found and placed in glass cases to be used in evidence at the trial, which was fixed at the High Court of Justiciary in Edinburgh, for 6th June, 1814. A request was made by the defence to have the trial behind closed doors, but this was not granted. The case was dismissed for lack of evidence as to who had done the deed, but Granville Sharp emigrated to America for several years.

In Govan Churchyard in the same year, a student, eventually an eminent surgeon, began work at a grave. He was about to disinter the corpse when the alarm was given, and he had to swim across the River Clyde to escape capture.

A family set a watch day and night at a relative's grave because surgeons had been unable to diagnose the cause of death and, as they had refused to allow a post-mortem, they suspected that a good deal of interest would be shown by the teachers of anatomy. At dusk they lit a lantern which they placed on the grave and settled down to watch. While members of the family were changing watch the doctor moved the lantern to another grave nearby. Unsuspecting, the ones whose turn it was to watch settled down and, as usually was the case, fell asleep. The doctor, who was desperate to exhume the corpse, moved quickly and was successful. However, while he was dissecting it he cut himself and later died of blood poisoning.

One night in 1813, a student was accidentally shot dead by a trap-gun at Blackfriars Churchyard, Glasgow. His two companions dragged his body to the gates, each tied a leg to one of theirs, put their arms around him and took him home. The two were almost caught later. They heard about a man who had died of a disease which had baffled even the respected surgeons, Dr Balmanno and Dr Cleghorn, and they set off the next night to the Mearns on the south side of the city to disinter his body so that they could investigate it further.

This time they went prepared with an old suit of clothes and a hat. They duly hired a horse and gig from a carter in the High Street and, on reaching the south side of the city, dug up the body and dressed it in the suit and placed the hat on the corpse's head.

The students, their task completed, then sat the 'man' in-between them and set off on the return journey. All toll-keepers were warned that they must pay close attention to every vehicle, so when they reached Gorbals Tollbar one of them paid the toll while the other spoke to the dead man. The toll-keeper held up his lantern to see who was in the coach, commented on how ill the 'puir auld bodie' looked and told them to drive carefully. They arrived at College Street to be greeted by applause for successfully carrying out such a daring raid.

If the bodysnatchers were disturbed, or if they 'lifted' the wrong corpse, or heard that it had died of an infectious disease, they would then happily abandon it and run. Rabbie Reid, at Campsie, was left half in, half out of his grave. On another occasion the bodysnatchers panicked while transporting the body of a child and abandoned it at Gilshochill. At Cadder Kirkyard, close to the Forth and Clyde Canal, the bodysnatchers did escape with the corpse despite the watch housed there. The watchmen gave chase and the bodysnatchers ran away carrying their spoil. The body was later found dumped in a farm dung-heap covered with straw.

Many of these violations were fictionalised and the general public were fascinated to read about the actions of the bodysnatchers, even though they disapproved of them.

> About this time there arose a great sough and surmise that some loons were playing false with the kirkyard, howking up the bodies from their damp graves, and harling them away to the College . . . I'll never forget it. I was standing by when three young lads took shools [shovels], and, lifting up the truff, proceeded to houk down to the coffin, wherin they had laid the grey hairs of their mother. They looked wild and bewildered like, and the glance of their een was like that of folk out of a madhouse; and none dared . . . to have spoken

to them. They did not even speak to one another; but wrought on with a great hurry, till the spades stuck on the coffin lid – which was broken. The dead-clothes were there huddled together in a nook, but the dead was gone. I took hold of Willie Walker's arm, and looked down. There was a cold sweat all over me; – losh me! but I was terribly frightened and eerie. Three more graves were opened, and all just alike; save and except that of a wee unchristened wean, which was off bodily, coffin and all.

Mansie Waugh, David Moir, 1828

The coffin was forced, the cerements torn and the melancholy relics, clad in sackcloth, after being rattled for hours on moonless by-ways, were at length exposed to uttermost indignities before a class of gaping boys.

The Bodysnatchers, R. L. Stevenson, 1884

The supply of bodies continued to be scarce and, in 1827, it was said that in summer they were stolen, salted and hung up in cellars 'like Yarmouth herring'. A medical student in Glasgow was attacked by a mob when he was seen carrying a parcelled baby. It had been stillborn and the fact that the mother had given him permission did not interest the mob.

The official graveyard staff and other informers who attended funerals also passed on information as to the cause of death, the position of the lair and details of the watch to the bodysnatchers.

The Professionals

Burke and Hare

The most infamous suppliers of bodies were technically not bodysnatchers. William Burke and William Hare, in 1818, hawked fish around the village of Ettrickbank. Their real purpose of taking a cart to the country areas was to procure dead bodies which they sold to anatomists in Edinburgh. This was to develop into a major trade for these men.

William Burke, from Ireland, and his partner Helen McDougall, from Stirlingshire, were friends of William Hare, also from Ireland, and his partner Margaret Log. In 1828, the latter pair kept a boarding house mainly patronised by tramps and down-and-outs. In December 1827 one of their clients, Donald, a pensioner, died owing them £4. To rectify this, Hare, with the help of Burke, filled a coffin with bark and buried it. They then arranged with students of Dr Knox (see p. 28) to sell the corpse. Dr Knox appeared and examined the body on delivery, offering £7 and 10 shillings (£7.50), realising a profit of £3 and 10 shillings (£3.50) for Burke and Hare. This was the first of many transactions but they grew greedy, and rather than waiting for their clients to die, they began helping them on their way.

An old woman, Abigail Simpson from Gilmerton, was their first victim. They invited her to have a drink with them then employed laudanum, putting it into her drink. While she slept they suffocated her by lying across the body, covering the nose and mouth and compressing her throat. Upon delivery of the body Dr Knox commented that it was fresh but asked no questions.

The next victim was Joseph, a miller, followed by that of an English match-seller; Effie, the old cinder-raker; and a drunken women handed over to them for safe-keeping by the police. After Mrs Hostler, for whose body they received £8, and Mary Haldane and her daughter Peggy, whom they sold for £12 and £14 respectively, Burke and Hare were congratulating themselves on setting up a successful business.

In about midsummer 1828, a grandmother and her grandson lodged with Hare. She was murdered during the night. In the morning Burke broke the back of the child, who then died. Their bodies were placed in herring barrels which were then stowed on a cart. At the Grassmarket the horse stopped, refusing to move on, and two porters then shouldered the load and carried the barrels to Dr Knox's establishment at 10 Surgeon's Square unaware of their true contents.

Ann McDougall, a relative of Burke's common-law wife, came on a visit from Falkirk, and even she became a victim. Mary Paterson, a homeless girl to whom the pair had offered lodgings, was almost their downfall as some of the students thought that they recognised her. Burke, however, assured them that he obtained her body from the house in which she had died. A student even cut off her long hair and gave it to Burke to sell to a barber for making wigs.

James Wilson, known as 'Daft Jamie', was extremely popular in Edinburgh. He was born in 1809 and, with his widowed mother, a street hawker, often visited people's houses, where he would be fed and given a dram. He was unfortunate, in October 1828, to be invited into the house in West Port and plied with drink by Burke and Hare. They, in turn, were foolish in their choice of victim, as he was well liked and well known. His disappearance caused a stir and the students of anatomy recognised his body. However, no action was taken against Burke and Hare.

Later that same month the Grays, former lodgers of Burke, discovered the body of a Mrs Docherty lying concealed with straw in Burke's house. They refused to be bribed into silence and reported their find to the authorities who immediately searched Dr Knox's dissecting room and identified the body, which was found still lying in a tea-chest.

> The ruffian dogs, – the hellish pair,–
> The villain Burke, – the meagre Hare,–
> Impatient were the prize to win,
> So to their smothering pranks begin.
>
> Burke cast himself on Jamie's face,
> And clasp'd him in his foul embrace,
> But Jamie waking in surprise,
> Writhed in an agony to rise...
>
> Now both these bloodhounds him engage,
> As hungry tygers fill'd with rage.
> Nor did they handle axe or knife,
> To take away Daft Jamie's life.
>
> No sooner done than in a chest,
> They cramm'd this lately welcomed guest,
> And bore him into Surgeons Square –
> A subject fresh – a victim rare...
> 'Elegiac Lines on the Tragical Murder of Poor Daft Jamie', J. P., 1829

Burke and Hare provided sixteen corpses before suspicion was raised. Hare and Log turned King's evidence, receiving pardons in exchange for information, much to the anger of the people. Hare blamed Burke and McDougall for the atrocities. The trial was held on 25th December, 1828. Burke was defended at no cost by the finest lawyers but even they could find no escape clause for such behaviour. Burke confessed, but in turn blamed Hare for thinking up the idea. These murders disgusted people, who could hardly believe that they had taken place in the capital city without anyone being aware of what was happening.

> The jury find the pannel, William Burke, guilty of the third charge in the indictment; and find the indictment not proven against the pannel, Helen McDougall.
> *Burke and Hare*, William Roughead, 1921

The jury were reviled for having permitted Helen McDougall to escape execution. She was mobbed if she showed her face and had to leave Edinburgh. It is believed that she emigrated to Australia.

Twenty thousand people attended the execution and began to chant 'Where is Hare?' Sir Walter Scott was present at the event and wrote in his journal:

The mob, which was immense, demanded Knox and Hare, but though greedy for more victims, received with shouts the solitary wretch who found his way to the gallows, out of five or six who seemed not less guilty than he.

Another description of the gathering states:

The day fixed for the execution of Burke, 28th January 1829, was looked forward to with savage glee. The gallows were erected at the head of Libberton's Wynd – cross stones in the roadway yet mark the spot – and instead of, as usual, there being a difficulty in finding men to execute the work, there was an eager competition among the carpenters for the privilege of being engaged upon it, while for the time being, the public executioner was the most popular man in Edinburgh. The malefactor on appearing at the edge of the scaffold was received with an appalling yell of execration, to which he returned a look of fierce and scornful defiance. 'Burke him', 'Give him no rope', were the grim directions to the executioner and as the body was cut down, the vast crowd stretching from the Lawnmarket to the Tron Church, gave three tremendous cheers.

Old Edinburgh Pedlars, Beggars and Criminals, 1886

Children were frightened into good behaviour by the threat that Burke and Hare would take them away. Bravely, as they skipped in their ropes, they chanted:

Burke an' Hare
Fell doon the stair,
Wi' a body in a box,
Gaun to Doctor Knox.

Traditional

The verb 'to burke', meaning to cover someone's mouth with a plaster, a method used by Burke and Hare, entered the language.

Hare is recorded several fates. He was supposed to have been blinded by being thrown into a lime pit, become a beggar in London, or stoned at Dumfries as he headed for Ireland with his partner, Margaret Log.

The part played by Dr Knox and his students is a doubtful one. If they had not been so delighted to receive such fresh corpses to experiment on, or had questioned how Burke and Hare could supply these so regularly, fewer victims might have been the result. Even when they recognised the corpses they took no action, so perhaps should be considered accessories after the fact.

Dr Carlaw

It was hinted that the local doctor at Maryhill was kept informed of burials. Indeed, it was suggested that his death occurred on his return from a raid. In October 1832, he had attended the presentation of a silver watch to John Andrew, a joiner, who had carried out sterling work during the cholera outbreaks. He is reported to have left the gathering at midnight, but at five o'clock the next morning, he was found lying dead on the path of his house. His funeral took place before anyone could examine the body. This, allied to the fact that Dr Carlaw had shown a spade – specially designed for lifting – to friends, aroused suspicions that he may have been present at New Kilpatrick churchyard on the night it was reported that students had been fired upon by watchers.

John Dallas

John Dallas, a boy of eight, died in Edinburgh on 3rd December, 1751. His father was out working as a sedan chair carrier and his mother was drinking in the house of a neighbour, Helen Torrence. Jean Waldie, one of the drinking party, left. She went upstairs, found the boy, who was ill, and took him into her house where she gave him a drink after which he died.

She then contacted some surgeon-apprentices whom she and Torrence had been promising since November to supply with the body of a child. They gave the two women 2/- and a dram of whisky for the body and later another sixpence to Torrence for carrying him to their premises.

Unfortunately for the women, after they dissected the boy's body, the apprentices dumped it in a lane where it was found four days later. The parents were at first accused, but later released. When the two women were tried their counsel pointed out to the jury that they could only be indicted for murder. Stealing the child was not a hanging offence and selling his dead body was not officially a crime. Helen Torrence and Jean Waldie, however, were sentenced to hang, on 18th March, 1752, in the Grassmarket for stealing and murdering John Dallas.

Others

There were many others who made money from this trade whose only crime was in removing bodies from their graves. Geordie Mill, a grave-digger at the Howff, as the churchyard at Dundee was known, was believed to supply Dr Knox of Edinburgh with bodies. He also traded bodies lifted from other graveyards in the city and surrounding areas. He was eventually caught in the act and charged with violation.

Here goes Geordie Mill, wi' his round-mou'd spade,
He's aye wishing for the mair folk dead,
For the sake o' his donal', and his bit o' short-bread,
To carry to the spakes in the mornin'.

A porter cam' to Geordie's door,
A hairy trunk on his back he bore,
And in the trunk there was a line,
And in the line was sovereigns nine,
A' for a fat and sonsie quine,
Wi' the coach each Wednesday mornin'.

. . . Geordie's wife says, 'Sirs, tak tent,
For a warning to me's been sent,
That tells me that you will repent
Your conduct on some mornin'.'

. . . Then they ca'd on Tam and Jock,
The lads wha used the spade and poke,
And wi' Glenlivet their throats did soak,
To keep them richt in the mornin'.

                                        Popular ballad

At Kirkintilloch in 1827, Will Monach was disturbed in his task, and was escaping over a wall when one of the watchers lifted a hedge-hook and lashed out. He lost his leg and wore a wooden one, which after his death was used as a heel stock by a local cobbler.

Mrs Purdon of Maryhill, near Glasgow, was lifted in 1827. While visiting her grave, relations discovered that a piece of cloth, which had been around the corpse's head, was lying on the snow. The bodies taken from this graveyard were usually carried over the moor and taken to the dissecting rooms at the university.

'Burke' Morrow got his nickname from the infamous man. He was a carrier who transported fish between Ballantrae and Ayr. One night in 1830 he halted at an inn at Maybole. A drunk man crawled onto his cart and fell asleep beneath the covers. Next morning, coming to and now sober, he decided to steal two fish for his breakfast. He pulled them from a box, but in doing so he dislodged a human foot. He ran post haste to tell the police constable, but by the time Morrow was apprehended, he was on the road to Ayr and the cargo was clear of any human remains.

Public Dissection

Through time, it became the norm when sentence of death was being passed for the judge to include that the corpse would be given for dissection to the nearest school of anatomy. The condition was that members of the public should be admitted, although this instruction often upset the criminal's relatives. Great crowds would gather, pushing and shoving their way to the front, eager to witness the experiments. In 1822, when two murderers were due to be hanged at Aberdeen, the father of one of them went to London to try to have that part of his son's sentence rescinded. He was not successful. Many criminals feared the idea of being dissected more than being hanged. Sometimes the experiment would go wrong, causing uproar amongst the spectators.

Matthew Clydesdale was a miner in Lanarkshire when he was arrested for murdering an old man with a pickaxe in 1818. His sentence was that he was to be hanged and his body 'shall be delivered up by the magistrates of Glasgow, or their officers, to Dr James Jeffrey, Professor of Anatomy in the University of Glasgow, there to be publicly dissected and anatomised'. Once the prisoner was dead, his dangling body was removed, placed in a cart and taken to the anatomy rooms at the university, guarded by a detachment of soldiers.

He was placed in the Anatomy Hall, which was crowded with students and citizens sitting in the tiered seats up to the roof watching intently as the fire was lit and the bellows began to blow. Clydesdale, still wearing the white cap that covered his face on the gibbet, with his hands in white gloves and his feet still tied with cords, was laid on the dissecting table. His body was then lifted and placed in an armchair facing the audience. An air tube containing a galvanic battery was put into his nostril, the bellows were blown and his chest began to heave. He drew breath. Another tube was inserted in his other nostril, and this time his tongue moved onto his lips, his eyes opened wide; his head, legs and arm moved and he appeared to rise up. He then stood upright.

The audience believed that he was resurrected. Some people screamed, some fainted and others clapped at the triumph of the galvanic battery. Dr Jeffrey then took his lancet and punctured Clydesdale's jugular vein.

A similar experiment was carried out at Aberdeen in November 1821 when, after being hanged, George Thom, who killed his father by poisoning, was taken under escort to Marischal College. His sciatic and spinal nerves were exposed and the galvanic battery switched on. To the astonishment of the onlookers, his body shook and then his hand closed.

On passing sentence on William Burke, the judge ordered that, after his execution, his body be given to Dr Munro for public dissection – a case of the punishment fitting the crime. There was nearly a riot as people fought to enter the dissecting room and upwards of 25,000 people passed by the dissected body. His skeleton remains in the Anatomical Museum at the University of Edinburgh.

CATTLE-LIFTING

The Borders

Scotland's border extended past Cumbria in 1242. The area was divided, in 1249, into marches. Each march was under the supervision of a warden. The East March was slightly more civilised, having an administration of justice, and the clans usually desisted from plunder and pillage. The Middle and Western Marches, however, were home to the moss troopers and cattle-lifters whose only law was their strength and their weapons. They were untameable and proud of the fact.

These bands of men were known in the Borders as Border reivers – 'reif' being a word for thief; moss troopers, after the wild inhospitable territory where they had their lairs; or simply as thieves. Often they were given hero status and tales of their daring deeds were passed down through the generations by word of mouth. Most of these tales appeared in poetic form. They were later written down and became known as the 'Border ballads'.

> They stole the beeves that made them broth,
> From Scotland and from England both.
>
> Traditional ballad

The freebooters were fearless, ruthless men who rode out to seize herds of cattle, horses, sheep and any other goods which they could find to drive home to their own fastnesses. If a few people were injured or killed in the process, or if homes or crops were set on fire, that was fair game. Strangely, for such a ferocious group they were also very superstitious and carried charms, relics and books of spells.

A charge of March Treason could be brought against freebooters. Geordie Bourne was attacked by the garrison of the East Marches under Sir Robert Carey, as he drove cattle to the border. Bourne was a friend of the Warden of the Middle Marches and had hopes of being freed but he was executed early in the morning before word could be taken to his supporter.

Up until the fourteenth century the Border clans had little dependence upon the Scottish Crown. They had their lands by right of occupancy, often having won them by force, and not by a charter from the king; this put them outside the reach of the law. Even as late as 1509, John Murray, the Outlaw, refused to bow the knee. He was challenged by a messenger of King James IV with the words:

> The King of Scotland sent me here,
> And, gude Outlaw, I am sent to thee;
> I wad wat of whom ye hald your landis,
> Or man, wha may the master be?

To the suggestion that that Ettrick Forest belonged to the king, Murray had a ready reply:

> 'Thir landis are mine!' the Outlaw said;
> 'I ken nae King in Christentie;
> Frae Soudron I this Foreste won,
> When king, nor his knights were not to see.'
>
> 'The Sang of the Outlaw Murray', Traditional ballad

He stuck to his guns and King James IV made him Sheriff of Ettrick Forest.

In the sixteenth century lawlessness reigned on both sides of the Scottish/English border and in the Highlands. The clan system throughout Scotland was based on a sharing of property so clan members did not consider taking what they required from another clan as a crime or accept that they were breaking any law. Clan warfare was fuelled by revenge, but clans treated raids on each other's property almost as a sport.

> It happened that three breekless bands
> O' caterans came frae distant lands,
> And took what fell amang their hands,
> O' sheep and duddies.
> Just like your reivin' Hielan clans,
> Or Border bodies.
>
> The Deil's Reply to Robert Burns, Anonymous, 1816

A proclamation was made in 1505 that the inhabitants of parts of Northumberland, Teviotdale, Liddesdale, Eskdale, Ewesdale and Annandale who were members of the 'broken clans' – clans having no chief to pledge surety for their members' good behaviour – such as the Elliots and the Armstrongs, should

> Put away all armour and weapons offensive as well as defensive, as jacks, spears, lances, swords, daggers, steel-caps, hagbuts, pistols, plate sleeves and such like and shall not keep any horse, gelding or mare, above the value of 50/- sterling or £30 (Scots) upon the pain of imprisonment.
>
> Proceedings of the Border Commissioners, 1505

Despite this warning, reiving was rife and, throughout the sixteenth century, people were attacked when going about their lawful business.

Often, the Wardens of the Marches were also clan chiefs. If they felt that proper redress of wrongs was not forthcoming they were entitled to embark on warden raids. This promoted their followers to legal status while carrying out their usual thefts. If a warden was appointed from outwith the clans and did not meet with their approval, he was often found murdered.

The Earl of Albany lured Lord Home to Edinburgh where he was tried and executed for treason. In retaliation, in 1517, the French cavalier, Anthony d'Arcey, who had been appointed Warden of the East Marches in his place, was trapped in Langton Merse by Home of Wedderburn who cut off his head, attaching it to his own saddle by the hair. In 1520, the Earl of Arran was appointed Warden of the East Marches, but the Douglases, Homes and Elliots did not approve and routed him at Kelso.

The chiefs supported their clansmen against the law of the land, which annoyed the lawmakers. In 1594, the Privy Council complained bitterly that the chiefs always sought revenge for perceived offences by raids rather than by recourse to the courts

> ... although it were ordour of justice, or in rescuing and following of trew mens gears [goods] stollen or reft.
>
> Statute, 1594 (cap 231)

Also, in 1594, the chiefs of the clans were ordered to pay bail, grant hostages and subject themselves under due course of law. Those clans who had no chief to ensure their conduct became outlaws.

Black-mail

The Borderers sometimes made money by running protection rackets as a sideline. This was called cess or black-mail and was often levied on the English. If it was paid, the receiver was then banned from injuring the payee and his followers, and also had to help him recover his property if a third party carried it off. If this pledge was broken, it was considered a dishonour.

In the Borders, Jamie Telfer of Selkirkshire was the victim of a raid by members of the clan Elliot of Liddesdale, which left him devastated. He ran ten miles on foot to Stobbs Hall where he protested against this to Gibbie Elliot, the owner, to whom he had paid black-mail, but he received no assistance. At several houses he pleaded his cause and gathered men around him, then set out to recover his goods.

It's I, Jamie Telfer, o' the fair Dodhead,
And a harried man I think I be!
There's naething left at the fair Dodhead,
But a waefu' wife and bairnies three.

'Jamie Telfer', Traditional ballad

He had the last laugh when, after a fight, the goods and cattle were
recovered, for instead of ten milk cows, he had thirty-three.

Debatable Land

There are numerous references to wardens on the English side
getting tough with reivers and hanging them, but lessons do not
seem to be learned from this, as in 1501 the sheriffs summonsed
seventy Armstrongs to trial at Selkirk for the slaughter of John
Blackburn. The Earl of Bothwell declared that they should be put
to death and to the horn – which meant forfeiting their goods and
property – for non-appearance, but nothing happened and the same
threats were made in 1504 when King James IV made another
justiciary visit.

The Turnbulls, whose members had been terrorising the area,
caused King James IV to ride to Jedburgh again in 1510, where he
surprised the clan who submitted to the king at the Water of Rule
where they handed over their swords. Two hundred of them had
halters put over their necks and were led away to be imprisoned in
Edinburgh Castle. Many were executed but a few were released
after giving assurances of good behaviour.

After the Battle of Flodden, a treaty was drawn up by England,
Scotland and France, in 1515, which made the land between the
River Sark and the River Esk, including the Cheviots, a no man's
land. This land was considered a neutral area and called the
Debatable Land. It was here that the reivers of both countries lived,
with no other means of support than cattle-lifting. The Debatable
Land was tailormade for the men from the broken clans of both
nations to carry out their lawless raids. The Armstrongs, Elliots
and Grahams (Graemes) were the chief clans who inhabited this
area.

Johnnie Armstrong of Gilnockie, a Robin Hood figure, was
considered a hero. In 1527, Lord Dacre, an English warden,
attempted to drive him and his 2000 followers from the Debatable
Land. Although Lord Dacre burned Gilnockie Tower, Armstrong's
stronghold, he was driven back over the border and reprisals were
immediately carried out.

Robert, Lord Maxwell, was accused of giving shelter and
support to the Armstrongs. King James V was irritated with

Maxwell because he had entered into an agreement with an English warden, the Earl of Cumberland, to bring peace to the Debatable Land, but Maxwell was not actively supporting it.

The king retaliated by imprisoning the Lords Bothwell, Maxwell, Home and Buccleugh in Edinburgh Castle. Then he appeared in Teviotdale proclaiming that the lives of all broken men who submitted to him would be spared. Johnnie Armstrong of Gilnockie answered the summons in good faith and was seized along with many of his men and was hanged at Caerlanerig Chapel on the high road to Langholm, ten miles from Hawick. This was seen as a terrible betrayal by the country people, who said that the trees withered and never bore leaves again.

> John murdered was at Carlinrigg,
> And all his gallant companie;
> But Scotland's heart was ne'er sae wae,
> To see sae mony brave men dee–
>
> Because they saved their country deir,
> Frae Englishmen! None was sae bauld,
> Whyle Johnnie lived on the Border syde,
> None o' them durst cam neir his hauld.
>
> 'Johnnie Armstrong', Traditional ballad

King James V then turned his thoughts to the question of the lawless marches. At Henderland he seized Piers Cockburn and Adam Scott of Tushielaw, who were taken to Edinburgh and executed. In the Debatable Land it was reckoned that there were around 3000 occupants. The people of the more peaceful dales were annoyed that their crops could be burnt or their herds stolen at will. The Moss of Tarras was particularly densely wooded and difficult, although it had several areas near the river which were high and dry. This was the stronghold of the Armstrongs and the Elliots.

The leader was expected to have a detailed knowledge of the lie of the land. He should be able to guide his followers safely through forests, avoid precipices, and know where to ford a river, even under cover of darkness. The clansmen were always on the alert and at the first sign of attack they left their homes and hid their spoils in the moss. Since the passing of the March Laws, in 1249, the power of the March Warden ceased when a rider reached the Moss of Tarras.

There was a saying: 'Elliots and Armstrongs ride thieves all'. In 1550, the Treaty of Norham was signed, which made the Debatable Land a buffer state that must not be inhabited, but this was difficult to enforce. In 1552, the new border between the nations of Scotland and England was set much as it is in the twentieth century. Canonbie was given to Scotland, Kirkandrews to England and Berwick fluctuated between the two.

In 1561, a shortage of ropes for hanging resulted in eighteen reivers being drowned in the river at Hawick. The Regent Moray swooped on Hawick in October 1567 and seized thirty-four moss troopers. He hanged or drowned nineteen, put ten in chains and took them to Edinburgh and released five on caution. Again, in September 1569, he arrived in Dumfries and duly tried men for reiving.

> To Liddesdale he did again resort,
> Through Ewesdale, Es'dale and all the dales rade he,
> And lay three nichts in Canonbie,
> Where nae prince lay thir hunder years befoir.
> Nae thief daured stir, they did him fear sae sore;
> And that they sud nae mair thair theft allege,
> Threescore and twelve he brocht of thaim the pledge,
> Syne warded thaim, whilk made the rest keep order;
> Than micht rash bush keep kye on the Border.
> > *Ane Trajedie in form of ane Diallog betwix Honour,*
> > *Gude Fame and the Authour,* Lepreuk, 1570

The Regent Morton, in 1573, went with 4000 men to Peebles where he was joined by the Earl of Argyll with a hundred horse-and-carriage-men. They set out for Jedburgh. Some reivers came to him there and gave pledges for good behaviour. Morton, meantime, had their crops burnt and their goods taken. This breaking of vows angered the Borderers, who retaliated with a spree of raiding and destruction throughout the country. A second expedition by the Regent Morton brought in 140 reivers, who were imprisoned in Edinburgh Castle and the Tolbooth.

King James VI held a Privy Council meeting on the first day of every month to hear complaints. Several complaints were received about the lack of control over the broken clans. Legislation was made, in 1590, that:

> Liddis-daill, Esk-daill, Annandaill and the landis of the Hielands – who have long continued disobedient, are to be removed out of their present dwelling on the orders quhair broken men has dwelt and presently dwellis, to quhilk roll, the 94 Act of this Parliament is relative.

The captains, chiefs and chieftains also had to find surety for them. With the Union of Crowns in 1603, a measure of peace came to the Borders but there were still those who clung to the old ways.

In 1606, the Earl of Dunbar, Royal Commissioner of the Borders, sentenced another 140 reivers to be hanged and reported to King

James VI that the district was now free of them, but in 1609 he returned again to hang many more. He put several chiefs 'to the horn'.

In 1608, Lord Home disposed of a number of reivers by hanging them at Jedburgh, although he had no direct evidence that these particular men had been involved in raids. This idea of hanging first and enquiring later became known as 'Jeddart Justice'.

In October 1663, Parliament declared that a reward of £10 sterling would be paid on conviction of a 'felon' to anyone who reported him. The Earl of Traquhair conducted a court, in 1666, at which he condemned thirty Border reivers to be hanged, five to be burned and fifteen banished. Forty were outlawed for non-appearance and twenty given a caution. Anyone having goods lifted must prosecute the thief or thieves, if discovered, and no-one must give them shelter.

Famous Raids

The Armstrongs were outlawed by both nations. Sir Robert Carey, warden of the West Marches, in 1588, complained to the King of Scotland that the town of Haltwhistle in Cumberland had been terrorised and later burned by reivers, believed to be Armstrongs. The king replied that they were no subjects of his and that Carey was at liberty to take revenge. He was given assistance by the garrison of King James VI housed at Hermitage Castle, Liddesdale. The Armstrongs, safely holed up in the Moss of Tarras, sent him word that he was like the first taste of a haggis, hot but blowing cold.

Carey laid three ambushes and at four o'clock one morning, with 300 horses and 1000 foot soldiers, set out to capture them, but the reivers had scouts or lookouts on the hilltops to give them warning. Carey succeeded in capturing five men and held them as hostages. The reivers had their revenge, for while Carey was besieging Tarras they sent out a party by a secret route to plunder his lands in England and gifted him one of his own cattle on their return.

A Liddesdale outlaw, Dickie of the Den, and his men went raiding in Teviotdale. Veitch of Dawyk and Tweedie of Drummelzier had little liking for each other. Dickie of the Den found a flock of sheep on Drummelzier's land and drove them off. He did not know that they had strayed from Dawyk land and that they belonged to Veitch. They heard the braying of the bloodhounds and Dickie and his men hid in haystacks. Veitch, finding his flock missing, had sent the dogs out to find them. One of the dogs worried away at a stack and refused to budge until

Veitch and his men tore it down to discover Dickie and his men. The outlaw, expecting to see Drummelzier's men, was taken aback and tried to explain that if he had known that the sheep belonged to Veitch, he would not have touched a hoof of them. Luckily for him, Veitch accepted his explanation but confiscated the flock.

Black Morrow, the outlaw, terrorised the countryside around Kirkudbright, hiding in the woods by day and plundering by night. His name was probably Murray and there was a price on his head. The people, fed up with his behaviour, found out where he had his lair and poured a barrel of spirits into the well where he drew water. He fell into a stupor. A MacLellan then took a dirk and killed him. With the award he bought an estate in Borgue. A head on a dagger appears on the MacLellan coat of arms.

> The Scots and moss-troopers have again revived their old custom of robbing and murthering the English, whether soldiers or other, upon all opportunities, within these three weeks. We have notice of several robberies and murders, committed by them. Among the rest, a lieutenant, and one other of Colonel Overton's regiment, returning from England were robbed not far from Dunbar. A lieutenant, lately master of customs at Kirkudbright, was killed about twenty miles from this place; and four foot soldiers of Colonel Overton's regiment were killed going to their quarters by some mossers who, after they had given them quarter, tied their hands behind them, and then threw them down a steep hill, or rock, as it was related by a Scotchman, who was with them, but escaped.
>
> *Mercurius Politicus*, 11th November, 1662

Wullie of Westburnfoot was an Armstrong. He was one of the last of the Border reivers. He stole ten cows in Teviotdale and drove them to the banks of Hermitage Water. They were followed and traced to Liddesdale where he was taken with nine men and brought to trial at Selkirk. He was sentenced on habit and repute to be executed. On hearing the verdict he broke up the oak chair on which he sat and tried to fight his way out of court. He was duly hanged. This was the last Circuit Court held at Selkirk.

Walter Scott of Harden, a noted freebooter, concealed his spoils from raids in a deep glen near the Tower of Harden. The cattle were kept and killed as required. When they were down to the last few, the lady of the house served at table a covered dish containing only a pair of clean spurs and said, 'Ride Rowly [Rowland] the houghs i' the pot'. This was a signal that another raid should be planned.

William Johnstone of Wamphray, nicknamed 'the Galliard', was a wild freebooter who hid his spoils in Teviotdale; the valley he frequented adopted the name of Galliard Faulds. He was involved in a raid which went wrong and he was hanged on a tree by Sim Crichton. His nephew, Willie of the Kirkhill, vowed to revenge his uncle's death.

> And out spoke Willie of the Kirkhill,
> 'Of fighting lads, ye'se hae your fill.'
> And from his horse Willie he lap,
> And a burnish'd brand in his hand he gat.
>
> Out through the Crichtons Willie he ran,
> And dang them down baith horse and man;
> O but the Johnstones were wondrous rude,
> When the Biddes-burn ran three days with blood.
>
> 'Now, sirs, we have done a noble deed;
> We have revenged the Galliard's bleid,
> For every finger of the Galliard's hand,
> I vow this day I,ve kill'd a man'–
>
> 'The Lads of Wamphray', Traditional ballad

This same Willie won himself the ownership of a five-merk land by cutting off the right hand of Lord Maxwell as a challenge.

Football

The game of football was a favourite in the Borders and drew large crowds. This gave the moss troopers an excuse to gather and make plan for further raids. During a match at Kelso on the 16th June, 1600, a murder was planned, under the nose of Sir Robert Carey, Warden of the West Marches.

Sir John Carmichael, Warden of the Middle Marches, a favourite of the Regent Morton, attended the match and later was murdered near Lochmaben where he was going to hold a Court of Justice. Thomas Armstrong (known as 'Ringan's Tam') and Adam Scott ('The Pecket'), 'ane of the most notalrie thieffes that ever rade', according to Birrel's Diary, were seized, taken to Edinburgh, sentenced to have their right hands struck off and were to be hung on the gibbet on the Burgh Muir.

Hostages

It was often the case that in order to gain release for any of their band who may have been captured, reivers were not averse to taking hostages. In 1528, Lord Dacre imprisoned a reiver at Dumfries. Dick Irwen, the reiver's companion, who had escaped, was quick

to retaliate by seizing Jeffrey Middleton, an innocent passer-by who
was returning from a pilgrimage to Whithorn, and detaining him
until the man's friends brought about the reiver's release.

The Salkelds were a powerful family in Cumberland. They had
captured the brother of Jock Graeme of the Peartree and thrown
him into Carlisle jail until he could be executed.
Jock was riding past Corby Castle, their stronghold, when he
noticed a child of the sheriff playing alone outside the gates. He
gave him an apple saying, 'Master, will you ride?'; the boy was
lifted into the saddle and carried off as a hostage. He kept the child
in Scotland until his brother was pardoned and released.

The most famous release was that of Kinmont Willie. The
Wardens of the Marches ensured that when they met the King's
Peace (or in this case, as the meeting was on English soil, in 1596,
the Queen's Peace) would be observed. William Armstrong of
Kininmouth was returning home from such a meeting when he
was attacked and taken prisoner. He was imprisoned at Carlisle by
the Depute of the West Marches, Lord Salkeld. The Lord of
Buccleugh, enraged at this breaking of the peace, gathered 200 men
and set out to storm Carlisle Castle.

> He call'd him forty marchmen bauld,
> Were kinsmen to the bauld Buccleugh;
> With spur on heel, and splent on spauld!
> And gleuves of green, and feathers blue.
> There were five and five before them a',
> Wi' hunting horns and bugles bright:
> And five and five came wi' Buccleugh,
> Like warden's men, arrayed for fight.
>
> And five and five, like a mason gang,
> That carried ladders lang and hie;
> And five and five, like broken men;
> And so they reached the Woodhouselee . . .
>
> We crept on knees, and held our breath,
> Till we placed the ladders against the wa';
> And sae ready was Buccleugh himself,
> To mount the first before us a'.
>
> He has ta'en the watchman by the throat,
> He flung him down upon the lead –
> 'Had there not been peace between our lands,
> Upon the other side thou hadst gaed.'
>
> 'Now sound our trumpets!' qho Buccleugh;
> 'let's waken Lord Scrope right merrilie!'

Then loud the warden's trumpet blew–
'O wha dare meddle wi' me?'

Then speedilie to wark we gaed,
And raised the slogan ane an a',
And cut a hole through a sheet of lead,
And so we wan to the castle ha'...

Wi' coulters and wi' forehammers,
We garred the bars bang merrlilie,
Until we came to the inner prison,
Where Willie o' Kinmont he did lie.

And when we came to the lower prison,
Where Willie o' Kinmont he did lie
'O sleep ye, wake ye, Kinmont Willie,
Upon the morn that thou's to die?'

'Kinmont Willie', Traditional ballad

The rescue completed, they sat him, complete with irons, on Red Rowan, a gallant steed, and headed for home chased by Lord Scrope. Once they had crossed the River Eden they felt safe.

Hot Trod

Hot Trod was the name given to the right to retrieve cattle or goods which were stolen. In 1398, the Commissioners of Scotland and England ordained:

That all manner of men of baith realms sal hafe freedome to follow their gudes that beis stolen or restit frae thaim with hind and horn.

Bloodhounds or sleuth hounds were used because they could trace the tracks of men or animals. The family affected blew a bugle and carried a burning wisp of straw on a spearhead then called out their slogan or war cry. When the cry was raised all the clansmen had to follow under penalty of death.

Just put a lighted peat on the end of a spear, or hayfork or sic like, and blaw a horn, and cry the gathering cry and then it's lawful to follow gear into England, and recover it by the strong hand, or to take gear from some Englishman providing you tak nae mair than's been lifted frae you. That's the auld Border law, made at Dundrennan in the days of the Black Douglas.

The Black Dwarf, Walter Scott, 1816

With the abolishment of heritable jurisdictions in 1747, and a national system of law enforced, many who had suffered felt that the new laws were unfair and preferred the law of the barons. One tenant is quoted as saying:

> Yerl John, was nae yerl, an' Yerl Alexander was nae yerl ava but Yerl James was the man! He'd hang them up just at his ain word an' nane o' yer law!
>
> *Hereditary Sheriffs of Scotland*, Vol 2, 18—

Nicknames

The Border reivers having the same surname, and often a common first name, had other means of identification. These nicknames were either taken from their place of origin or their land: 'Jock o' the Syde', 'Archie o' Ca'field', 'Will o' the Wa' '; father's name or an occupation: four Robert Elliot's were thus known, 'Clement's Hob', 'Vicar's Hob', 'Mirk Hob' and 'Elder Will'; or a characteristic: 'Sleep'ry Sim', 'Snoring Jock', 'Toppet Hob'.

Slogans

These were cries which were used as clans went into battle or into a fight. They were usually based on the name of the leader of the clan, the symbol on the standard or the rallying place. For example, 'A Douglas! A Douglas!', was the cry of the Lowland clan Douglas.

Gibbie Elliot of Stobs married a daughter of the Hardens. He could not take her home for a month, so her parents demanded the plunder taken at the first harvest moon for her keep. The motto and slogan of the Hardens was, 'We'll have moonlight again'. They also had the moon and stars on their coat of arms. 'A Bellandaine!' was the cry of the clan Scott from Bellendean, their rallying place near Borthwick and 'Loreburn!' the cry at Dumfries from the lower burn where the men of Dumfries gathered.

War cries were often adopted as mottos and added to the clan crest. 'Wha daur meddle wi' me?' appears on the crest of Buccleugh and 'Thou shalt want ere I want' on that of the Cranstouns. The Johnstons have 'Light thieves a' – a reference to the command to the reivers used by the chief of the clan during the time he was Warden of the Western Marshes, when he demanded that they dismount and surrender.

CATTLE LIFTING

The Highlands

In the Highlands, the same type of behaviour as that of the Borderers was common. The perpetrators were known as caterans, reivers, freebooters and robbers. The clans raided each other's territory for the possession of cattle, which was a sign of wealth and was necessary for a daughter's dowry. They also took delight in raiding their Lowland neighbours. The Laigh of Moray, Strathspey, Grampian, the Mearns, the Lothians and the Lennox were plagued by these bands of robbers.

In many cases, because of marriage agreements, land taken by force, lands granted to nobles by the king in exchange for pledges of men to fight for him if required, or forfeiture of lands through their owners being put to the horn, clans (or branches of them) were often driven into areas where there were fewer resources. In such places, the only way to obtain wealth, or even to have enough to eat, was to 'lift' cattle. This was the term used, never 'steal', because they did not see any harm in what they were doing and often felt that it was their right.

In 1459, Robert Lindsay of Piscottie, in his *History of Scotland from 1436–1604*, gives a report of a host of Highlanders who raided the area between Loch Lomond and Stirling. They came over the Lennox Hills by Strathblane, Campsie and Kilsyth, and lifted hundreds of cattle. They were not averse to committing murder, and several people in Clachan of Campsie were killed attempting to defend their property.

The farmers of the Lennox suffered constantly from raids. In 1515, the MacFarlanes of Arrochar raided the widowed Lady Haldane's lands of Boturich, near Balloch.

> Ane messenger cam speedilie
> From Lennox to that Ladie
> And schew how that Makfarlane
> And with him mony a bauld baron
> His castell had tane perfors,

And nowther left hir kow nor hors
And heryit all that land aboute.
> *Ane Satyre of the Thrie Estatis*, David Lindsay, 1570

The MacFarlanes carried out their raids by moonlight and the moon was known as 'MacFarlanes Bowat' (lantern).

Duncan Laudasnach – the name Laudasnach means 'lord' – was a descendant of a younger son of the MacGregors of Glenstrae; a wild, lawless man, he terrorised Perthshire. He lived on an island in Loch Rannoch and, in 1542, raided the lands of the MacLarens, wiping out twenty-seven members by 'fire and sword'. He obviously returned, as a tombstone in Balquhidder Churchyard records:

> The Chief of whom, in the decreptitude of old age, together with his aged and infirm adherents, their wives and children, the widows of the departed kindred – all were destroyed in the silent midnight hour by fire and sword at the hands of a banditti of incendiarists from Glendochart AD 1558.

The MacFarlanes, in 1543, again raided all the area around the Gareloch carrying off not only cattle, goats, sheep and horses, but also eighty stones of cheese. On that occasion they murdered nine people.

The Regent, Mary of Guise, held a court at Inverness in 1555 'to quiet the Highlands and punish caterans and political offenders'(*Gazetteer of Scotland*, Robert Grose, 1888).

The Earl of Caithness, in the same year, was imprisoned in a dungeon because he had given shelter to caterans.

In 1590, the Colquhouns of Luss, the lairds of the land stretching from the shores of the Gareloch to Loch Lomond, raided and lifted from the Dennistouns of Colgrain, probably as an act of revenge. Yet on other occasions, the Colquhouns, Dennistouns and MacAuleys combined to raid Lowland neighbours.

In 1592, on the shores of Loch Earn, Alistair Stewart of Ardvorlich went cattle-lifting in style. He raided lands near Killearn and Drymen and invaded his neighbours' territory, not by stealth, but headed by two pipers, their 'bagpypis blawand befoir thame'. He managed to remove 300 sheep, 66 horses and 254 cattle.

John Drummond-Ernoch, the king's forester, caught a party of MacGregors from the Lowlands who had paused to kill some deer in the Royal Forest of Glen Artney on their way home. Instead of bringing them before the sheriff for trial, he had their ears cut off. In retaliation they slew him and cut off his head, wrapping it in a plaid. His sister was the Lady of Ardvorlich. The raiders paid her a visit and she offered them hospitality. She served bread, cheese and oatcakes, then left the room. On her return she saw the head of her brother sitting on her table with a piece of bread and cheese in his mouth.

The area around Dalmore, Invercauld and Balmoral was pestered with caterans. In 1638, a commission by King Charles I was issued 'In favour of Robert Farquharson of Invercauld, for trying certain caterans' (*Records of Invercauld,* 1726). These were members of the Clan Cameron, who are described as 'broken men', and who came under cover of darkness and terrorised the Lordship of Mar with pistols and shotguns, taking the money gathered for taxes from the town stent or assessor's house.

Clan Gregor

The clan Gregor was a broken clan known as 'the Children of the Mist'. Their exploits came to the attention of the Government in Edinburgh. On 3rd February, 1590, the Lords of the Secret Council outlawed them and condemned them to death. Letters of 'fire and sword' were granted to the Earl of Huntly by the Privy Council. John, Lord Drummond and Stewart of Ardvorlich sought out the MacGregors of Balquhidder and slew twelve men at Inverenty.

When Alasdair of Glenstrae, the young leader of the clan, needed protection for his clansmen, Archibald the Grim, Earl of Argyll, took responsibility for them at a price – Alasdair was forced to harry Argyll's enemies. He refused to attack those who had been friendly to the MacGregors and at one point was sent as a hostage to the Royal Court at Dunfermline.

Two raids took place in 1602. Alasdair of Glenstrae and his brother, Ian Dubh, and an outlaw, Neil Campbell called 'the Traitor', lifted 120 cattle in Glenmulchen, during a daytime raid. Then Duncan of Glenstrae raided Glen Finlas, leaving little behind and injuring many Colquhouns.

The Colquhouns, angered by constant harrying, approached the Privy Council in December 1602 with a complaint against the MacGregors. With a little subterfuge, using 222 women of the clan to pose as widows and carry blood-stained 'sarks' or shirts, they journeyed to Edinburgh where, in the presence of the king, the chief was granted the right to deal with the MacGregors as he saw fit.

This licence to punish infuriated the MacGregors. Alasdair of Glenstrae, head of the clan, rallied his followers and, with Ian Dubh and members of other clans, crossed Loch Lomond, marched down Loch Long and fought with a force of Colquhouns in Glen Fruin on 8th February, 1603. The MacGregors killed forty men and only lost two. Colquhoun had support from farmers and merchants, but horses were of little use in the boggy land of the glen. Many of those taken prisoner were massacred by a MacDonald of Glencoe in whose guard they had been placed. The law, however, was on the side of Colquhoun, Laird of Luss, and the man admitted putting forty prisoners to the sword and was tried for this dishonourable crime.

The victorious MacGregors and their hangers-on went on a spree of destruction, burning and plundering and driving off hundreds of cattle. Ian Dubh was slain in the fight. The name of MacGregor was proscribed. All those who bore it had to change their name or face a death penalty. They became outlaws and all their goods and property were forfeited to the Crown. In 1613, the penalty of death was declared on any MacGregor found in the company of more than four people.

Alasdair was trapped by his 'protector', the Earl of Argyll, at whose instigation he had carried out the raid on the Colquhouns. He had surrendered to him and been promised that he and his men would be sent out of Scotland. They were escorted over the border but were almost immediately brought back to Edinburgh and tried, by the Justice-General – the Earl of Argyll. The charge was treason and doom was pronounced.

> That the said persons be tane to the Mercat-Cross of Edinburgh, and there to be hangit on the gibbet while they be deid; and therafter their heids, legs, arms and remanent parts of their bodies to be quarterit and put upon public places, and their hale lands, heritages, annual-rents, taks, steadings, rowmes, possessions, corns, cattle, guids, gear, and sums of money pertaining to them to be forfaultit, eacheat, and inbrought to our sovereign lord's use, as convict of the said treasonable crimes.
>
> *Records of the Court of Justiciary, Edinburgh, 1604*

Alasdair was instantly taken from the court to the gallows and was hanged.

James of the Knoll

In 1615, James Grant of Carron was visiting a fair at Elgin when his brother was attacked by a Grant of Ballindalloch who bore a grudge against the Carron side of the family. James defended his brother, but in doing so the other party was killed. James was outlawed and set out with a band of followers to raid Strathspey. A price of 5000 marks was placed on his head. A cunning plan was hatched by James Grant of Ballindalloch to force James of the Knoll into the open. He and his men killed John Grant of Carron at Abernethy, hoping to bring the outlaw there to avenge John's death, but he failed to capture his prey. In 1630, James of the Knoll was caught by the Earl of Moray, who made a pact with some Macintoshes, broken men, who found the outlaw, slew four of his men and succeeded in capturing him and wounding him with eleven arrows. He was imprisoned in Edinburgh Castle for two years. The four others captured with him were hanged.

He escaped in 1632 with the aid of ropes which his wife had smuggled in to him hidden in a cask of butter. The Privy Council again put out a reward, and his old rival, Grant of Ballindalloch, set a trap and captured him. Grant of Ballindalloch kept him tied up in a kiln near Elgin for three weeks under constant guard. Somehow James of the Knoll again escaped and killed sixteen cattle, but unfortunately he chanced to beg for food at the hangman's house at Strathbogie and was recognised. During the trial it was established that his original crime was committed in defence of his brother, and eventually he received a pardon and died a natural death in 1639. Thomas Grant, the owner of the kiln, was hanged for harbouring an outlaw.

Patrick Dhu Ger

This cateran was a MacGregor who was hired by James Grant of Ballindalloch, in October 1630, to track down and kill James of the Knoll. He found the outlaw with his natural son at home in Carron and surrounded his house.

> James Grant, hearing the noise, and seeing himself so beset...shot out arrows at two windows, [so] that few did venture to come near the door, except their captain [Patrick Dhu Ger]...whilk James perceiving and knowing him well, presently bends a hagbut, and shoots him through both thighs, and to the ground he falls. His men leave the pursuit and loup about to lift him up again; but as they are at work, James Grant, with the other two, loups frae the house and flies, leaving his wife behind him. He is sharply pursued, and many arrows shot at him; yet he wan away safely to a bog near by with his two men. Patrick Ger died of the shot, within [a] short while, a notable thief, robber and briganer, oppressing the people wherever he came, and therefore they rejoiced at his death.
>
> Memorials of the Troubles in Scotland and England,
> Vol 1, John Spalding, 1850

Gilderoy

'The Red Lad' was the nickname of this MacGregor who preyed on the people of Strathspey, Braemar and Cromarty. His band not only carried off cattle and goods, but also took the householders and held them to ransom. He had as his hideout a cave in Glenmuick shaped like a vat. In February 1636, Stewart of Athole captured seven of his men and hanged them. In revenge Gilderoy set fire to several houses. A price of £1000 sterling was put on his head and he was eventually caught by the Marquis of Argyll, along with another nine men, and brought to trial at Edinburgh.

His brother, John Dhu Roy, and his half-brother, John Graham, were also taken. All three were drawn backwards on a hurdle, a raft-like object made by weaving tree branches, to the Cross of Edinburgh, and hanged. Gilderoy and John Forbes, one of his men, were hanged on a gallows 'ane degree higher' than the other eight who were hanged with them. Their heads and right hands were cut off to be exhibited on the city ports, or gates, as a deterrent to others. A popular broadsheet of the time lionised Gilderoy.

> My love he was as brave a man
> As ever Scotland bred,
> Descended from a Highland clan,
> A catter to his trade.
> No woman then or womankind
> Had ever greater joy
> Than we two when we lodged alone,
> I and my Gilderoy.
> And now he is in Edinburgh town,
> 'Twas long ere I came there;
> They hanged him upon a pin,
> And he wagged in the air:
> His relics they were more esteemed
> Than Hector's were at Troy–
> I never love to see the face
> That gazed on Gilderoy.
> Of Gilderoy sae fear'd they were,
> They bound him meikle strong;
> Till Edinburgh they led him there,
> And on a gallow's hung;
> They hung him hie aboon the rest,
> He was sae trim a boy;
> There died the youth whom I loved best
> My handsome Gilderoy.

A Collection of Old Ballads, J. Roberts, 1724

Greysteel

Caithness was a wild and isolated area. There, in a castle near Loch Rangag, this ferocious cateran reigned supreme. He enjoyed torturing his victims both in Caithness and Sutherland. He killed a Sinclair, then threw his body into the loch. The Laird of Dunn, near Watten, set out to revenge his friend's death. Legend says that he borrowed a talisman, a sword believed to have magical properties, from an old woman and succeeded in killing Greysteel.

The Halkit Stirk

Donald MacDonald, known as the Halkit Stirk – 'the white-faced young ox' – was active in Grampian and Moray in 1660. He was caught by the Laird of Grant to whom, in recognition of this deed, the Committee of Estates granted the right to raise a watch of forty men to seek out Highland reivers. The Halkit Stirk was passed from one set of magistrates to another, going from Aberdeen to Montrose, then to Dundee, Cupar and Burntisland. All had cases against him. He finally reached Edinburgh but was released on bail of £1000 sterling. In 1671 he was again apprehended, tried and incarcerated in the Tolbooth for many years.

James MacPherson

MacPherson's mother was a gipsy and he travelled with a band of about thirty other gipsies throughout Moray. His trademark was the two-handed sword he always carried. He was also an accomplished fiddler. He and his followers broke into hen-houses, stole horses and cattle which they sold at fairs in Banff, Elgin and Forres. They were often accompanied by a piper. Another band, led by captains Peter and Donald Brown, was also active in the area. The people were angry at the way in which these reivers flaunted the law.

They were further abetted by the rivalry between the Duff, Laird of Braco, who wanted them brought to justice by the courts, and his neighbour the Laird of Grant, who wanted to preserve his right of hereditary jurisdiction and try them himself. Finding them at the Summer's Eve Fair at Keith, the Laird of Braco determined to capture them. He succeeded and locked them up but was challenged by the Laird of Grant, with thirty men, demanding access to them.

The Laird of Braco immediately found two justices of the peace and fenced a court which sentenced them to imprisonment. He formed a guard of sixty men and marched them to the jail at Keith.

James MacPherson, Peter Brown and James Gordon were then charged with 'masterful bangstrie [violence] and oppression' by the sheriff at Banff in November 1700. A procurator appeared for the Laird of Grant demanding that they be bound over to him for trial by the Baron's Court of Regality. He was overruled and Gordon and MacPherson were sentenced to be hanged next market day. This was carried out with rope that cost the burgh £1 sterling.

The ballad version is more romantic and suggests that as he was marched to the gallows tree MacPherson played the fiddle tune MacPherson's Rant, which he had composed in prison:

> I've spent my time in rioting,
> Debauch'd my health and strength;
> I squandered fast as pillage came,
> But fell to shame at length.
> But dantonly and wantonly
> And rantingly I'll gae,
> I'll play a spring and dance it roun',
> Beneath the gallow's tree.
>
> *Collection of Scottish Songs*, Herd, 1776

Robert Burns later refined it as 'MacPherson's Farewell'.

MacPherson is alleged to have offered his fiddle to anyone who would play it over his dead body but as no-one came forward he broke it over his knee before throwing himself off the ladder.

Rob Roy MacGregor

The most famous of the caterans was Rob Roy – 'Red Robert' – MacGregor. He was the subject of a novel of that title by Sir Walter Scott and was usually called 'the Scottish Robin Hood'. Born in Glengyle in 1671, he was a cattle dealer well known at the fairs and trysts of the Lowlands. However, in 1691, his father, Donald of Glengyle, was in prison and a ransom was required for his release. To raise the money Rob Roy turned to cattle-lifting and took 250 cattle from Buchlyvie.

Rob Roy also had legitimate business dealings with Lowland lairds who did not relish having to trade in the Highlands themselves and who trusted Rob's judgement in buying cattle, but in 1712 he stood accused of embezzlement.

> That Robert Campbell, commonly known by the name of Rob Roy MacGregor, being lately intrusted by several noblemen and gentlemen with considerable sums for buying cows for them in the Highlands, has treacherously gone off with the money, to the value of £1000 sterling, which he carries along with him. All Magistrates and Officers of his Majesty's

forces are intreated to seize upon the said Rob Roy, and the
money which he carries with him, until the persons concerned
in the money be heard against him; and notice be given, when
he is apprehended, to the keepers of the Exchange Coffee-
house at Edinburgh, and the keeper of the coffee-house at
Glasgow, where the parties concerned will be advertised and
the seizers shall be very reasonably rewarded for their pains.
Edinburgh Evening Courant, 18th–21st June, 1712

Sometimes the MacGregors were so short of food that they
plundered the grain from the Duke of Montrose's girnels or
granaries. They also took not just cattle and goods but the tenants
as well and then demanded a ransom for their release.

The skilful, raiding MacGregors were an annoyance to the
authorities. During the Jacobite Rising of 1715 they seized all the
boats they could find and hauled them across Loch Lomond to
Inversnaid. One hundred naval seamen accompanied by Volunteer
Rifle Brigades from Paisley and Dumbarton took to long-boats
and were towed up the River Leven to Luss where they were joined
by the Colquhouns. They went on to Inversnaid where they landed
and searched for the MacGregors. They stood on mountain tops
and beat their drums but could find no trace of them. This became
known as The Loch Lomond Expedition.

After the Jacobite Rising of 1715, Rob Roy was at Falkland
garrison with fifty of his men. He robbed a funeral party and took
their intended food for his own men. A price of £1000 sterling was
placed on his head.

Rob Roy had an ongoing battle with the Duke of Montrose,
which came to a head when Montrose evicted Rob's wife, Mary,
from their home at Inversnaid. Rob stepped up his reiving and did
everything he could to annoy the duke. In 1716, Rob Roy was on
his way from Inversnaid to Aberfoyle when he heard that a widow
MacGregor would be unable to pay her annual rent to Graham of
Killearn, the Duke of Montrose's factor. Rob Roy lent her the
money and told her to obtain a receipt. Rob and his men hid at the
inn where he knew the factor went for a refreshment and when he
arrived he was relieved of the twenty pounds. Rob got his money
back and the widow had proof that she had paid her rent.

The same year, the factor was collecting Martinmas rents for
His Grace when he was seized by Rob Roy and taken to an islet on
Loch Katrine. Rob Roy moved him around for a week, relieved
him of the rents, then demanded a ransom of 3400 merks, about
£1000 sterling, from the duke for Graham's release. The duke raised
a band of farmers and set out to meet him but they were harried by
a group of MacGregors under Gregor of Glengyle and relieved of

their weapons. The duke did capture Rob near Balquhidder but on the way home Rob managed to escape by sliding from a horse as it forded a river and hiding beneath the water.

In 1717, Rob Roy was captured by the Duke of Atholl at Logierait, where he held his justiciary courts and had his prison. Rob was put in jail but entertained his guards with whisky and got on with them so famously that, when the door was opened, he escaped by jumping on a horse and riding off to one of his hideouts. On another occasion when Rob had been captured, he escaped by grabbing a branch of a tree, clambering up a hill and disappearing through the bracken across the land he knew so well.

At Inversnaid, a garrison was set up. The Duke of Montrose first suggested this in 1716 in a letter to the King's Advocate.

> I had my thoughts before of proposing to government the building of some barracks, as the only expedient for suppressing these rebels, and securing the peace of the countrie; and in that view I spoke to General Carpenter who has now a scheme of it in his hands; and I am persuaded that will be the true method for restraining them effectually.

A fort was built and existed from 1721 to 1792. It was raided and burnt down on several occasions. After its third rebuilding, it was commanded by Thomas Wolfe, later General Wolfe of Quebec.

> Keppoch, Rob Roy and Daniel Murchisan,
> Cadets or servants to some chief of clan,
> From theft and robberies scarce did ever cease,
> Yet 'scaped the halter each and died in peace.
> *Wade's Roads in Scotland*, 1737

Rob Roy MacGregor Campbell died at Balquhidder on 28th December, 1734, and was buried in the churchyard on Hogmanay.

Caetharnach Dhu

James of the Fat Cheeks, a MacKenzie of Dalmore, raided Lochaber and lifted some gold which he first buried at Braeriach, but later moved beneath a tree, then under a large stone on Carn Geldie where, legend has it, it lies to this day. The Lochaber caterans had a hiding place known as The Robbers' Thicket. They had lifted cattle in Gleney, in 1726, and James of the Fat Cheeks went up the glen to challenge them.

He told his sons to watch him carefully and, if he should raise his hand to his brow, it would be a signal for the sons to shoot at the caterans. Caetharnach Dhu, captain of the band, offered to do a deal on payment of some money. James raised his hand without thinking and his sons fired a volley, killing the sentry at the door of the bothy. Caetharnach Dhu, a MacKenzie of Dalmore, leader of the Lochaber caterans, seized the sentry's rifle and shot James of the Fat Cheeks. Both his sons were also killed in the fight which followed.

Sandy Bane

In Wester Glenalmond, Alistair Bane, known as Sandy, had his hiding place at the Thieves' Cave. Like many caterans he had originally been a drover but he led, in the 1750s, a band of up to sixty men who terrorised the area. He was caught at Perth, charged with sheep stealing and hanged.

Heather Jock

On the day that his mother hanged herself, John Ferguson of Dunblane cut her down, then took the rope and stole a cow. The owners caught him and found the cow shut up in the press bed.

> Jock kent ilka bore an' bore;
> Could creep through a wee bit hole;
> Quietly pilfer eggs and cheese,
> Dunts o' bacon, skeps o' bees;
> Sip the kirn an' steel the butter;
> Nail the hens without a flutter,
> Na! the watchfu' wily cock
> Durstna craw for Heather Jock.
> Jock was nae religious youth;
> At the priest he threw'd his mouth;
> He wadna say a grace nor pray,
> But played his pipes on Sabbath day;
> Robb'd the kirk o' baan and book;
> Everything wad lift, he took;
> He didna lea' the weather cock,
> Sic a thief was Heather Jock.
> *Vagabond Songs and Ballads,* edited by Robert Ford, 1904

He was imprisoned in the Tolbooth at Perth and tried by a Circuit Court of Justiciary in 1812. Lord Meadowbank presiding said that he should be punished to deter others and, on 18th April, he was charged with regularly stealing cows and black cattle and was convicted and transported to Botany Bay. Years later he returned and carried on as before.

Scrapies

The scrapies of Falkland were very poor. They carried goods from village to village to earn a living and owned a few cows which they grazed on the Lomond Hills. They had a horse and cart and often helped themselves to produce from the fields.

Watches

In 1666, the Marquis of Montrose appointed Mungo Stirling of Glorat and Milton of Campsie, as watch to keep the peace in Cowal. In 1679, the Privy Council proclaimed that no Highlander was permitted to travel in a group or hold meetings, as these were only excuses and occasions for stealing. However, in 1690, the 'happie revolution' saw the Highlanders still raiding all their old haunts.

The Highlands swarmed with caterans and, because of the lack of roads and local knowledge, the Government were powerless to protect property. In 1693, an Act for the Justiciary in the Highlands was passed but it was not until General Wade's roads were built in the 1730s that access was improved.

In 1723, the heritors of Ross-shire met to discuss the raising of a Highland Watch of thirty men and three overseers. Each man was to receive £2 per year for wages, shoes, clothes and six bowls of meal. The overseers were to be paid £20 per year and every tenant would contribute 2/- per year.

> It's not doubted that all the tenants in the county will voluntarily agree to such a small thing, to be sure of their cattle all the year over, being, by the thieves turning so very insolent, as in great danger at home as in the hills.
>
> *Chalmer's Mss*, Advocates' Library

At Nairn, a local watch was formed out of desperation and they succeeded in capturing four caterans, or *cearnochs*, and imprisoning them at Ruthven. Euan MacPherson of Cluny also set up his own watch to preserve the area, but the caterans were cunning and stole cattle, then took them by boat across Loch Ness instead of by their usual route. MacPherson then set guards on the ferries and succeeded in returning cattle to their owners as far off as the Lennox.

The six independent companies of the Black Watch were beginning to cut down the instances of reiving, which pleased the people of the Lowlands. However, in 1739, the government moulded them into a regular regiment and sent them on foreign service. This benefited the Highlanders, who were immediately up to their old tricks, robbing day and night and killing anyone who put up resistance.

Black-mail

In 1724, it was stated that, when the people were almost ruined by plundering, the leaders of the caterans would offer to protect them on payment of a sum of money. To refuse meant leaving themselves open to plunder; so they paid up. In 1724:

> the garrison at Fort William, Killicummin and Inverness proved ineffectual to restrain the system of spoilation, or to put down a robbers' tax called black-mail [nefarious rent], which many paid in the hope of protection.
>
> *Domestic Annals of Scotland*, Vol 2, *From the Revolution to the Rebellion 1745*, Robert Chambers, 1874

In *Rob Roy*, Sir Walter Scott has Bailie Nicol Jarvie explain black-mail to Mr Obaldistone.

> It grieved him [Rob Roy] to see sic hership [devastation] and waste south o' the Hieland line, why, if ony herotor or farmer wad pay him four pund Scots out of each hundred punds of valued rent . . . Rob engaged to keep them skaithless [unharmed] – let them send if they lost sae muckle as a single cloot [head of cattle] by thieving and Rob engaged to get them again, or pay the value – and he aye keepit his word – I canna deny but he keepit his word – a' men allow Rob keeps his word.

The *First Statistical Account for the Parish of Campsie* records that, in 1744, the farmers still paid black-mail to MacGregor of Glengyle. The arrangement was that Rob's son promised to pay them should any more than seven sheep be stolen or 'lifted'. Under this number the crime was known as piking and was fair game.

Thieves' Road

The Caterans' Road, or Thieves' Road, goes from Lochaber through Rothiemurchus and along the shore of Loch Morlich. It was used by the Camerons and MacIntoshs from Lochaber, the MacPhersons from Cluny, and others, to drive away the cattle stolen from Moray. Another Thieves' Road is located near Peebles, and many other traces of such well-used paths remain.

COMMON PUNISHMENTS

The hangman or executioner had other tasks. A variety of forms of punishment existed, many of which amounted to torture. It was the duty of the executioner to see these carried out. Many accounts books give details of the materials needed for various punishments.

> For tow for binding Catherine McCulloch to the tron, 2/- Scots
> For a penknife for cutting off her ear 3/- Scots
> *Stirling Burgh Records*, March 1722

Torture was not forbidden as a means of examination for guilt in Scotland or as a means of punishing crime until the Treason Act of July 1709. To modern eyes, the treatment at the hands of the magistrates was not far different from that issued out by the detested barons. The saying 'as well to be hanged for a sheep or a lamb' was applicable because there was no set scheme of punishments, unlike in England where, by the eighteenth century, each crime had an assigned penalty. A person convicted of a trivial crime, such as stealing a web of linen or a horse, was as likely to be hanged or drowned as one who committed pre-meditated murder.

In 1855, capital punishment was still effective in Scotland for twenty-five crimes for which it was no longer inflicted in England and Wales. Capital punishment was abolished for a five-year trial by the Murder (Abolition of the Death Penalty) Act 1965 and was later abolished permanently.

Branding

> For cords . . . to bind a woman when she was burned on the cheek – 2/-
> *Edinburgh Accounts Book*, 1554–55

A red-hot branding iron was used to mark the face, hand or other parts of the body. This was often with a letter, such as 'T' for thief. In 1705, Anne Harris had been branded so often on her hands that there was no room for more letters. Branding also acted as a device for recognising anyone who tried to return after having been banished from the town. In Dunfermline, a Burgh of Regality, 'DR' was burned onto the hands of its offenders.

Drowning

Drowning was a favourite punishment for women but was also used for men. The Sheriff's Kettle at Gavrock, Kincardineshire, saw John Melville of Glenbervie, Sheriff of the Mearns, thrown into it and drowned by his fellow barons in 1421. Edinburgh's Nor' Loch, now Princes Street Gardens in Edinburgh, was frequently the scene of the drowning of felons, especially after evening courts when it was felt necessary that justice should be swift. In 1675, James Mitchell was drowned in the Nor' Loch between four and five o' clock in the morning, for the crime of bestiality.

Ducking

Ducking was reserved for women. The apparatus consisted of a stool on which the accused sat. This was attached to a beam which had a weight on the other end to make it act like a see-saw and the woman was ducked. Betty Trot, a hawker, was to be ducked four times in the Nor' Loch at Edinburgh for stealing, 'to ken the differ between what wis her ain gear an' ither folks'. When the hangman tried to fasten her to the stool she pushed him into the water. She ran along the shore and jumped into a boat which she pushed out. Other boats gave chase and everyone ended up in the water, much to the amusement of the onlookers. This episode ended safely but, in 1663, a woman being ducked was accidentally drowned and an Act was passed to prohibit this punishment.

Hanging and Hangmen

Many felons were executed by a single rope, a loop made by a slip knot, being hung over the branch of a tree often known as the 'dule tree' or 'tree of sorrow'. They were often made to stand in a cart so when the horse was pulled away, the body was left suspended by the neck. Later gallows were built consisting of two uprights and a cross beam. A ladder or double ladder was placed against this. The criminal climbed up and stepped off, his weight tightening the slip knot which throttled him.

In Glasgow, in 1757, three men were hanged for trivial offences: one for stealing a piece of cloth from a bleachfield and two for robbing a surgeon at the west end of Argyle Street.

Scaffolds with platforms were erected in towns and the criminal was brought either on foot, in a cart or tied to a wattle sledge drawn by a horse to the foot of the place of execution. The criminal was often permitted to make a farewell speech before he was hooded or blindfolded. The noose was placed around the neck and the prisoner indicated readiness for the bolt to be drawn by dropping a handkerchief. The neck was then dislocated and the spinal cord snapped. Occasionally, the criminal did not die immediately and means had to be taken to finish off the job properly. In 1594, Hercules Stewart, brother of the Earl of Bothwell, was hanged at the Cross in Edinburgh. He was suddenly cut down and taken to the Tolbooth where he was strangled, as the rope had not finished him off.

Criminals were sometimes hung in chains. If he or she had no friends, the corpse could remain hanging until it gradually decayed, leaving only the skeleton. The body was usually attacked by birds who picked at its flesh. This sight was considered a powerful warning to others to keep them on the straight and narrow. The body would swing in the wind which led to people avoiding gallow hills at night, as the eerie creaking put the fear of God into them. The last person in Glasgow to be exhibited in this way was Andrew Marshall, who was executed on 25th October, 1769, for the murder and highway robbery of Allan Robert. His body was removed by friends and smuggled away during cover of darkness.

In 1675, at Inveraray Circuit Court, Duncan McKawis was convicted of being caught in an act of bestiality 'with a whyte mare' and was sentenced to be strangled at a gibbet, cut down and his body burned to ashes. The mare was also killed and burned. In 1751, on a visit to Banff by the Justices at the Circuit Court, Alexander Geddes was accused of repeated unnatural acts with a mare and suffered the same punishment.

Public hangings, which took place wherever the gallows was traditionally erected, and which attracted crowds of up to 20,000 people, were the norm until 20th May, 1868 (see p. 83), after which they took place within the prison walls. Most public executions were carried out between two and four o'clock in the afternoon. The bodies were taken down around nine o'clock in the evening and were often taken immediately to the nearest school of anatomy to be used for dissection.

When hangings took place within prison compounds, inmates used to shout and make noises by banging on anything they could find or by shaking the doors of their cells. A bell was tolled and a black flag was run up to let the crowd – a large number usually gathered at the gates – know that the deed had been done. Executed bodies were buried in chloride of lime within the prison grounds.

Hangmen

Hangmen were often notorious criminals or rascals who had fallen on hard times. Many towns found it difficult to persuade anyone to take on the job, which involved not only hanging, but also whipping, ducking, burning and organising other punishments. A gruesome job was the preparation of the bodies of hanged criminals for display. Heads and quartered parts of the bodies were treated by being placed in hot water to which salt and preservative, often cummin seed, was added. They were then parboiled.

It was an exectioner's job to ensure that there was bran to soak up the blood that was splattered all around. The Maiden, a kind of guillotine, was introduced in 1566 at a cost of £25, but in Edinburgh, in 1583, two hundredweight sacks of bran were still needed at one execution. Another task of the hangman was to receive English-made cloth which was against the monopoly and which had to be publicly burned by him. An Act of Parliament in 1694 demanded that Scots linen must be used for garments in order to protect the local industries and, in 1705, another required that only woollen cloth woven in Scotland be used.

Edinburgh

In 1682, Andrew Cockburn was appointed Edinburgh's hangman and saw away many martyrs of the Covenant as they went 'singing to God in the Grassmarket'. He murdered a blue-gown beggar and was himself hanged in 1682 by McKenzie of Stirling.

Donald Monro, the executioner at Edinburgh in 1684, was dismissed for beating a beggar with undue severity to the threat of his life. He was thrown into the Thieves' Hole, as the prison was called. George Ormiston of Melrose, from a wealthy family, had squandered his money when he accepted the position of hangman at Edinburgh in 1684. He was detested as it was his misfortune to hang many noted Covenanters. He eventually committed suicide by throwing himself off a cliff in the King's Park; the cliff is now known as Hangman's Crag. His son, John, was appointed in his place.

Another contender was John Dalglish, who was so disliked that he was always sure of having a pew to himself at the kirk and a separate act of Communion, as no-one would share the cup with him. John High, usually known as Jock Heich, became hangman at Edinburgh in 1784 to escape being punished for stealing poultry. He was said to beat his wife.

Glasgow

'Set a thief to catch a thief' was Glasgow's motto when appointing a hangman in 1605. John McClelland was himself under sentence of death for theft when he was offered the post on condition that he was bound over for good behaviour and, should he fall foul of the law, he would be hanged without trial. The Council put out a warning that should anyone annoy him by word or deed they would be fined £5 Scots. Fathers were responsible for the behaviour of their children and masters for that of their servants. The fines were directly payable to McClelland.

Jock Sutherland did not hold a sinecure as hangman at Glasgow in the 1770s.

> In those days there was scarcely a Glasgow Ayre (sic) which closed its sittings without two or three unhappy persons being left for public execution, and frequently for crimes which now-a-days, would be visited with a few months imprisonment; while the Bailies of the day, under the advice of their learned assessor, Mr John Orr of Barrowfield, were ordering many to be drummed out of the City – sentencing others to the pillory – and what was worse, condemning not a few to torture and degradation of public whipping through the town.
>
> *Glasgow and Its Clubs*, John Strang, 1855

He is described as being a man of ordinary height but with a small head, pock-marked face, and spindly legs which he covered by wearing white stockings with buckles at his knees and on his shoes. He wore a coat of blue cloth with collar and cuffs of scarlet, a cocked hat with a white edging and frills at his skinny wrists which 'reached to the knuckles of his skeleton-like fingers, which wielded the cat-o'-nine-tails'.

Tam Young came from Berwick to Glasgow and worked as a labourer. He became hangman in 1814 and lived with his wife and family in two apartments of the Justiciary Buildings. He received one guinea per week, coal and a candle plus a salary of £1 per week with bonuses for hangings. He was the last official hangman in Glasgow. After he retired in 1837, the Town Council at first employed John Murdoch on a casual basis then later sent to England when they needed an executioner.

Other Towns

Hangmen throughout Scotland had built up a fine line in perks. The hangman was often referred to as the lockman, so called from the free handful, or lock, of meal to which he was entitled. At

Dumfries, the hangman had a special iron ladle which held the recognised amount. Hangmen were, by right, allowed to choose the best fish, peats and pecks of meal without charge. They were given clothes, shoes, coals and candles, provided with a house or at least rooms within the tolbooth and, in addition, they had a salary.

William Kirk, an old man, was hangman at Kirkcudbright when, in 1699, he petitioned his masters the Provost and Magistrates:

> To the Right Honorable my Lord Provost, Baylies and Cownsell of the Royal Burgh of Kirkcudbright. Humbly showeth, that you Honors pachioner [petitioner] is in great straits in this dear time and lik to sterv for hwnger, and whan I go to the cowntrie and foks many of them has it not and others of them that has it say they are overburdened with poor fok...they bid me go hom to the town to maintain me and cast stanes at me.
>
> *Town Records of Kirkcudbright*, 8th July, 1699

The reply published in the Treasurer's Accounts was to allow him a special payment of six shillings forby his weekly allowance.

Through time, few towns in Scotland had their own hangman, and men like William Calcraft came from England, for a fee of about £20, to carry out the deed. In 1862, Dumfries had even to borrow a scaffold from Edinburgh when a crowd of over 3000 gathered to see Calcraft dispatch Mary Timney. She had killed a neighbour in a fierce quarrel. She had four children and called out from the scaffold for them. Another famous hangman who came from the south was William Pierpoint. In 1908, he hanged Joseph Hume at Porterfield prison, Inverness, the first there for over seventy years.

Place-names

The place-names Gallow Hill, Gallowgate, Gallowmuir, Gallowbank, Gallowlea, Gallow's Haugh, Hangman's Brae, Hangman's Hill and Tom-na-Croich indicate that these were places of execution. In Edinburgh, at the east end of the Grassmarket, the Gallow's Stone stood. It was a large block of sandstone with a hole at its centre into which the gallows fitted. It was in use up until 1784.

Jougs and Pillory

There are many reports of women being put into the jougs, when they had to stand for a given time with a metal ring placed around their neck. In the case of scolds or gossips, this often had the addition of a piece of metal which would restrict their tongue and was called a scold's bridle.

In towns and major cities, the sound of the drum beating was almost a daily occurrence and the local folk dropped everything and rushed out so as not to miss the spectacle of the hangman marching the convicted to stand at the pillory. This meant that the criminal was exhibited at the market cross or other public place. She stood for two to three hours on market day with a paper round their neck on which her crime was written.

At Glasgow on 3rd June, 1589, a pair of jougs were ordered to be set up at the pillory to silence 'monifauld blasphemies and evill wordis usit be sundrie wemen'.

The Maiden

A device similar to the guillotine, which was used during the French Revolution, the Maiden was brought to Scotland by the Earl of Morton after he had seen it in use at Halifax, Yorkshire. Its sharp blade dropped down and severed the head from the body. Ironically, he was to discover its effectiveness for himself when, in 1581, he was beheaded for his part in the murder of Lord Darnley. His head

The Maiden

was placed on a spike on one of the gates of the Capital. The use of the Maiden was discontinued in 1710.

Nose-pinching

Another favourite punishment of the crowds was nose-pinching.

> Children played truant from school, the weavers left their looms, women threw down their spindles, and ran to watch some creature having her nose pinched – a process performed with an iron frame with clips which held secure the cartilage of the victim's nose.
>
> *The Social Life of Scotland in the Eighteenth Century,*
> H.G. Graham, 1899

Stocks

In 1577, for as trivial a 'crime' as pulling thistles and other weeds from another man's land without leave, the punishment was to stand in the stocks. This was a wooden contraption which could imprison the hands and head of the offender. Standing in the stocks was usually an invitation for the youth of the town to throw eggs and other things at the offenders who could not escape.

Pressing

Heavy objects were sometimes piled upon the prone bodies of prisoners until they were crushed to death.

Put to the Horn

This meant that the person was outlawed and forfeited his land and possessions, usually in addition to other punishments. The forfeited possessions were often taken by the establishment and given out to favourites. Many families, who in later times prided themselves on their 'nobility', gained their land and titles in this way.

Slavery

Vagrants, considered as idle and vicious criminals, could legally be 'captured' by any British subject. A law passed in 1649 gave such permission and captors could demand that the vagrant work only for 'meat and cloth'. In 1662, King Charles II gave the Earl of Eglinton the exclusive privilege of arresting vagrants in Galloway, Ayr and Renfrew and sentencing them, without trial, to work for fifteen years without pay in his woollen factory.

Criminals could escape hanging by being gifted as slaves. In 1650, eighteen 'rebels', the followers of Montrose, were gifted to General Leslie and six to Sir James Hope to work in his lead mines. The Duke of Atholl and the Earl of Mar were given criminals for their collieries.

Alexander Steuart was found guilty of theft at Perth in December 1701 and was given by the justiciaries as a slave to Sir John Areskin [Erskine] at Alva to work in his silver mine in the Ochils. Steuart drowned hinself in the River Forth and his slave collar, with its inscription intact, was recovered in a fishing net many years later.

Torture

The penalty for murder was usually death by hanging, but convicts were often tortured before execution. Occasionally, they had a hand cut off or their tongue pulled out. Sometimes the arms and legs were encased in iron bands and a cap filled with hot tar was placed on the prisoner's head before he took his place on the scaffold. The offending limb was often pinned to the gallows above the prisoner's head. This was done to warn others not to stray from the narrow path of righteousness, as seen by the Establishment.

The rack was a table to which the prisoner was tied by the arms and legs. It had a turning device which was used to stretch the body until the limbs came out of their sockets. In 1591, John Dickson was excommunicated for denying the slaughter of his natural father. He was taken to the Cross at Edinburgh where he was broken on the rack. He was then strangled and taken to the scaffold at the Burghmuir to be hanged.

The rare punishment of being broken at the wheel was suffered by Robert Weir at the Cross of Edinburgh, in 1604, for conspiring with Lady Jean Warriston in the murder of her husband. This was a horrific punishment and amounted to torture. A cart wheel was used and the offender was tied by the wrist and ankle to it. While it was being turned, the person was constantly hit with a heavy object until dead. Many others awaiting death were disembowelled, or had fingers and legs broken before climbing onto the gallows.

Whipping

A whipping through the town always attracted a good crowd, interested in the proceedings but rarely taking heed of the warning not to try anything similar. The whip, named the cat-o'-nine-tails,

had nine leather tails because of the belief that the magic formula
3 x 3 = 9 would make it more effective.

> Item to Andro Davie, lockman, for scurging of Katherine Smyt
> through the town for gettin' a bairn with a souldeor.   12.0
> Item to Andro Davy, lockman, for his whipping of Allaster
> McAlpine through the towne for steiling of herring.   6.0
> *Dumbarton Common Goods Accounts*, 1614–1660

George Nicol, a treasurer to King Charles I, tried to warn the king
in 1634 that his aristocratic followers were stealing from the public
purse. For his pains he received sixty lashes on his naked back and
banishment from Edinburgh. In 1671, Marion McCall of
Mauchline, for allegedly drinking the health of the devil, was taken
to Edinburgh to be publicly whipped from the Cross to the
Netherbow. Her tongue was bored, her cheek burned with an iron
and she was banished from Ayrshire under pain of death should
she attempt to return.

In Glasgow, in 1775, all carts for hire stood in the Trongate and
it was generally on the tail of one of these that the culprit to be
whipped was attached. First, Jock Sutherland, the hangman, would
appear dressed in his uniform of blue cloth. He wore a long coat
with cuffs, collar and facings of scarlet, white stockings on his
spindly legs, many frills at his wrists and a cocked hat with a white
edging. He would halt at the Cross to apply several strokes of the
cat-o'-nine-tails to a bared back. The procession then moved off,
headed by the town's officers, each carrying a stave. They went
down a crowded Saltmarket, along the Bridgegate, up Stockwell
Street and back by the Trongate to the Cross. At each crossing, the
cart halted and the hangman administered more strokes of the whip.

At Peterhead Prison, up until 1948, an offender was tied by the
wrists and ankles to a triangle. A belt, waistcoat and collar were
worn to prevent injury before being lashed with the cat-o-nine-
tails or the birch. The cat was for those over twenty-one and the
birch for those younger. The Criminal Justice (Scotland) Act 1949
abolished whipping.

CONCEALMENT OF PREGNANCY AND CHILD MURDER

Whilk gart some aft their leeful lane
Bring to the warld the luckless wane
And sneg its infant thrapple

Poems, Allan Ramsay, 1777

Concealment of pregnancy and child murder was forced on many young women because of the disgrace which was brought upon them by the attitude of the church to illegitimacy. Although efforts were made to discover the name of the father, it was only the woman, if found guilty of the deed, who suffered punishment.

In Glasgow, in 1599, the two town midwives were ordered not to attend any unmarried woman in labour during the daytime until they had first informed the magistrates or a minister of the Church. If it was through the night they had to make the woman swear on oath the name of the father before they would give her assistance, or they would in turn be answerable to God and the Kirk Session.

The Act Against Concealment of Pregnancy was passed in 1690:

> If any woman shall conceal her being with child during the whole space, and shall not call or make help of assistance in the birth, the child being found dead or missing, the woman shall be holden and reputr the murderr of her own child, though there be no appearance of bruise or wound upon the body of the child.

The penalty was death. This statute remained in place until 1803 when the punishment was reduced to transportation. Because of the increase in the number of charges for child murder, in 1751 the General Assembly ordered the Act to be read as a reminder in every parish church:

> In consequence of the great increase of the crime of child murder, both from the temptations to commit the offence and the difficulty of discovery, a certain set of presumptions must be enacted, which in the absence of direct proof, the jury are

to be directed to receive as evidence of the crime having been committed that the woman concealed her situation during the whole period of her pregnancy; that she should not have called for help at her delivery . . . and that the child should be found dead or missing.

The Scottish Statute Book, 1690

The view of the Church of Scotland was that a woman carrying an illegitimate baby required the severest punishment. Those who sinned openly should be rebuked openly, according to the Bible, and women who concealed the fact that they were pregnant or who refused to reveal the name of the child's father suffered the shame of standing at the pillar. Many preferred to kill their child rather than suffer this punishment.

Baby Farming

Because an illegitimate child was a stigma for a family, many who did survive were immediately given to a baby farmer. These women also often acted as midwives. Most families paid money to them for the child and eventually profited further when they arranged for the child to be adopted. One advertisement could bring twenty or thirty replies.

Mrs Macpherson [Jessie King]

Elizabeth Campbell gave birth to an illegitimate boy on 20th May, 1887, and died seven days later. Before she died she told her sister, Janet Anderson, that the father was David Finlay of Leith. Her sister looked after the child, called Walter Anderson Campbell, for three months and volunteered to adopt him. However, Finlay advertised him for adoption and told her that a couple called Stewart would call to collect him. The Stewarts took the child away, together with his birth certificate and vaccination papers. They were given £5 and the father dismissed his son from his mind. The boy was never seen again and murder was suspected, but his body was not found on or around the premises of the 'Stewarts', or as they were better known, Macphersons.

Euphemia Mackay, a midwife, attended Catherine Gunn, an unmarried mother, in Edinburgh on 1st May, 1887. She delivered twin boys. The mother was a domestic servant and unable to rear her sons, so when they were four days old she placed them with a Mrs Henderson, where they remained for eleven months. The mother then advertised them for adoption and the boys were separated. Alexander, known as Sandy, went to a Mrs Macpherson with the sum of £2. The midwife, Mrs Mackay, called to see Sandy at Mrs Macpherson's house on two occasions and he seemed to be well in the care of a young girl, Janet Burnie. When the child disappeared, a variety of contradictory explanations were given to different people. (Later, at Mrs Macpherson's trial for child murder, it was reported that he had been given neat whisky to drink.)

In June 1888, Alexander Brown, and a group of boys were playing in Cheyne Street when they found a bundle wrapped in a waterproof coat. They kicked it and it opened to reveal the dead body of a little boy. It was decomposed.

The Macphersons moved house after this event. In August 1888, an unmarried mother named Alice Tomlinson gave birth to a daughter in Edinburgh Maternity Hospital. At four weeks old, the child was placed with a woman who said that her sister, Mrs Macpherson, wanted a daughter. The woman was given £2 and £25 towards the baby's keep. Alice tried several times to see her child, whom she called Violet, but was unsuccessful and was told that it was in the country at the home of the Duke of Montrose's piper. Alice next saw her child when she was summonsed by police to identify her six-week-old daughter's dead body.

The Macpherson's new landlord, James Banks, became suspicious when he heard of the death of Sandy Gunn and informed the police that the child who had lived in his house was no longer to be seen. James Clark, a constable, searched the house and on opening a locked coal cellar found a child's body, wrapped in canvas, on the bottom shelf. Dr Harvey Littlejohn and Dr Joseph Bell examined the bodies of both children and, from forensic evidence, believed that they had been strangled.

Jessie King, alias Macpherson or Pearson, had been paid to adopt these children but could not afford to keep them. She tried to place them in Miss Stirling's Home, which sent children abroad, but the children were refused because they were illegitimate. After that, she strangled the children, wrapped the bodies in a cloth and placed them in a box which she put in a cupboard.

In February 1889, at the High Court in Edinburgh, she stood in the dock, a small and respectable looking woman, accused of three charges of child murder. She pleaded not guilty, but was convicted on two of the three counts and placed in the Calton Jail in Edinburgh to await her execution. Twice she attempted suicide with strips of material torn from her skirt. She was pronounced sane and an unsuccessful appeal for leniency was made to the home secretary. She was executed on 11th March, 1889, the last woman hanged in Edinburgh. Her body was buried in the Calton Jail. There was a public outcry and eventually a law was passed which made such adoptions illegal and put paid to the slaughter of innocent children.

Common Punishments

A public drowning took place at Aberdeen, in 1586, when three women were found guilty of conspiring to poison an illegitimate child. The father was also convicted and he was hanged, his head being exhibited at the Justice Port.

At Cadder, in 1592, three women were accused of 'smooring bairns' in the night and sent to the Session to be tried. They were given two Sundays standing in sackcloth at the kirk door, a very mild punishment. It can only be assumed that the baby was accidentally smothered in these cases. This seems to have happened on occasions when the mothers were drunk. The baby would be in bed with them and when they turned over the child could not breathe.

The Parochial Records of Leith for 10th January, 1605, note that Janet Merling and Margaret Cook, her mother, made public repentance on the next Sabbath morning for concealing for twenty weeks an unbaptised girl, who they called Janet.

In June 1614, at the High Court of Justiciary in Edinburgh, Janet Brown was accused of concealment of pregnancy and child murder. A midwife had helped her to deliver the baby in a field near Biggar and Janet had immediately strangled it and placed it in a hole in a dry-stone wall and covered it with peat turf. She denied the charge saying that the child died of natural causes, so 'she earthed it in the grun' in a turf stack'. The Chancellor, William Fleming, pronounced doom, saying that she was to be taken to the Castle Hill of Edinburgh and hanged and that her goods were to be taken for the Crown. This was the fate of many young women found guilty of murdering their babies; others were taken up the Castle Hill and burned at the stake.

In 1646, some men discovered a baby still alive in Biggar Moss. Eventually the mother was detected and she confessed to smothering the child. She was put in prison, and the King's Advocate decreed that she should be sent to Edinburgh for trial by the Lord Justice-General. The Kirk Session of Biggar minuted the matter but no conclusion was recorded.

Margaret Tait, in 1681, pleaded before Lord Fountainhall that the shame of facing public rebuke on the cutty-stool forced her to kill her newborn child. This was related to the Duke of York, who was investigating the death penalty. The duke believed that the death penalty should not be used for 'drunkenness, sabbath breaking, lying or other enormities', and decreed that he thought that the penalty should be reduced to loss of goods and gear and a whipping.

Notwithstanding the duke's advice, four women were hanged in Edinburgh in January 1681 for murdering their illegitimate babies and, in April, another was hanged for the same crime. At Balquhidder, the mother of an illegitimate child was scolded in private before the Kirk Session but the father was pilloried in public. The books of the majority of Kirk Sessions tell similar tales.

In 1689, Margaret Craig carried her baby all the way from the north of Scotland to Peebles in search of her seducer. In despair she drowned the child in a burn. The body was discovered by fishermen and she was thrown into prison. Later, by order of the Privy Council, she was moved to the Tolbooth in Edinburgh where she remained until her trial, three years later when she was condemned to be hanged.

Margaret Dickson was sentenced to death for child murder in 1690. The hanging took place and she was released from the gibbet and her body given to her friends for burial. When they were taking her along the road on a cart she came to life again and went free.

On 8th December, 1690, Christian Adams bore a baby out-of-doors without a midwife. She had told no-one that she was pregnant because her lover, a married man, would have been ruined had his infidelity come to light. Rather than name him, she suffocated the baby, covered it with a cloth, wrapped it in leaves and buried it in a field. She was afraid that if it was discovered she would be hanged or transported. The body was found and she was executed with two other women for the crime of child murder at Edinburgh in 1691. Her hanging was described as 'giving the ministers much satisfaction'.

One of the other women, Bessie Turnbull, was so disturbed by what she had done that she voluntarily confessed. The other, Margaret Inglis, annoyed them by not repenting and being defiant even as she mounted the scaffold.

Investigators into the deaths of illegitimate children were more appalled by the lack of morality than the actual social causes behind the deaths.

At Aberdeen, in 1705, four women were imprisoned in the Tolbooth for this crime, and the bailies complained to the authorities about the cost to the town. In 1706, the Privy Council was petitioned by Bessie Muckieson of Fife that she had suffered two years in Edinburgh Tolbooth. She blamed the death of the child on Robert Bogie, the father. Their Lordships were lenient and passed a sentence of banishment out of Scotland under penalty of death should she return.

As late as 1752, Christine Phren, a farm servant near Aberdeen, murdered her illegitimate baby and threw its body on to a fire in order to destroy any evidence. Nevertheless she was caught, tried and sentenced to death. She was also forced to carry the baby's charred remains through the town in her apron before she was publicly hanged in chains as a warning to other girls. After her death, her body was stolen by students of anatomy for dissection.

Heart of Midlothian

Sir Walter Scott based his novel *The Heart of Midlothian* on an actual case of concealment of pregnancy. In 1736, Helen Walker and her younger sister, Isobel, lived with their widowed mother near Dumfries. In October, the Cluden Water was in flood and the body of a male child was washed up on its banks. Isobel Walker was accused of having drowned the child and the Ordeal by Touch was administered. When the child was placed on her knee she panicked and denied that it was hers but a handkerchief tied around its neck was known to belong to her.

Grave of Helen Walker ('Jessie Deans') (within railings).

She was tried at Dumfries and sentenced to be hanged six weeks later. She was imprisoned in the Tolbooth. Her sister, Helen, was a devout woman who, when asked if her sister had disclosed to her that she was pregnant, answered 'No!' She could not tell a lie even to save her sister from the gallows because she had sworn on the

Bible to tell the truth and dared not perjure her soul. However, she set out for London, a journey of fourteen days, to petition the King for a pardon. She arrived at the home of the Duke of Argyll, who used his influence to secure a reprieve and a remission, provided Isobel went abroad within forty days.

Murder of Children

Many children were disposed of, for various reasons, by murder. Occasionally, parents who were members of a Friendly Society were tempted to dispose of a child as though it had died from natural causes. Since death in childhood was a common occurrence, few questions were asked before they could claim insurance.

Agnes Johnston, of Airth, attempted to drown herself in a well at Clackmannan, in 1674, after having cut the throat of her grandniece because she believed that a spirit guided her to commit the deed as revenge on her relatives who refused to acknowledge that she suffered from fits. She was tried in Edinburgh and hanged in the Grassmarket.

Robert Irvine was tutor to the sons of Mr Gordon of Ellon and resided with them in Edinburgh. His charges saw him behaving with impropriety with their mother's maid and he decided to murder them. In 1717, the New Town did not exist and the ground was covered in broom and whins. He took them for a walk along a path which was overlooked by the Castle Hill. There he disposed of them by attacking them with a knife. The Baron of Broughton witnessed the deed from above and pursued the tutor and arrested him. Two days later, Irvine was executed at Gallowlee having first had his hand cut off by the same knife with which he had murdered his charges. He was left hanging in chains and his right hand was nailed above his head.

Helen Rennie

Helen Rennie, a well-educated Glasgow girl, had been seduced by Jonathan Atwood and had fallen pregnant. She had her child, a son, fostered by a couple in Gorbals where she visited him regularly on a Sunday for the first five years of his life. One Sunday she took him for a walk along the banks of the Paisley Canal and returned him, as usual, to his foster parents. That night he vomited, took convulsions and died.

On examination of the child, traces of arsenic were found on his clothing and it was discovered that Helen Rennie had bought a mixture of sulphur and arsenic at a nearby dispensary. She was arrested and charged with murder. The public flocked to her trial at the High Court and a military presence was provided to keep order. Within the Court of Justice, a juryman protested at the treatment of the accused. The public benches cheered and clapped and the judge, Lord Succoth, fumed. Soldiers with drawn bayonets were summonsed to clear the gallery.

> At nine o'clock on Monday morning, the 22nd of April 1822, the bells of the city began to ring anew, announcing that the procession of the Judges was coming forward from Garscube House, to finish the trial of Helen Rennie. The magistrates and military went out towards the Cowcaddens Toll, to meet and escort them with pomp and circumstance into the city. Precisely at ten o'clock, the Judges took their seats once more in the Old Hall. The Court was again surrounded by infantry and dragoons, and every inch of it crammed by palpitating mortals, young and old, to hear the doom of Helen Rennie...it was the rule of law, in all capital cases, for the Jury, after being enclosed whether for a short or long period, to return a written verdict, under an envelope, duly signed and sealed by their Chancellor, who again was to deliver it into the hands of the Justiciary Clerk, sitting beneath the Judges, and by him communicated to their Lordships. If the verdict was a guilty one, the envelope containing it was generally sealed with black wax – if otherwise, conveying a verdict of not proven or not guilty, as the case may be, the envelope had its seal of red . . . If black, the black cap was very soon to hand; if red, the prisoner and his or her friends might get ready with their peons of congratulation . . . the Jury . . . had found the prisoner not guilty! What a cheering and clapping of hands then took place.
>
> *Old Reminiscences of Glasgow and the West of Scotland,*
> Vol 1, Peter Mackenzie, 1890

Despite a recommendation of guilty by the judge, this personable young woman had charmed the jury who decided to be lenient and she escaped the noose.

Jamie Glen

Jamie Glen, a hauler on the Forth and Clyde Canal, was arrested and brought to trial in 1827. He had drowned his illegitimate daughter in the canal. When the body was discovered, near Firhill, it was buried at Maryhill Churchyard. The child's mother worked at Dunn's Textile Mill at Duntocher. She had been fobbed off for some time by Glen about their daughter's whereabouts. Whenever she enquired after her daughter he told her that 'the wean was a' richt'. Suspicious, she forced the authorities to agree to open the child's grave. She identified her daughter by the print frock in which she had been buried. Jamie Glen, dressed in white clothes bound by black braid, was hanged by Tam Young, on 12th December, 1827.

Jeannie Donald

Helen Priestley's body was found in a sack, in the close where she lived in Aberdeen, in April 1834. It had been made to appear that the motive was rape but a neighbour, Jeannie Donald, a Salvationist, with whom the family were on bad terms, was accused of murder and was sentenced to death in July 1834. Ten years later the charge was reduced to culpable homicide and she was released on special licence. It was believed that the child had given her cheek and that she had given the child a shake which had caused her to be sick. Helen must have choked on her own vomit but, in panic, Jeannie hid the body and tried to falsify the motive.

Robert Smith

The last public hanging in Dumfries took place in May 1868 (see p. 67). Robert Smith had attacked, robbed and murdered a little girl who was going shopping in Annan. She was taken into a wood and assaulted, then strangled with a shoelace. Alarmed that he had been seen with the girl, he went to the house and attempted to murder the witness with a large knife, but he was disturbed and escaped. Later that day he was arrested in Dumfries whilst with another young child.

Robert Duff

At Perth, in 1910, Robert Duff kicked his four and a half-year-old step-daughter to death, then tossed her body over a fence. A witness confirmed that he had kicked the child three times and the jury found him guilty. An appeal was successful in proving that his intent had not been to kill the child and he did not hang.

COVENANTERS

The 1680s were known as 'the killing times'. 'Covenanters' was the name given to those religious zealots opposed to an Episcopalian form of religion being foisted onto a mainly Presbyterian country. They were prepared to die as martyrs for their cause; many people suffered for their beliefs and paid for them with their lives. The Test Act, a red rag to a bull, was introduced in 1681. This was an Abjuration Oath of loyalty to the king acknowledging his authority in matters temporal and ecclesiastical. The heritors tended to outwardly accept the Test, while at the same time offering help and hiding places to those who opposed it.

> Here in this shire I find the lairds all following the example of a late great man and considerable heritor among them [Sir John Dalrymple who was deposed as Lord President for refusing to take the Test] which is to live regularly themselves, but have their houses constant the haunts of rebels and intercommuned persons, have their children baptized by the same, and then lay blame on their wives.
>
> Letter from John Graham of Claverhouse to
> Lord Queensbury, 5th March, 1682

The populace aged sixteen to seventy, especially in Galloway which was strong in opposition, fought it fiercely. In 1684, people were forced to attend a meeting at a given time to sign the Test Act of 1681. The court was guarded by soldiers since the Government expected trouble. Those who refused to sign the hated Act were interrogated, in the manner of the Spanish Inquisition, by Robert Grierson of Lagg and 'Bloody' Clavers, Graham of Claverhouse, two of the greatest tyrants to support the Government.

If anyone continually refused to sign they had their ears cut off, their thumbs crushed by the thumbscrew or their legs crushed by the boot, a contraption of iron or lead which fastened around the leg and into which smaller metal wedges were hammered to tighten it. Hundreds refused to take the Test. Their homes were burned down and they were tortured and killed. There was no trial and no defence.

I sent out a party with my brother Dave three nights ago. The first night he took Drumbui [Mackie of Drumbui was outlawed in 1679] and one McLellan and the great villain McClorg, the smith at Minnigaff that made all the clikys [hooked knives used by the rebels to cut the bridles of the cavalry], after whom the forces have trotted so often . . . I am resolved to hang him; for it is necessary I make some example of severity, lest rebellion be thought cheap here. There cannot be a more wicked fellow alive.

Letter from John Graham of Claverhouse to
Lord Queensbury, 13th March, 1682

Six men were seized near Girthon on 4th December, 1684, and four were shot. The other two were taken to Kirkcudbright for trial and were later hanged, then beheaded and their heads placed on spikes. The bodies of the four men were buried in Dalry by friends but Claverhouse, hearing of this, ordered them to be exhumed, as the bodies of traitors had by law to be displayed publicly after execution.

The fate of John Bryce, in 1685, was typical of many. He was taken from his home to Mauchline where he was executed, then buried in a hole in the earth. Others were shot on the spot or were fined, imprisoned at Edinburgh, Blackness Castle or on the Bass Rock, and were transported to the plantations.

Ministers, forced from their churches, became outlaws and had to go into hiding or live rough on the moors. They held services in the open air which became known as 'conventicles'. These were illegal but were attended by hundreds of people. Anyone conducting or attending such a service was liable to severe punishment if caught. The Government sent spies to infiltrate these meetings and report on the whereabouts of the gathering places.

The Martyrs of Wigtown

Margaret McLachlan and Margaret Wilson, one a woman of sixty-three and the other a girl of eighteen, refused to take the Test, in 1685, so Lagg had them tied to a stake at the Water of Blednoch in Wigtown. Drowning was a form of death often used for women and, by placing them where the tide was slowly rising, Lagg may have hoped that they would be so terrified that they would agree to take the Test.

Margaret McLachlan's stake was a good way beyond that of the young girl's and she was first to be led out into the water. Margaret Wilson was led out next and refused to be coerced into taking the Test. She began to sing a psalm and then to pray. The water began to cover her. When asked, by Lagg, to take the oath,'God save the king', she replied 'God save him, if he will'. Some people thought that this would save her but both women perished. The strange thing about this event was that at the eleventh hour, the Privy Council in Edinburgh granted a reprieve, but it mysteriously disappeared and never reached Wigtown.

Prisoners

In 1679, 100 prisoners taken at the Battle of Bothwell Bridge were confined within a walled section of the Greyfriars Churchyard in Edinburgh. They were chained two by two. They had nothing to lie on, were poorly clad, and had only four ounces of bread per day and some water. They were guarded by day by eight soldiers and by night by twenty-four. If they allowed any prisoner to escape the soldiers would, by cast of a dice, themseves be executed. If a prisoner stood up at night he was immediately shot. Many died or signed papers promising to renounce the Covenant. Four hundred remained there for five months. As winter approached shingle huts were built to give them shelter.

After the battles such as Aird's Moss, Drumclog and Bothwell Bridge, fought in the 1670s, the 'heretics' were often taken to Edinburgh.

> David Hackston of Rathillet, who was wounded and made prisoner in the skirmish of Aird's Moss at which the celebrated [Richard] Cameron fell, was, on entering Edinburgh, 'by order of the [Privy] Council, received by the Magistrates at the Watergate, and set on a horse's bare back with his face facing the tail, and the other three laid on a goad iron [rods of iron], and carried up the street. Mr Cameron's head being on a halberd before them.
>
> Note in *Old Mortality*, Walter Scott, 1829

Many Covenanters were taken to Edinburgh for trial, imprisoned in the Tolbooth and brought into the Laigh Hall of Parliament for questioning. There, 'Bluidy' Mackenzie, the Lord Advocate, or the Duke of Lauderdale, conducted the 'trial'.

> A dark crimson curtain, which covered a sort of niche...rose at the signal, and displayed the public executioner, a tall, grim and hideous man, having an oaken table before him, on which lay thumbscrews, and an iron case, called the Scottish Boot, used in those tyrannical days to torture accused persons . . .
>
> The executioner, with the help of his assistants, enclosed the leg and knee within the tight iron boot, or case, and then

placing a wedge of the same metal between the knee and the edge of the machine, took a mallet in his hand and stood waiting for further orders.

Old Mortality, Walter Scott, 1829

When Covenanters were being executed in Edinburgh's Grassmarket they always sang psalms. The sentence of execution became known as 'glorifying God in the Grassmarket'. After execution, the more 'famous' Covenanters had their head placed on a spike with their hands, which had been cut off and laid together, palms pressed as though in prayer.

James Renwick, one of the staunchest Covenanters, was seized and taken to be hanged at Edinburgh on 17th February, 1688. The authorities were afraid that an attempt would be made to rescue him and commanded the drums to beat to drown out his voice as he spoke from the scaffold. He was twenty-six years old.

Transportation

Many religious prisoners were transported, condemned on hearsay by the Bishop's Court of High Commission. They were placed in irons and then herded together to the ships heading for the American colonies, where they were handed over to merchants who sold them into slavery.

Cromwell came north in 1650 to suppress the Covenanters who, although rebels, were also Royalists. They wanted a king who would recognise their right to worship as they chose. Cromwell crushed them at the Battle of Dunbar. Many were angered when General Monk rounded up 500 prisoners, many of them captured at Dunbar, and sold them into slavery in Barbados.

After the Battle of Bothwell Bridge, in 1679, 300 prisoners were crammed onto a small ship heading for Barbados. Two hundred and nine of them drowned during the journey.

Six men, Mungo Eccles, Thomas Home, John McWhirter, William Rodger, John MacHarvie and Robert MacGarron, became known as the Martyrs of Maybole because they were below deck with the hatches battened down when the ship struck rocks on 10th December, 1679, and all six perished. In 1684, 200 small heritors were banished to the plantations for refusing to take the Test.

Others were shipped to Virginia. The Provost of Glasgow, Walter Gibson, owned a company which traded in the colonies. He made a great deal of money by using his ships to transport large numbers of Covenanters, sentenced to slavery for their part in the battles of Aird's Moss and Bothwell Bridge, to the plantations in America.

In 1685, George Scott of Pitlochie was given prisoners from Dunnottar Castle:

> It was a most disastrous voyage. Partly because of the reduced and sickly state of many of the prisoners at starting, but more through deficiency of healthful food, and want of air and comfort, a violent fever broke out in the ship before she had cleared Land's End. It soon assumed a malignant type and scarcely any individual on board escaped. The whole crew excepting the captain and boatswain died; Pitlochie himself and his lady also sunk under the disease. Three or four dead were thrown overboard every day . . . Fifteen long weeks were spent by this pest-ship before she arrived at her destination.
>
> *Domestic Annals of Scotland*, Vol 2, *From the Reformation to the Revolution 1745*, Robert Chambers, 1874

Seventy had perished. A few were released and managed to return home.

In 1688, William Milroy had his ears cut off and with 190 other Covenanters was put into the hold of a ship berthed at Newhaven. The voyage lasted three months and thirty-two prisoners died. The survivors were sold as slaves in Jamaica.

In 1689, an Act for the Securing of Suspect Persons was passed. Graham of Claverhouse was soldiering in the north in the service of King James VII, but Sir Robert Grierson of Lagg was arrested by Lord Kenmure and imprisoned in the tolbooth at Kirkcudbright for several months before being taken to Edinburgh where, in August 1689, he was released on bail. Both these tolbooths had been filled by him with prisoners for over a decade. He was held from June to August 1689 before his release; he died in Dumfries in 1733.

There is a legend that just before his death, a vessel sailing on the Solway during a storm was overtaken by black clouds. When they passed, the sailors saw in the moonlight a black coach drawn by six black horses. The skipper called out to the coachman, 'Where bound?' The answer came, 'To tryst with Lagg, Dumfries from Hell.'

By 1690, Presbyterianism had been declared as the religion of Scotland and the Church of Scotland as its national Church, though some tolerance was permitted. Those who were devout Cameronians remained a separate sect and Scottish Episcopalians worshipped in their own church. Through time, Quakers, Baptists and Roman Catholics could also follow their faith, but they could not hold office in Government.

The influence of the Church over the secular judicial courts waned after the Disruption of 1843, but the ethos was so deeply ingrained within the Scottish psyche that, until the Second World War, there was still a strong Protestant ethic in society which was reflected in the decisions of the judiciary and jurists.

CRIMINAL JUSTICE

In Scotland crimes were tried by a variety of courts. Up until the sixteenth century, the only crimes for which prosecution was initiated by the Crown in Scotland were those of treason, blasphemy and crop firing. Those found not guilty –'cleansit' – were set free. If guilty, the person was declared as 'fylit' or 'convickt'. As punishment, a woman was often 'drownit' – drowned. Both sexes could be sentenced to be 'hangit' – which usually meant being hanged, drawn and quartered; this often included beheading. These were the official verdicts until 1680 when, under the Government of King Charles II, the judges changed this and restricted the jury to declare the act proven or not proven.

Their reason for this was that the judges then retained the right to assess whether or not the act charged was a crime. The jury were only allowed to make a general verdict on the guilt or innocence of the accused as proved by evidence.

Lord Robert Dundas was Lord Advocate from 1720 to 1725, when he resigned to enter politics. In 1728, he introduced, through an Act of Parliament, the right of the jury to use the terms guilty and not guilty, but the verdict of not proven, a verdict peculiar to Scots Law, was also retained. This verdict implies that a majority of the jury find that there is suspicion of guilt but that the evidence is not strong enough to prove this beyond reasonable doubt. The accused is given an unconditional discharge.

The ancient laws of Scotland were written, in the fifteenth century, in the Scottish tongue as well as in Latin. In 1609, the ancient laws of Scotland, entitled *Regiam Majestatem*, were published. The chief court for all trials up until 1672 was the Court of Session, where it was said that 'the De'il wad hae been at hame'.

Under Scottish criminal procedure in the sixteenth century, if anyone was murdered or violated, the crime was not investigated and the perpetrator would go free unless the victim or his or her family raised a private prosecution making a charge against the accused. Bail had then to be paid to the court to ensure that he or she would appear on the day of the trial.

The trial was conducted by prosecutors who were advocates, the Scottish title for a barrister, acting privately for the victim. There was no need to produce evidence and no witnesses were called, and if twelve people swore that the accused was innocent he could go free. Under the rule of private revenge the accused was permitted to offer to pay money to the accuser, or in the case of murder, the family, which if it was accepted absolved the accused from trial. In return, the accused received a Letter of Slaines acknowledging his 'inward repentance' and forgiving him, giving an assurance that hereafter:

> All malice, rancour, grudge, hatred, envy of heart, and all occasions of actions, civil and criminal, [and receive him] in such amity, friendship, and hearty kindness as if the crime had not been committed.
>
> *The Lord Advocates of Scotland*, Vol 1,
> George W. T. Omond, 1883

This arrangement deprived the Crown of revenue, so an Act was passed in 1587, when King James VI reached the age of twenty-one, which appointed the King's Advocate and Treasurer to act as Public Prosecutor.

> That the Treasurer and Advocate persew slaughters and utheris crimes althoucht the parties be silent or wald uthwerways prively agree.
>
> *The Lord Advocates of Scotland*, Vol 1,
> George W. T. Omond, 1883

This action changed the perception of criminal acts. The community, in general, wished to punish crime to prevent further acts being committed. Acts were considered to be criminal when they endangered public peace, deprived someone of property or led to commercial distrust. Private interests differed from those of the public and the wish for revenge or reparation was often uppermost in these cases. It was decided that in the case of an acquittal, the informer had to pay a sum of money to be shared between the Crown and the accused.

Those accused could have an advocate to plead for them but, although the accused could plead not guilty, the counsel was not permitted to contradict the facts provided by the King's Advocate.

The chief judge was called the Lord President. The bench was semicircular, the president in the centre with seven judges on his right, called the 'east wing', and seven on his left, the 'west wing'. The decisions were announced as 'adhere', meaning that the judges agreed with the judgement, or 'alter', meaning that they disagreed.

The summons for trial at the High Court of Parliament in Edinburgh was made at the local market cross in the town of the accused – the panel in Scots Law – by the relevant pursuivant – the King's Messenger. There was no Habeas Corpus Act in Scotland and there was no limit to the time a prisoner could be held without trial. In 1701, the Lord Advocate, Sir James Stewart, introduced the 'Act for Preventing Wrongous Imprisonment and Against Delays in Tryals'. This Act deliberately excluded colliers, coal-bearers and salters, all of whom belonged to their owners. After the Union of Parliaments in 1707, Scotland retained its separate system of law based on the Parliament of Paris.

'Writers to the Signet' was the name given to the clerks of the Lord Secretary, also known as Keeper of the Signet – the King's seal – which was used to make documents official. They acted as clerks to the Court of Session and recorded the proceedings of all trials. When the Court of Session closed in March, 'vacance time', they took off to spend time at their country retreats.

> Tir'd o' the law, and a' its phrases,
> The wylie writers, rich as Croesus,
> Hurl frae the town in hackney-chaises,
> For country cheer:
> The powny that in springtime grazes,
> Thrives a' the year.
>
> Ye lawyers bid fareweel to lees,
> Fareweel to din, farewell to fees,
> The canny hours o' rest may please
> Instead o' siller:
> Hain'd multer hads the mill at ease
> And finds the miller.
>
> *The Rising of the Session*, Robert Fergusson, 1773

In 1873, training was made compulsory and examinations had to be passed to become a writer, the Scots name for a solicitor.

Doomster, or dempster, was an official position which required the appointee to repeat and record the sentence of the court. The use of the words, 'And this I pronounce for doom', legalised the sentence. It was often held in tandem with the post of executioner. This led to the name doomster or dempster being applied to the hangman. Through time, the court post was abolished, the sentence being read by the Clerk of Court who had to be a Writer to the Signet.

Bribery

Advocates were often accused of taking money from their clients to grease the palms of the judges and ensure a happy outcome for the accused. An Act of 1579 prohibited them 'be thame selffis or be their wiffis or servandes, to tak in any time coming, buddis, brybes, gudes or geir, fra quhatever persone or persones having...any actiones or caussis pursewit befoir thame, aither from the persewer of defender, under pane of confiscation'.

If the judge proved impossible to bribe, it was sometimes the case that he could be persuaded not to appear, either voluntarily or by direct action. In 1601, Sir Alexander Gibson of Durie, Lord President of the Court of Session, was kidnapped at St Andrews by George Meldrum the Younger of Dumbreck and taken to Harbottle in Northumberland, where he was detained for eight days until the trial of Lord Bothwell for the assassination of Lord Darnley was over.

The men-of-law regularly received gifts of barrels of herring from the various town councils for whom they tried criminal cases. After an execution, a celebratory feast was held for the dignitaries who had taken part. This was called the 'deid-chack'. On the occasion of the shrivelled head of Montrose being removed from its spike to be buried, in 1661, the Lord Advocate, Sir John Fletcher, gave a feast at which one of the guests became so drunk that he collapsed and died of alcohol poisoning. The custom survived in Edinburgh until Provost William Creech abolished it in 1790.

In the 1660s, Sir John Fletcher, King's Advocate, demanded bribes and the money had to be delivered to his house by the servants of the accused. Prisoners were often left to rot in chains because the Lord Advocate, Sir John Nisbet of Dirleton, had not been bribed to free them.

Another ploy was for the presiding judge to change the order of cases so that a fellow lawyer who thought to oppose him was unable to be present and a relative or placeman of the presiding judge would act for the defence. This was prohibited by an Act passed by King Charles II, in 1688.

There was a toast attributed to Lord President Forbes, ' Here's to such of the judges that don't deserve the gallows', and in the nineteenth century they were also referred to as 'fine villains in scarlet'.

Courts

Admiralty Court

The First Admiral of Scotland had power to hold courts for piracy and maritime disputes, both civil and criminal, up until 1828 when these powers were transferred to the Court of Justiciary. Peter Heaman and François Gautier killed their captain by bludgeoning him to death. They attempted to dispose of witnesses by suffocating them. The ship anchored at Barra where the spoils were divided out. They were tried at the High Court of Admiralty in Edinburgh, in June 1821, and sentenced to hang within the flood mark at the Sands of Leith.

A large procession accompanied them from the prison on Calton Hill to Leith, where the admiral and magistrates joined it as the bell tolled their doom. It was estimated that around £40,000 people witnessed their demise. Their bodies were given to Dr Munro, at Edinburgh, for dissection.

Burgh Courts

King David I tried to curb the power of the barons and pleased the growing merchant class by designating some towns Royal Burghs or Burghs of Regality. These towns received a charter from the king in return for direct taxation. Amongst other privileges was freedom from the authority of the baron or nobleman, and the right of the whole community to appoint councillors, magistrates and bailies, who could administer justice and hold courts.

They could impose fines, decree punishments and sentence offenders to imprisonment. Burgesses could demand trial by their peers and, in Galloway, escape a charge by the oath of twelve loyal burgesses that they were innocent. Other types of burgh were called Burghs of Barony and were under the jurisdiction of the laird. Some burghs had the archbishop or the abbot of the monastery as the superior and the courts were designated Abbot's Courts. The Abbot of Scone was given the island in the River Tay for trial by water, hot iron or duel.

The Nor' Loch, now Princes Street Gardens, Edinburgh, was frequently the scene of the drowning of felons, especially after evening courts, when it was felt necessary that justice should be swift.

Circuit Courts

The circuit courts, held twice per year in each county, had almost ceased by the beginning of the sixteenth century. The criminal court was only being held in Edinburgh, an inconvenience to many people. The King's Advocate represented the king and influenced the court. As demands on him grew, it necessitated the appointment of Depute-Advocates. All fines and forfeitures now fell to the Crown. By an Act of Parliament, in 1587, the circuit courts were restored

The Justice-General appointed eight deputes who held courts in each county in April and October. Justice Ayres was the original name for the courts which met twice per year in April and September. At these courts two Lords of Justiciary presided. They tried all criminal cases except the crime of high treason.

Judges held courts in Jedburgh, Dumfries, Ayr, Glasgow, Inveraray, Stirling, Perth, Aberdeen, Dundee and Inverness and the judges talked of 'going on circuit'. They set out in parties, mounted on horseback, their cloaks fluttering in the wind and their wigs going awry. Papers, books and a change of clothing were carried. In 1610, it was decreed that all advocates, clerks and scribes should wear black gowns in the judgement hall and in the streets.

The courts were attended by the sheriffs of the particular county, the Lord Provost, if appropriate, the magistrates of the district, the macers and other officers from the High Court of Justiciary in Edinburgh. These officials rode out to meet the judges and escorted them to their place of residence.

The roads left much to be desired, especially if it had been wet, and were rutted and stony. The judges often needed to drink several bottles of claret to clear their heads after such a journey. At Glasgow, they sat in the magistrates' refectory at a vast round table tippling till midnight. The judges lodged also at the Saracen Head Inn, Gallowgate, where the punch bowl held four gallons of toddy.

> O'er draughts of wine the beau would moan his love,
> O'er draughts of wine the cit his bargains drove,
> O'er draughts of wine the writer penned the will,
> And legal wisdom counselled o'er a gill.
> Alexander Boswell, 1771

Lord Cockburn described going on his first circuit to Stirling as a young man:

> After the circuit dinner, and when drinking had gone on for some time, I observed places becoming vacant in the social circle but no-one going out of the door. The individuals had dropped down under the table . . . [Next morning] The judge and some of his staunch friends coolly walked upstairs, washed their hands and faces, came down to breakfast and went to court quite fresh and fit for work.
> *Memorials of His Time*, Lord Cockburn, 1830

At Perth, the judges resided at the Royal George Hotel and, after attending church, they held a soirée for local magistrates. This was the habit in most towns.

> Payed to the watch the first night the commissioners
> came to the toune att the Justices Court   1/-

Payed to Bessie Maxwell ffor wyne and aille druken
by the judges when they came from the Tolbooth   2/6

Payed ffor ane horse and a cairt to cairie Keitt of
Kraigielands to the ald gallows   7/-
    Treasurer's Accounts, Burgh of Kirkcudbright, 1650

There had been no circuit court held at Inveraray for twenty-one
years when on Friday 21st August, 1908, Lord Johnston arrived
and was ceremoniously met by the provost and magistrates and
taken to his lodgings in the Argyll Arms Hotel. Lord Johnston
was guarded by two halberdiers. Later, an old fashioned
entertainment was held in the hotel for the dignitaries. On the first
day of the court, there was a procession to the courthouse led by a
battalion of the Argyll and Sutherland Regiment, two town officers
in scarlet uniforms carrying halberds, the Duke of Argyll, the Lord
Lieutenant of the County and the prisoner, guarded on each side
by two halberdiers.

    The Porteous Roll was a list of offenders who were summonsed
to appear at the circuit court. There were coroners, who were the
guardians of pleas of the Crown, and who received the list denoting
the name and the offence. The Porteous Roll was, literally, a roll of
paper which could be carried under the arm. The coroner's job was
to either arrest every person named or else take bail from them.

Colliery Court

At the Colliery Court at Tranent, miners were sentenced to be
taken down the pit. There they stood all day with an iron collar
around their neck with a chain attached which was nailed to a
pit-prop. For more serious offences, the miner had his hands tied
to the gin horse and was forced to go round and round as the
horse winched the coal up to the pithead. To give the horse a rest,
the man was attached at times directly to the gin handle and had
to turn it himself.

Dirt Court

A bailie sat in Edinburgh every Monday at Outer Parliament House
to hear cases of scandal and defamation or 'tulzies' – as
disagreements which usually came to fisticuffs were known. The
washerwomen and the ale-wives attended, greatly enjoying the
spectacle. A list of the cases was hung on a pillar at Parliament
Square in the area known as Scoundrel's Walk. The law agents met
their clients there to discuss their defence.

Dusty Feet

A special court, the Court of Dusty Feet, was held during the time of the local fairs. Anyone causing trouble after the fair was 'cried' was immediately tried and punished:

> That there is a muckle fair to be hadden in the Muckle Toun o' Langholm on the 15th day of July, auld style...a' land-loupers, and dub-scoupers, and gae-by-the-gate swingers, that come here to breed hurdums or durdums, huliments or buliments, hagglements or bragglements, or to molest this Public Fair, they shall be ta'en by order of the Bailie and the Town Council, and their lugs shall be nailed to the Tron wi' a twal-penny nail; and they shall sit down on their bare knees and pray seven times for the King, thrice for the Muckle Laird o' Ralton, and pay a groat to me, Jamie Fergusson, Bailie o' the aforesaid Manor, and aw'll away hame and hae a barley banna and a saut herrin' to my denner by way o' the auld style.
>
> HUZZA!   HUZZA!   HUZZA!
>
> *The Local Festivals of Scotland*, F. Marian McNeil, 1968

One benefit offered to bondsmen or slaves was that should they escape to a burgh during a fair, they could not be re-captured.

Fishing Company Courts

A Scottish fishing monopoly was established, in 1632, one of its aims being to give employment to 'lazie and ydle people' and four judges were appointed to administer justice to 'insubordinate workmen'. They could imprison those who displeased them and there was no right of appeal through the ordinary court. If an 'offence' occurred at sea, a judge-depute was appointed during the voyage by the masters to deal immediately with it. This usually meant flogging.

Galloway Justice

Galloway retained its own code of criminal law up until 1426, when it came under the general law by an Act of Parliament. The judges of Galloway differed in their ways of determining guilt. Trial by ordeal meant that the accused was forced to plunge his arm into a vat of boiling water until it was scalded or to grasp a rod of iron heated on an anvil until it was red hot. If the wounds healed quickly the accused was declared innocent. If they did not heal then a verdict of guilty, usually followed by execution, was declared.

If the King's Peace was broken then the accused must give to the king twelve score of cattle and three horses, or he could agree to a trial by battle, which meant duelling with his accuser. Whoever won was innocent. If caught red-handed, a robber could be instantly beheaded by a Sergeant of the Peace.

Master Courts

The Incorporated Trades individually held their own Master Courts. These were conducted by the Deacon and Masters to discipline any member who caused trouble. Men, women and apprentices were regularly fined for slander, fighting, swearing, blasphemy and drunkenness, and threatened that they might never hold office if they should repeat the offence.

The Master Court could recommend that certain workers be kept separate from each other to try to prevent a recurrence. As part of their punishment they had to drink the health of the deacon. A weaver, John Paterson, in November 1621, was forced to his knees in public during a service at the High Kirk to beg forgiveness for having sworn at his deacon by saying 'the devil tear the skin off him'. He was also fined £4 Scots. He offended again in December 1622 and was again fined and lost time by being discharged from his loom until it was paid.

In extreme cases, the deacon had the power of 'punishment of the persone', presumably whipping and imprisonment, but this was rarely used. A Glasgow weaver, Charles Snyp, was jailed for forty-eight hours in August 1644 for having disobeyed and wronged his deacon.

> The Deacon and Masters of the Glasgow Weavers were reprimanded in February 1665 for attending meetings and burials without wearing a hat. A motion was passed that should any of them be found breaking this law a fine of £10 was to be paid to the poor of the craft.
>
> *Records of Old Glasgow Weavers*, 1905

Sheriff Court

Sheriffs and Sheriff-Substitutes were appointed for each county. They were the guardians of the public peace. The Sheriff did not need to live in the sheriffdom but the Sheriff-Substitute did and was only allowed to be absent from it for two weeks each year. The Sheriff Court could prosecute on criminal matters of theft, poaching and the lesser crimes, subject to the review of the Courts of Session and Justiciary. In the seventeenth century, the post of

Procurator Fiscal was created in every Scottish county. The post still exists and is the public prosecutor for cases heard in the Sheriff Court in Scotland – the equivalent of an English coroner in the Crown Court.

Stayt

The Court of Justice of the Earl of Strathearn was held out of doors. The Steward, appointed by the earl, heard cases at the Stayt or Skait, an old burial mound south of the town of Crieff. It was said that the Earl of Strathmore executed a man on the first of every month to ensure that his feudal rights of pit and gallows were kept intact.

University Court

At the University of Glasgow, in the Old College in High Street, the Rector, Sir William Fleming of Farne, presided at the University Court on a charge of murder. The Procurator Fiscal of the University and a member of the victim's family were present. Robert Bartoune was charged with the murder of Jonnett Wright in her own home by 'the shoot of ane gun'. The fifteen strong jury found him not guilty.

The Old College in High Street had a steeple in which students could be imprisoned after being tried in the University Court. Students could be imprisoned, or even sentenced to death, without any right of appeal to the Magistrates Court, since the university had its own jurisdiction.

On one occasion, in 1667, John Satcher was in the cell when other students broke down the door and released him. They were fined 18/- sterling. If students were discovered breaking glass windows, they were publicly whipped and expelled.

Water Bailie Court

King Charles I established the post of Water Bailie of Glasgow, Leith, and Edinburgh by Royal Charter. The magistrate held a court to deal with civil and criminal cases appertaining to the river. Other towns had water bailies who were mainly concerned with the crime of poaching.

Works Courts

At Newmills, Haddington, in 1707, there was a prison built inside the textile factory walls. Any worker who tried to desert was forcibly brought back and imprisoned. Several collieries also held their own courts. At Alloa, there existed a Colliery Bailie Court, or

Court of Equity. This unique institution was established, in 1760, by Lord Erskine of Mar to settle quarrels and other offences which took place in his mines, initially to save time lost by his workers having to attend the Baron's Court. Twelve names were submitted to Lord Erskine by the oldest coalface workers and five miners were selected by him to serve as judges, the chief one being given the title of Head Bailie. No-one was allowed to appear before the court wearing working clothes.

The interesting point of this court was that it was men being judged and sentenced by their peers at a time when they were still serfs. The abolition of slavery in Scottish collieries did not take place until 1775.

Jury System

In 1324, King Robert the Bruce introduced the jury system, but it was often flawed because the jurymen could be influenced by their superiors. Forty-five names could be summonsed and the only objections to the suitability of a juror were if insanity was known, they were under the age of sixteen or on the poor roll. It was not until the nineteenth century that other objections could be raised. Jurors were fined for non-appearance. An Assize of Error could be held against the jury if the outcome was not to the prosecution's liking. If the King's Advocate had issued a warning against the acquittal of the accused, the jury could then go on trial.

The jury appointed a foreman before leaving the courtroom. They were locked in a room and no visitors were allowed, neither were they permitted to leave for any reason. If this rule was broken, the prisoner could immediately be acquitted. The verdict had to be written down and given to the judge. It was 1814 before a spoken verdict became acceptable.

Another ploy used by those with wealth and power was to have the sheriff bribed so that sufficient suitable men could be found to form a jury and the case was dismissed.

Up until 1612, no witnesses were called for either side. Lord Oliphant, the Lord Advocate 1612–1628, was the first judge to examine witnesses in the presence of the accused. He also permitted witnesses to be examined for the defence. Before this, statements were taken from witnesses before the trial and the jury decided if the evidence tallied with their statements. Prisoners could be witnesses in their own defence.

Evidence consisted mainly of word of mouth, unsubstantiated statements. No items of evidence were exhibited in court or information correlated, and there was no forensic or medical evidence available. Circumstantial evidence was acceptable, however unsupported. The counsel for the accused was allowed to sum up such evidence as he could muster on their behalf and be the last speaker before the jury withdrew to consider their verdict.

It was only after the establishment of the High Court of Justiciary, in 1672, that prisoners were given a list of Crown witnesses and jurymen, and could cite witnesses for their defence; warrants were issued for these people to attend the trial. This was the supreme court of criminal justice in Scotland and was housed in Edinburgh. It tried cases from Edinburgh and the three Lothians, and also those cases of serious crime referred from the rest of Scotland.

Justices of the Peace

These were unpaid appointees who were often the local lairds; and they could try the less important cases. At Milngavie, in 1827, the justices of the peace held a court in the Black Bull Inn; this lent a new meaning to being called to the bar and 'Time, Gentlemen, Please'.

A laird from Renfrewshire, having been appointed as a magistrate, met the local minister. He cracked a joke with the minister that, as he was riding on horseback, he was more ambitious than his master, Jesus, who was content to ride on an ass. The minister replied, 'They canna be gotten noo, they've a' been made Justices o' the Peace.'

Another similar appointment was County Keepers. These men seem to have been a type of travelling Justice of the Peace. They were keepers of a county and rode on horseback with a sword and pistols. Four constables, carrying staves or batons, attended them on foot. Robert Scott (Rob the Laird) held this post in Peebles, Selkirk and Roxburgh, while Patrick Gillespie, a gipsy chief, held it in Fife in 1812. He and his gipsy companions were sworn into office at Peebles Town Hall.

Places of Judgment

Place-names indicate where courts were held and judgment passed out-of-doors centuries ago. Barons' courts were held on Baron's Hill, now often shortened to Barnshill; Mute, Moot or Mote hill, mute meaning a plea is another popular name; Court hill – Corsehill, Stewarton being a corruption of this; Law park or muir; Towe hill and Tom a' Mhoid – 'hill of the assembly in Gaelic' – are also indications of an area having been used as a meeting place for the trying of criminals. Later courts were held in or near a castle, perhaps on the castle hill. Other judicial points were called Sheriff's Know or Knowehill.

HIGHWAY ROBBERY

Highwaymen have been romanticised out of proportion to their behaviour, which was usually based on greed and not on the idea of robbing the rich to give to the poor. The term is almost a misnomer as the state of the roads in Scotland was atrocious until the advent of General Wade's roads after the 1745 Jacobite Rebellion, and later the Turnpike Acts which led to metalled roads from the 1750s onwards.

However, those carrying money about their person, especially after a successful day at a fair or tryst, were often attacked by ruffians as they made their way homewards. There was often only moonlight to light the rough paths and tracks through woods, which were best avoided at night. Not all robberies took place at night and many footpads were bold enough to attack by daylight. By haunting lonely areas they were able to escape quickly, either on foot or on horseback. In the late seventeenth century, there was an upsurge in this crime and reports of it continue into the nineteenth century.

Highway robbery crime was even carried out by members of the landed gentry and officers of the Crown. One of the earliest known robbers was Bertram de Shotts who, in the fourteenth century, terrorised the area around Shotts. By public proclamation the Government notified that whoever should apprehend him or bring him to justice should be rewarded by the gift of his lands.

John Muirhead, Laird of Muirhead, set out during daylight hours to surprise de Shotts and on the east side of the Kirk o' Shotts ran him through with a sword. Muirhead cut off the highwayman's head and took it to King Robert II, at Edinburgh. The king awarded him the lands of Lauchope and the honour of adding three acorns and two hands clasping a sword to his coat of arms.

Andrew Cockburn set out on horseback in the seventeenth century to deliver official letters between Cockburnspath and Haddington. He had reached Hedderwick Muir when he was attacked by two masked men. They appeared to be well-dressed and riding fine horses. They held pistols to his head and demanded the packets, the black-box and by-bag which he was carrying. James

Seton and John Seaton of Garlton House, Haddington, were later accused. Robbing the post was punishable by death and all the accused's goods and gear could be forfeited to the Crown.

In December 1692 a drover, William McFadyen, had had a successful day at Dumfries and had set out for home carrying £150 in his pocket. All seemed quiet but just as the sun rose, he was joined by two well-dressed men. One of them was mounted on a dark-grey horse and wore a coat of scarlet with gold buttons. McFadyen noticed that he had a wart as big as a nut above one of his eyes and that the pinkie of his left hand was permanently folded towards the palm.

The other, probably his servant, was also on a fine horse and carried a gun. This man turned to McFadyen after half a mile and said that they were going through the moor and that he should accompany them. He refused and the servant hit him over the head with the butt-end of a gun. The master whipped out a pistol and threatened to use it if McFadyen would not agree to go with them. Although he was wounded, they forced him to travel about a quarter of a mile before cutting loose his saddle bag and taking his money.

The Privy Council, angered at the growing number of robberies, told Sir James Leslie, commander-in-chief of His Majesty's Forces, to find out if there was any officer in his regiment who fitted the description given by McFadyen. Sergeant Fae was appointed to search. His investigation revealed other footpads, two of whom were convicted. For his success he was awarded £10 and promised £5 for every subsequent footpad he might discover. An instruction was also sent to the Earl of Leven to enquire amongst the officers who came from Flanders to find recruits for the armies of the King of Denmark and Gustavus Adolphus, but the man was never identified.

Another group who found highway robbery a useful way of adding to their income was the gipsies. An army officer, riding from Linlithgow to Stirlingshire, was crossing the Sandyford Burn when a man caught the horse's bridle and demanded money. The horseman fired his pistol at the robber who fell to the ground. He did not let go of the bridle and was dragged along. The assailant of the officer was the captain of the local band of gipsies. Members of his band carried him home and the next day announced that he had died suddenly of a fever.

Sometimes gipsies would give protection to those who did them a favour. Robert McVitie was at a fair at Broughton, in 1726, when he was approached by Robert Baillie, whom he recognised as a leader of the gipsies. Baillie asked him for a loan of two guineas.

Unwilling to cross such a man McVitie obliged and, in return, Baillie gave him a brass token which he was to show to anyone who attempted to molest him.

One night, as he travelled from Elvanfoot to Moffat, he was overtaken by two suspicious looking characters. They turned and challenged him to give up his money. As he put his hand into his pocket he felt the token and, unsure whether or not they were gipsies, warily let it be seen. One of the men seized it and examined it by the light of the moon. When he was satisfied he returned it and let McVitie pass on his way unharmed. Some time later Robert Baillie returned the loan with one guinea interest.

Alexander MacDonald and his brother-in-law, James Jamieson, were notorious gipsy robbers who, like Robin Hood, enjoyed robbing the rich to give to the poor. They also gave tokens to those with whom they were friendly. When they needed to visit the country areas, the butchers of Linlithgow carried these, as did the local shoemakers when they travelled around the markets. They were eventually turned in by a member of their own band and sentenced, in 1770, to be hanged at Linlithgow Bridge.

The authorities feared that an attempt at rescue would be made when the men were being transferred from the Tolbooth in Edinburgh to the jail at Linlithgow. They posted all the Rifle Volunteers of West Lothian along the route. Great crowds of people gathered from far and wide. The prisoners were bound hand and foot in irons and placed in a cart accompanied by the Sheriff-Depute on horseback. The officers of court were armed with broadswords and marched on either side. The prisoners were housed overnight in the jail and taken at three o'clock the next afternoon to be hanged at the end of Linlithgow Bridge. McDonald seemed to expect to be rescued stating that 'the hemp was not grown that would hang him'. However, when he realised that it would not happen he turned to John Livingston, the hangman, saying, 'Now, John, don't bungle your job.'

Their nephews, Charles and James Jamieson, attacked and robbed the post-boy guarding the Kinross mail when he stopped at an inn for refreshment. Their mother had wanted them to attack him on the road and kill him but they disagreed. The highwaymen escaped but were traced to a house near Stirling. One of them attempted to escape by climbing up the chimney, the other attacked an officer with a knife. They were secured and placed in irons. They were executed on 18th December, 1786.

The *Edinburgh Evening Courant* reported, on 10th December, 1729, that a gentleman travelling south was attacked on Soutra Hill by two men armed with bayonets. They ordered him to surrender his purse. The gentleman put his hand beneath his jockey-coat as though assenting, then he whipped out a pistol and asked his attackers whether that or his money appealed to them more. They begged that he spare their lives since they had never robbed anyone except another country gentleman an hour before, when they had obtained six shillings and eight pence (about thirty-four pence). The gentlemen offered them a choice: either they receive his bullets or they cut off each other's right ear, which is what they proceeded to do.

During 1756, an Edinburgh lady who travelled regularly to London in her own carriage insisted that her manservant rode beside it with a pair of loaded pistols and a sword at the ready, while she also had a pair of pistols to hand. Once, the carriage was approached by footpads but she waved the pistols at them and they fled, leaving her unharmed.

There were many rogues living in the Highlands. In the eighteenth century, when vagrants were being banished throughout the Lowlands, after having been burned on the lobe of their ear, they gravitated north and formed themselves into bands who attended fairs. They watched the people enjoying themselves and noted what they bought, then at night they followed them onto the lonely ways, attacked them at knife-point and robbed them. If they were caught they were hanged. There was a spate of highway robberies in the late eighteenth century when men and women were dragged from their coaches, knocked down and stripped, not only of their wealth but of their clothes, which the robbers later pawned.

Several people were attacked around Glasgow in the early years of the nineteenth century. In 1814, two Englishmen, William Higgins and Thomas Harrold, were caught and sentenced to be hanged. Unfortunately, at that time the position of city executioner was vacant and they had to send to Edinburgh for a man to do the deed at a cost of £40 sterling.

David Loch was a carter in Biggar. On the Wednesday afternoon of 23rd November, 1814, he was asked to return a hired horse to Edinburgh. He set out between one and two o'clock with four pound notes, twenty shillings of silver and a tobacco pouch made from calfskin, which he had repaired by putting a stitch in a slit in the inside. He also had a twopenny loaf.

He had almost reached his journey's end and was riding down the hill towards Morningside when, at the entrance to the Hermitage of Braid known as the Brigs o' Braid, two men approached and asked him for the time. 'I dinna ken,' he replied, 'but it'll likely be aboot sax.' They seized his horse's bridle, dragged him to the ground and tossed him into a ditch. He called out 'Murder! Murder!' and one of the men hit him across his head with the butt of his pistol to quieten him. Loch had broken several ribs and was in pain, but the man threatened that if he did not keep quiet he would shoot him.

Andrew Black, a blacksmith, and his companion, Samuel Payne, were walking towards Edinburgh when they heard Loch's cries. They stopped to investigate and the two men ran off across the fields. One of them turned and fired a pistol at them. They found David Loch in the ditch and helped him to a nearby house.

The homes of Thomas Kelly and Henry O'Neil at the West Port were searched and the booty of several robberies was found. They appeared on three charges at the High Court of Justiciary. The first of robbing William Welsh, schoolmaster of Stenton in November 1814, secondly with attacking James Leigo and Thomas Wilson, farm servants at Haddington, and lastly with attacking David Loch. His purse was shown in evidence and he was asked if he could prove that it belonged to him. He described the stitch he had recently sewn into it. The Lord Justice-Clerk pronounced doom and, because the crime of highway robbery was growing, he declared that they would be taken and hanged at the spot where the attack took place.

Although it was snowing heavily, people walked the three miles from the city centre to view the hanging on 25th January, 1815. The procession headed out of Edinburgh at a quarter past one, led by the high constables and supported by the city officers carrying halberds. They were followed by magistrates, church ministers and two priests – since the men were Irish Catholics – the hangman and the criminals in a horse-drawn cart. The men were hung in chains as an example to others; later their bodies were cut down and taken to be buried in the Greyfriars churchyard. The gallows was erected in the road set into two stones, which can still be seen.

William Gordon, an Irishman, thought that he had managed to get away with murder. In November 1821 he was refreshing himself at Canonbie when he met a young pedlar. By telling him that he knew of a shortcut to Moffat he enticed the young man to a lonely place where he attacked and robbed him, leaving him for dead. He then travelled north. The case was reported in the newspapers and a man sitting in a hotel at Nairn read it and gasped as the man fitting the description appeared before his eyes. Astonished, he called his name and, caught off guard, Gordon turned. He was arrested and taken to Dumfries for trial.

William Thomson was executed at Dalkeith in 1827. Originally, he was accused of robbing a farmer returning from Dalkeith market the previous November. His brother, John, and another labourer, John Frame, were tried as accomplices and sentenced to death.

However, since they had been kept in the Calton Jail in Edinburgh for several weeks, they received a reprieve. On 1st March, at Dalkeith, the large crowd, who relished a hanging and treated it as an entertainment, watched as William Thomson swung on the gibbet.

On a cold, blustery day in the early months of 1831, the driver of the Glasgow to Edinburgh coach, Jock McMillan, had only one outside passenger, James Smith, a messenger. His luggage, an old tin box, was secured in the boot. Two workmen came aboard between Coatbridge and Airdrie. They travelled on the top outside seats of the coach and passed the time cleaning a greasy chain. A gentleman and his companion, a young lady wrapped in ermine against the snowy wind, joined the coach a few miles after Airdrie for the short journey to Armadale Toll. The two workmen left the coach at Bathgate.

On arrival at Uphall, James Smith was to exchange places with another messenger who would convey the box to Edinburgh. He asked Jock if they might just open the boot to check that all was well. They were astonished to find that the padlock had been forced and that the box was empty. Entry to the boot had been forced through the wall of the coach and the £6000 being transferred by the Commercial Bank from Glasgow to Edinburgh had vanished. Suspicion fell on the two passengers and their presumed accomplices, the two workmen.

The young 'lady' had been George Davidson, clerk to the Sheriff-Substitute of Glasgow, and the 'gentleman', George Gilchrist, the owner of the coach who had known of the transfer. George Davidson escaped execution by a clever ruse planned by his parents. A religious service was requested to be held in the condemned cell of Glasgow's Tolbooth. They attacked the turnkeys and he was released from his chains and smuggled to the Broomielaw where, in disguise, he boarded a ship bound for Australia. George Gilchrist was hanged on 3rd August, 1831, the last person to be hanged for this crime in Scotland.

A song popular in the bothies and amongst the 'light-fingered brigade' was about Bold Brannan, the Dick Turpin of Scotland.

The first of my misfortunes was to list and desert;
The way for to rob, boys, I soon found the art;
Over hedges and ditches I soon found my way,
And I went a-robbing by night and by day.

As Brannan was walking on yon mountains high,
A coach with four horses he chanced to espy;
With a blunderbus alone in his hand,
He made the guard and horses at once for to stand.

As Brannan was riding up on yon mountains high,
A coach and six horses he happened to spy;
He robbed from the rich and he gave to the poor,
He's over the mountains and you'll see him no more.

But oh, do you see yon crowds a-coming,
And oh, do you see yon constables a-running,
And oh, do you see yon high gallows tree;
They're hanging bold Brannan for highway robbery.

Vagabond Songs and Ballads of Scotland,
edited by Robert Ford, 1904

A case occurred at Garscube Bridge to the north of Glasgow, in 1860, when two men set upon a traveller. One was sentenced to two years' imprisonment but the instigator received four years' penal servitude.

As roads improved and there were more varied means of travel, such as by canal and railway, which provided protection by guards and other staff, the number of cases of highway robbery fell.

ILLICIT STILLS

Whisky, usequebah, moonshine – call it what you will – was originally a fairly rough and ready drink distilled by the Scots in places where water and peat were plentiful. It was a far cry from the famous national drink which became renowned throughout the world.

All over Scotland, but especially in the Highlands, the illegal production of whisky was a growing trade in the late eighteenth century. After the Jacobite Rebellion of 1745, it replaced rum as the popular drink. One of the most popular was the unlicensed 'Ferintosh', as it was known, after the distillery of Forbes of Culloden. Forbes's licence to distil was reneged after the Jacobite Rebellion and his whisky was declared illegal. However, it or the produce of other stills flowed down the welcoming throats of the populace in ever greater amounts.

> Thee Ferintosh! oh, sadly lost,
> Scotland lament frae coast to coast;
> Now colic grips and barkin' hoast
> May kill us a',
> For loyal Forbes's charter' boast
> Is ta'en awa'.
>
> Thae curst horse-leeches o' th' Excise,
> Wha mak the whisky stells their prize!
> Haud up thy han', Deil! ance, twice, thrice!
> There seize the blinkers!
> An' bake them up in brimstane pies
> For poor damned drinkers.

Scotch Drink, Robert Burns, 1785

Illicit distillers were even more respected than smugglers and did not believe that they were committing a crime. They believed that any violence that occurred was justified as self-defence.

> The keg of smuggled whisky that had been sent to him from the 'Black Bothy' (it was really a bribe; for the wherebouts of the illicit still was well known to the shepherds), but that if it

was presented to Mr. McInroy (the minister of the parish) there would be a kind of sanctifying it to good uses.
The Wise Woman of Inverness, William Black, 1885

When a minister tackled a smuggler and questioned him about his trade, the reply was that he never allowed a man to swear at his still and he saw no harm in it. At Inversnaid, The Tea Pot Inn served illicit whisky poured from tea pots into cups. At Kilmarnock, there were twelve known stills in operation and eventually the Government put a revenue cutter on Loch Lomond. In Glenlivet, in 1787, there were reputed to be 200 stills. They were also numerous in Kintyre.

In the late eighteenth century, the MacGregors came upon an illicit still while lifting cattle in the Campsie Valley. They secured the cattle in a field and proceeded to enjoy the whisky. The local farmers from whom the cattle had been taken were watching them and, when they were drunk and many were asleep, they attacked the MacGregors and killed several of them. The cattle were rescued and the field from then on was called the Field of Blood.

The area of the Campsie hills was popular with distillers, the name Smugglers Plantin' remains. There were seven stills working there in the early nineteenth century. All materials for the stills had to be taken up on horseback. Most stills were of copper, but a few were made of tin.

Not all stills, however, were in glens; many operated in towns. In Edinburgh, 400 stills were manufacturing at this period. They were buried in the ground, often in a cellar with some form of chimney to convey the smoke away.

In 1787, it was reckoned that 300,000 gallons of distilled whisky had passed into England without a penny paid to the Customs and Excise. The practice was rife and of economic value to the farmers and crofters who carried out the trade.

Near the sea, the smugglers loved a windy day, which blew the water of the falls about and hid the smoke coming from the stills. The revenue cutters tried to detect the smoke through telescopes while they patrolled the coastline.

> The distillation of whisky presents an irresistible temptation to the poorer classes, as the boll of barley, which costs thirty shillings, produces by this process, when the whisky is smuggled, between five and six guineas.
> *A Tour in the Highlands and Western Islands*,
> John Leyden, 1800

While on a tour of the Highlands with the Lighthouse Commissioners in August 1814, Sir Walter Scott noted in his diary that, as their ship approached the the Isle of Eigg, the people seemed unfriendly until they realised that they were not revenue men. Excise officers had recently raided the nearby island of Muck seizing all the stills, the pot-stillers' goods and even confiscating the bedding of the islanders.

Smugglers, as the distributors of the illicit whisky were known, took orders for special occasions such as weddings and funerals. Tin cans filled with whisky were strapped around the waist of the delivery man. Excisemen attempted to intercept the deliveries and several of the excisemen were murdered as they carried out their duty. This encouraged others to turn a blind eye.

In 1815, the revenue cutter *Earl of Moira* was anchored off Lochranza on the Isle of Arran, where some signs of illicit stills were found. William Mason, the boatswain, launched a small boat and, with four of a crew, sailed along the coast of Kintyre and noticed some sacks on the shore. On investigation, they discovered that these contained barley; two excisemen set off to search for a still. The boat sailed on and encountered a small smack which they thought was behaving suspiciously. They recognised some of the crew as smugglers and gave chase.

The boat threw several casks overboard before heading for the nearest shore, where one of its crew seized another cask and disappeared into a wood. Mason fired a gun and demanded that the boat be handed over in the name of the king. A fight began and Mason and his crew were injured with cutlasses. The smuggler on shore had been joined by woodcutters. Mason had to give in and head out to sea without a single cask of the whisky he needed for evidence.

The excisemen could search for the stills or they could try to capture the goods in transit. They would set up a watch if they believed that a consignment was on its way to the inn or nearest town. However, as the excise officers did not have a big staff and had to cover the whole of Scotland they could easily be fooled.

It was quite usual for the exciseman to pay his respects to the dead by doffing his hat as a funeral passed by. The coffin, on being unloaded at the graveyard, would then be emptied of its cargo of whisky by the 'mourners'.

The smugglers were watchful and would often change their route. Sometimes a decoy was used. They would carry some harmless cargo, such as straw, and lead their horses in the opposite direction to draw the excisemen away from the still.

Another trick was to fill bags with sawdust or other ballast to fool the 'gaugers', as the excisemen were called. One or more decoys would appear to realise that they had been seen and take to their heels carrying a sack on their back. The gaugers would give chase and be led a merry dance away from the still. This allowed their colleagues time to bury the evidence. It became a game and many miles might be covered before the gaugers gave up.

Women were also involved in this trade. They would be sent out to deliver whisky, which was concealed in bladders attached to a band around their waists and hidden by voluminous skirts. A woman, at Torrance, was folding blankets into a chest when the excise officer appeared at her door. In front of her was a flagon of whisky. She moved eagerly towards him and, as though by accident, knocked him over into the blanket chest, while her son removed the evidence. Other tales are of women filling their aprons with stones and pelting the excisemen with these to distract them while the goods were smuggled away. Excisemen sent to search could easily be frightened away by tales of infectious disease in the house.

In the two statistical accounts of Scotland, ministers record their disgust at the amount of spirits which were drunk. Many hostelries did not pay duty on all their stock and were happy to encourage the illicit distilling by purchasing from the smugglers.

There were ale-houses, often more than one in every village, where much of their stock evaded the excise tax. In 1816, in Dunbartonshire, the country areas such as Roseneath, Luss, Bonhill and the islands of Loch Lomond were home to moonshiners who supplied Glasgow inns with whisky.

'Flaskers' was the name used for the Irishmen who operated in Dunbartonshire, going as far as Arrochar for supplies. They also visited Tayside, in around 1800, to buy whisky from the crofters, who could pay their rents from the profits made from this supplementary trade. These flaskers would lead trains of ponies south laden with cans of whisky, which they sold in Glasgow for a profit. Occasionally, they were caught and imprisoned. Their goods would be forfeited and sold for revenue.

In 1787, three men were fined for the private distillation of 'aqua vitae', another name for whisky, at the Sheriff Court at Kirkintilloch, while John Liddel was also fined for assaulting an excise officer.

Officers of excise at Troon seized, near Irvine, a still at work of about 45 gallons content, and destroyed upwards of 400 gallons of mash, some malt, a few gallons of low wines and about 30 gallons of yeast, with all utensils. There were seven men and three women attending the still, who made some considerable resistance, but from the determined conduct of the officers they judged it prudent to resist.

Glasgow Herald, 1st June, 1818

Act to Eliminate Illicit Distilling, 1825

The 'sma' stills at Glenlivet considered themselves superior to the Lowland distillers. After the passing of the above Act in 1825, a licence to distil whisky cost £10 for a forty-gallon still. The first licence was held by George Smith, Drumin, Glenlivet, and in 1880 the High Court of Justiciary agreed that only the products from his distillery could legally be described as Glenlivet.

The Act did not manage to stop the trade entirely and for many years reports continued of seizures of stills. Sometimes the pot-stillers fled, leaving behind their utensils. In the Aberdeen area, in 1886, an excise officer discovered a large enterprise, including casks and tubs of fermenting malt, the remains of the still and a spy-glass. Warning of his approach must have been given and they were abandoned.

In Glen Quaich near Corriemuckloch Inn, an exciseman surprised several crofters who were transporting whisky south to Glasgow. In panic, they buried the casks in a peat bog and ran away to hide in the glen. Since the exciseman was on his own he could do little to stop them and he had lost the evidence against them. This was a common practice and, in many places, when bogs were being dug for roads or canals years later, perfectly drinkable whisky was found, much to the delight of the navvies. As late as 1907, in Ross-shire, five stills were found. Some of the utensils were hidden in a bank of peat.

At Campsie, in 1822, Dougal, the Ranger, ambushed a smuggler. He was attacked at Lennoxtown later in the day by overzealous smugglers and, in the end, he was murdered and buried at the side of the Crow Road.

There was a double smuggle when malt was run to the illicit stills by wherries landing along the Clyde coast. The deed was done during the hours of darkness. On occasions, the runners were captured and taken to jail in either Greenock or Dumbarton. In 1820, fifteen men were caught and placed in the tolbooth at Dumbarton. A gentlemen came to inspect the jail and was astonished at the respectability of the prisoners. He left money to treat them to a dinner of broth, beef and potatoes, ironically washed down by a dram of whisky.

No social occasion was worth its salt if there was a lack of whisky, including wetting the newborn baby's head or a tinker's wedding.

> The drink gaed dune before their drooth,
> That vexed baith mony a maw and mooth,
> It damped the fires o' age and youth,
> And every breast did sadden, O;

Till three stout loons flew ower the fell,
At the risk o' life, their drooth to quell,
And robbed a neebourin' smuggler's stell,
To carry on the waddin, O.

Wi' thunderin' shouts they hail'd them back,
To broach the barrels they werna slack,
While the fiddler's plane-tree leg they brak,
For playin' 'Fareweel to Whisky', O.
      Vagabond Songs and Ballads, edited by Robert Ford, 1904

KIDNAP

There are many reports of young ladies being abducted, not so much kidnapped for a ransom, but usually to be forcibly married because they were heiresses to a fortune. The 'macaronis', as young bucks were called, having lost heavily at cards or spent their allowances unwisely, had no scruples about seeking out young ladies. Ladies with even a modest inheritance would be swept off their feet, often literally, if there was no legitimate way of gaining their hand in marriage.

Marion Crichton, step-daughter of Isobel Borthwick, was sent to be educated by her uncle, Harry Stirling, at Ardoch. On a June night, in 1524, Robert Crichton, her own brother, with Patrick Graeme of Inchbrakie, led a band of armed men to abduct her, burgle the house and carry her away. For not returning her they were declared outlaws but she was never traced.

It was passion, however, which ruled the Duke of Lennox when, on 19th April, 1591, he went to Easter Wemyss in Fife and forced Lady Sophia Ruthven, daughter of the late Earl of Gowrie, onto his horse and rode all night until he arrived home where he married her in front of a priest, 'contrair the ordinance of the kirk'. Unfortunately, she died the next year.

On Sunday 10th June, 1593, a young lady, daughter and heir apparent to John Carnegie, was seized under armed guard by James Gray. He was a gentleman of the king's bed-chamber and was accompanied by Lord Hume, one of King James VI's chief courtiers. This was their second attempt at abducting her. The two men dragged her down an alley to the Nor' Loch where they crossed by boat to where ten men were waiting. They put her on a horse and galloped off.

When the Edinburgh magistrates went to Holyrood to complain to the king they found him in the company of Lord Hume and all knowledge of such an incident was denied. The magistrates left, realising that they would not find any justice at the Royal Court.

A spate of abductions followed. Margaret Hay, a girl of fourteen, was taken from her mother's house at Peebles on 14th August, 1594, by a relative, Thomas Hay. She was rescued by Cockburn of

Skirling but, instead of returning her home, he kept her for himself. Christian Johnston, a widow, was carried off from Edinburgh by Patrick Aikenhead in August 1595. The town bells were rung and she was recovered. The daughter of George Carkettle was seized in Edinburgh, in 1600, and taken to East Lothian. John Kincaid came to the Water of Leith on 17th August, 1600, and raped and took away a widow, Isobel Hutcheon. He took her to Craighouse. A party headed by the Earl of Mar was in the vicinity and threatened to burn down his house if he did not release her. Kincaid was fined 2500 merks (£1000) and a brown horse.

In September 1631, a young girl named Lady Catherine Grahame and her sister named Lady Beatrice, whose father, John, Fourth Earl of Montrose, was dead, were taken to live with their elder sister, Lilias. Lilias had married Sir John Colquhoun of Rossdhu. He was besotted with Lady Catherine and, with his valet, Thomas Carlippis, spirited her away. Her sister approached the king for help in tracing their whereabouts.

King Charles I wrote to the Earl of Strathearn demanding that they be found and Colquhoun arrested. It was generally believed that Carlippis was a sorcerer and that Sir John had been in league with witches and sorcerers for charms and incantations which were used to force his young sister-in-law to go with him. There was talk of love potions and enchanted jewellery, especially one of a gold piece set with diamonds and rubies which had magic powers. A sentence of death was passed on them in their absence and Colquhoun's estates were declared forfeited. The Presbytery of Dumbarton excommunicated Sir John, who was never traced. Whether Catherine went of her own free will or was bewitched was never discovered. Sir John's brother, Humphrey, eventually managed to regain the family estates.

Another cause of abduction, in the case of Anna Gibson, heiress of the late Alexander Gibson of Durie, was that since she was a minor she required a curator for her inheritance. On 7th May, 1668, an orphan aged eleven, she was taken to the Highlands, supposedly by Viscount Stormont, her mother's brother, to influence her choice of curator and to prevent her father's family gaining the upper hand. In order to safeguard her inheritance, it was decided by the Privy Council to make a clause stating that if any man should marry her they must pay a fine of £20,000 Scots. The Council also issued a warrant for a search to be made to find her, but no action was taken against Stormont.

On 11th February she was found and placed in Edinburgh with the family of Alexander Gibson, a clerk to the Council, until she was twelve and ready to name the curators. In August 1669, a compromise was reached between the families and members of both her mother's and father's sides were named to settle her affairs. An heiress with a large fortune, she eventually married.

The late Laird of Ayton, Berwickshire, had charged the Countess of Home with looking after his heiress, his orphaned daughter Jean, to whom he had left his entire fortune. Home of Plendergast, who had expected to be his heir, decided to marry her to a member of his family to gain what he considered to be his inheritance.

When Jean was twelve, Plendergast petitioned the Privy Council to appoint curators of her fortune. The rest of the Homes were so determined not to allow Plendergast to get his hands on her fortune that, on the appointed day in December 1677, with the agreement of the countess, Jean was taken across the border and paraded around to find someone prepared to pay them to marry her. Eventually, they brought from Edinburgh a poor relation, George Home, and he married her that day. The ceremony was conducted by an English minister.

This slighted the Scottish clergy who fined them for a clandestine marriage. They were ordered to pay 1000 merks (£100) to Plendergast, and the young couple were imprisoned in Edinburgh Castle for three months.

Sir John Johnston belonged to Fife and was serving as an officer in Ireland in 1690 when he paid his addresses to Miss Magrath of County Clare, a young lady with a dowry of £10,000. She was besotted with Johnston and, since her father would not agree to the wedding, planned to elope with him. However, her father got wind of the plot and when Johnston arrived at the meeting place, instead of his intended, there was a crowd of young men armed with cudgels who beat him mercilessly until he agreed to depart from Ireland.

He was not put off heiress-spotting and he next attempted, with Captain James Campbell and the Earl of Argyll's brother, to carry off Miss Mary Wharton, a thirteen-year-old with an annual income of £1500 and prospects of a large inheritance when she came of age. She, being a minor, lived with a guardian in London. She was seized at her guardian's house and thrust into a waiting coach drawn by six horses and taken to a rendezvous where she was forced into going through a marriage ceremony against her will. They were pursued and she was rescued in time. The Campbells escaped, but John Johnston was arrested, tried and convicted. He was executed at Tyburn in 1690.

Simon Fraser was a rogue. In 1692, when he was a captain in Lord Tullibardine's regiment, he resigned his commission in order to pursue his claim to be head of the clan Fraser. He determined to marry the heiress of Lord Lovat. Emelia was nine years of age, but was already engaged to be married to the son of Lord Saltoun. Lovat obtained the services of a gang of thugs who seized Lord Saltoun and his son and, taking them to a gibbet, threatened to hang them both if the son did not give up all rights to the hand of this young lady. They were so surprised and terrified that they agreed. Simon Fraser then set out to abduct the girl but, unable to find her, he seized her mother, the Dowager Lady Lovat.

He raped the dowager, then absconded with her and forced her into a marriage before a priest. An alarm was raised and he abandoned her and escaped to France via Skye, where he joined the Jacobite cause and received a commission. Later, he switched sides and supported King William of Orange. In his absence he was sentenced to death in Edinburgh and was seized in France and thrown into the Bastille. He eventually gained his freedom by taking Holy Orders and becoming a Jesuit priest. He lived until he was eighty when, after his trial at Westminster for being a Jacobite, he was imprisoned in the Tower of London. In April 1747, he was beheaded for high treason at Tower Hill. He was so large and ungainly that he had to be carried up the steps to the platform by three men. There was a vast crowd and several people were killed when the scaffolding collapsed.

KIRK MISCONDUCT

Vice obsessed the minds of those connected with the early Church of Scotland. They wanted to stamp it out and make everyone conform to a life of drudgery with no unseemly or frivolous behaviour whatsoever. This was a reaction to the leniency in such matters which had been allowed to develop in the latter days of Catholicism before the Reformation.

In 1581, King James VI asked for suitable people to form a Commission for Punishing Vice to combat social delinquency and petty crimes. In Glasgow, in 1581, the bailies held a court every month and appointed ten people as an Inquisition for Rottenrow, Drygate and the Cross, nine people for the Inquisition for the Gallowgate and Trongate, and six for the Inquisition for the Briggait to uphold this Act. Those found guilty of breaking these Acts could be sent to prison.

The king's interest in the efficiency of Sessions in the Kirk's disciplinary structure arose from his hopes of applying some of its features to the secular judiciary system and even of integrating the Kirk's work into the Crown's own system of criminal justice.

> The topics on which the visitor had to elicit information relate, in part, to the detection of sexual irregularities liable to disrupt social harmony: those considered to have committed adultery or incest were to be reported to the crown; so, too, were witches, unrepentant communicants, known recusants who superstitiously undertook pilgrimages to shrines of old. If convicted, all were guilty of transgressing secular as well as ecclesiastical law liable to punishment by church and state alike.
>
> *Visitation of the Diocese of Dunblane and other churches,*
> *1586–1589*, edited by James Kirk, 1984

The secular courts were also under the influence of the General Assembly of the Church of Scotland. In 1577, the statute against Sunday markets was passed. The penalty was goods being forfeited. Seven people were fined for 'slaying of flesche and working on the Sondaye, contrar the statutis' and again, in 1580, the Privy Council passed an Act against:

Disturbance of kirks in time of divine service, the holding of markets and labouring on Sunday, or playing and drinking in time of sermon, requiring householders to have Bibles and psalm books, the punishment of strong and idle beggars, and the relief of poor impotent persons.

This was a case of the law of the land enforcing the law of the Church. Magistrates were only appointed if they were also elders in their own parish, so civil offenders, such as brewers of illicit ale, could be fined 8/- Scots in the civil court and have to agree to sit on the cutty stool in their kirk for a given number of Sundays. Gossips and clypes stood in the branks, petty thieves were whipped at the market cross and placed in the stocks, and harlots, for a first offence, were carted through the town. Female thieves had their noses pinched and were branded with an 'M' for malefactor. In addition, they were often, either before or after civil trial, also forced to do penance in the kirk.

Until the Reformation, Scotland, like most of Europe, supported the Roman Catholic religion. The religious reformers made Scotland a Protestant country in the sixteenth century. The chosen system was, in the main, Presbyterian although there were pockets of Episcopalianism. A mixture of these doctrines co-existed until 1690. The Presbyterian doctrine was influenced greatly by the laws of the Old Testament of the Bible and these were adhered to in detail. The cruel punishments which were carried out in the presence of ministers and with the full authority of the Church stem from this adherence.

Each parish had its own minister, at first chosen by patronage, but later democratically chosen by the congregation. Every house had at least one Bible and access to its teachings was aided by ensuring that everyone would be taught to read in the parish school. All ages were expected to learn the catechism, on which they would regularly be tested by the minister or elders. Morning and evening worship was to be conducted by the head of each household, and the Sabbath observed by everyone as a day of rest broken only by attendance at church.

The elders were the Old Testament rulers and administrators of the law. After the Reformation, Scotland was divided into parishes and each parish church was the responsibility of the elders, always men, who made up the Kirk Session. They sat at the front of the church close to the pulpit. They ensured that vice was condemned and appointed a Session Clerk to record the minutes of their meetings. Many of these records have survived, giving a valuable resource and account of the importance which they attached to searching out, and punishing, sin.

The elders took their duties seriously, believing that they were solemnly sitting as a judicial court, seeking to elicit the truth and administer justice, and dealing with erring ones falling under the discipline of the church.

The main concerns of the Church courts, headed by the General Assembly of the Church of Scotland, were to search out moral offenders. They hunted for those who did not keep Sabbath observance, who took part in adultery, were incestuous, oppressors of children, witches, sorcerers, papists, superstitious persons, swearers, scolds, blasphemers and any other form of unnatural behaviour. These were more moral transgressions than crimes, but those who sinned in the eyes of the kirk were often ostracised more than if they had committed a secular criminal act.

The minister and the ruling elder also served on the Presbytery, the court of all the churches in the parish, in front of whom 'sinners' could be ordered to appear if the Kirk Session was not 'satisfied' that they had repented.

Because many of the leading churchmen were of the landed classes, Oliver Cromwell tore down the jougs and abolished other means of church punishment in 1653. In 1654, he abolished the General Assembly of the Church of Scotland. Cromwell also refused to permit the secular courts to uphold church punishments.

The General Assembly of the Church of Scotland was re-instated in 1690 after the Revolution and the defeat of Episcopalianism. A minister was chosen and elected by his fellow men to be Moderator of the General Assembly of the Church of Scotland for one year. The parish ministers and elders attended an annual meeting held in Edinburgh. This meeting made decisions affecting the whole country and its Court of High Commission acted as the highest church court. It set out to punish 'all that are scandalous in life, doctrine or religion . . . contumers of church discipline, blasphemers, cursers or swearers'.

There were procedures laid down by the General Assembly for the members of the Kirk Session to follow. These recorded the punishments which applied to every sinful act. The greatest fear of the ordinary person was that of being excommunicated from the Church. This was a severe punishment for it debarred the person from the 'benefit of the church'. As people were required to have references of good will from the Kirk Session for almost every important action, this curtailed their social and working life, depriving them also of the sacraments.

In 1708, an officer was appointed at Banff 'to cite all stranger servants within the paroch to bring in the testimonials to Session', *Morton Kirk Session Records*, 1708.

At Leith, the Bailie of St Anthony, a Kirk Session official, was appointed to ferret out those who broke Church laws and bring them to trial. This was challenged by the Sheriff of the County, but upheld by a higher court.

In order to be received back into the fold, the sinner had to show remorse. The phrase used to satisfy the congregation that the sinner was repenting was to say 'tongue thou lee'd'. A severe and public ritual had also to be gone through on the appointed Sunday before the morning service.

> He is to pass from his dwelling house to the Hie Kirk every Sunday at six in the morning, at the first bell, convoyed by two elders or deacons or any other two honest men, and stand at the kirk door, barefooted and barelegged, with a white wand in his hand, bareheaded, till after the reading of the text, and then in the same manner to repair to the pillar till the sermon be ended, and then go out to the door again till all pass from the kirk; and after this be received.
>
> *Glasgow Kirk Session Minutes*, 26th December, 1583

Being called 'before the Session' was an ordeal which often included public humiliation, and it was expected that repentance or regret should be shown in order to receive a rebuke and avoid further punishment. Every Sunday, members of each congregation were forced to repent of their sins. They were called by name and rebuked by the minister who read out details of their lapse from accepted behaviour and crimes against God.

The pillar, or pillory, was a wooden platform raised almost to the height of the pulpit. It could hold eight to ten people at once and was often filled. In some churches it was a cutty stool or stool of repentance on which the 'sinner' had to sit in front of the congregation.

> The dreaded Sunday morning came, and the delinquent kept an appointment from which there was no escape. The stool of repentance, a substantial piece of church furniture, made of tough ash or oak, and large enough to accommodate more than one person, if necessary, was placed in front of the pulpit. Arrayed in a covering of unbleached sackcloth, the offender was brought in from the session-house by the beadle, and ordered to mount the stool in the face of the assembing congregation.
>
> *The Auld Kirk and Its Worthies*, Dean Ramsay, 1912

Bessie Ruchat, the wife of a miller, summonsed Janet Hogg of Lenzie, in 1579, before the Kirk Session for slander, whereupon

Janet had to stand for several Sundays and be rebuked. She then had to go down on her knees and beg Bessie's forgiveness. She also had to shake Bessie's hand in front of the congregation.

It was not unknown for ministers or beadles to be forced to mount the stool themselves if found guilty of false witness. In 1601, speaking ill of the dead was punishable by standing two Sundays at the pillar and fined 'at the will of the session'. Offenders were often imprisoned. In 1604, in Glasgow, Blackfriars Church steeple was made into a wardhouse for offenders. One man was incarcerated for eight days on bread and water for being a 'Kirk delinquent'.

At Dunblane, young boys were often told off for making a disturbance during the sermon and, in 1701, the treasurer was asked to supply a whip with a long handle. At Fordyce, in 1721, stones and divots of earth were dropped from the 'loft', or upstairs seats, on the people below. This led to the Court of Regality passing an Act forbidding such behaviour. At Keith, in 1723, members were fined and made to sit on the cutty stool for cutting up and passing round apples during the time of the sermon.

Women were committing a crime if they sat in church with their plaids covering their heads, because the elders could not see if they fell asleep in time of sermon. If charged and found guilty of such behaviour, they could be tarred. In 1643, the Kirk Session of Monifieth provided their officer, Robert Scott, 'with ane pynt of tar' for that purpose.

On several occasions, fights broke out between worshippers, usually over the possession of a creepie stool, or over who was to lean against a pillar for comfort as they watched the sand slowly drop through the timer and listened to the long sermon. Few churches installed pews until the nineteenth century.

Many churches had jougs – iron collars with a lock attached – fixed to the outside of the church doorway. The sinner stood there before and after the time of Sunday services as the congregation was gathering and dispersing. The collar was placed around the neck of the offender. This was often the punishment meted out to slanderers.

It was often women who wore the jougs as punishment for scolding their husbands or taking part in slanging matches. In some churches, an iron tongue was attached to a collar with a headpiece. This was placed in the mouth to keep the sinner silent and it was known as the scold's bridle.

Dancing was frowned upon, especially 'promiscuous dancing', which meant a man and woman dancing together, probably because it encouraged a lack of control and self-discipline. The punishment was to stand at the pillory in the church on a given number of Sundays, be rebuked by the minister and repent in front of the congregation, promising never to do it again.

Many pipers were forced to stand 'barefoot and barelegged' at the door of the church for the offence of playing at a penny wedding. Before a wedding took place, the bridegroom had to leave a sum of money or a pawn, any valuable item, as a security against wild festivities at penny weddings and especially against promiscuous dancing taking place at the celebration. It was not until the Disruption, in 1843, that such fines were officially abolished.

Another punishable offence was to visit Holy or healing wells believing that they could cure diseases: 'Ane universall abuse rinnyng to Christis well fra all places in May time' or consulting a charmer for the same purpose.

> This day J.B. appeared in face of the congregation, confessed his sin in consulting Donald Ferguson, the charmer, for the relief of his children, whereby he cast off much of the fear of God and yielded to Satan.
>
> *Kirk Session Records*, Balfron, 1700

Other complaints were that many people still held May Day, took part in Robin Hood plays and performed rituals which were pagan in origin. Bakers were not to bake Yule bread at Christmas. Bonfires were frowned upon and adult guising became a matter to be reported to the Kirk Session by the elders.

MURDER

Murder, or the premeditated slaughter of a citizen, is a crime of so deep and scarlet a dye, that there is scarce a nation to be found in which it has not, from the earliest period, been deemed worthy of capital punishment.

The Life of Sir Walter Scott, J. G. Lockhart, 1893

Thou shalt not kill. Taking another person's life has always been considered a heinous sin. Murder can be premeditated, opportunist or accidental, but the fear of discovery or panic at the deed usually leads to the perpetrator ensuring that an alibi is available, all evidence destroyed as soon as possible and an escape route put in place.

Throughout the centuries, murder has been committed for a number of motives and in a variety of ways: personal gain, whether property, person, money or possessions; the removal of an inconvenient obstacle, often wife, husband or child, or someone who is an obstacle to the murderer gaining an inheritance or heart's desire, jealousy; taking revenge for an action, or revolting against authority for political gain.

High-fliers, rogues, psychopaths and seemingly ordinary people commit murder. A few thoroughly enjoy the plotting, planning every move, and the challenge of not being discovered, while others find that a fight or disagreement simply gets out of control and are astonished to find that they have killed someone.

Various methods have been used. Poisoning was popular, while stabbing, bludgeoning, strangling, suffocating, shooting, garrotting and arson, have all been effective. (Poison is dealt with in a separate chapter, see pp. 159-167.) Detectives, in the modern sense, did not appear until the late eighteenth century and murderers were usually caught red-handed, by chance or through enquiries by those close to the victim.

On occasions, there have been miscarriages of justice and people have been blamed, even hanged, in error. Circumstantial evidence can lead to the wrong conclusions. Forensic science was still in its infancy in the mid-nineteenth century and took many years to become acceptable as evidence in court. Nowadays it is the main method of detection.

Blunt Instruments

Many murderous weapons are described in court as 'blunt instruments' to distinguish them from sharp or body-piercing instruments. Murderers could find solid items in any household which would, if the blow was severe enough, cause death.

The Arran Murder

Two young men interested in hillwalking met in Rothesay at the Glasgow Fair in 1889. Edwin Rose from London was staying with other friends at the Glenburn Hydro, while John Laurie, having adopted the alias of John Annandale, was in digs at Port Bannatyne. Laurie and Rose and two others decided to visit the Isle of Arran and sailed on the teetotal steamer, the *Ivanhoe*. Laurie and Rose decided to stay on and climb Goatfell while the other two returned to Rothesay. They organised digs and set off. Only Laurie returned, slept the night and took off early in the morning without paying his bill.

When Rose failed to arrive home in London, his family were worried and one of his brothers arrived in Arran to find out what had happened to him. On 4th August, the body of Edwin Rose was discovered in a cairn. He had been hit on the side of his head with a stone and severely beaten around the head and face and was hardly recognisable.

Laurie played games with the press, sending letters from Liverpool and Aberdeen but he was discovered near Hamilton and arrested and charged with the murder. In his defence at the trial in Edinburgh, in November 1889, he insisted that Rose had fallen heavily. However, Rose had been robbed and his body concealed, which did not suggest that he had fallen.

Laurie was sentenced to be hanged at Greenock, much to the dismay of the officials there who had to hire a black flag and flagpole, gallows from Glasgow and James Berry, the Bradford hangman. Two days before the execution, Laurie was reprieved and sent to Perth Penitentiary. He died in Perth Criminal Asylum in 1930.

Joseph Hume

Joseph Hume was a deserter from Fort George who found lodgings near Elgin with John Smith in 1908. He repaid the kindness by murdering Smith with a hammer, then robbing his house of money and a gold watch and other items. He ran off, locking the door behind him. Hume tried to pawn the watch in Edinburgh but the pawnbroker checked it with the police. He again moved on but was arrested in Stirling. He was tried at Inverness and sentenced to be hanged. His was the first execution there for seventy years and, as a concession to the local people who had lost their taste for witnessing hangings, the Home Secretary allowed the tolling of the bell to be cancelled but the black flag was hoisted as soon as the deed was carried out within the walls of Porterfield Prison.

The Railway Murder

Bishopbriggs was a small village when the Glasgow to Edinburgh railway line was constructed. In 1841, there were many Irish labourers working as navvies. John Green was murdered by being hit on the head; three men – Dennis Doolan, Patrick Reeding and James Hickie – were accused of the deed. James Hickie was found as being 'art and part' involved and received mercy, but the other two were sentenced to be hanged at Crosshill.

A crowd of 75,000 lined the route from the jail at Glasgow Green by the old Tolbooth at the foot of High Street along the Inchbelly Turnpike, which came over Balgray Hill, past Huntershill, the home of the Reformist, Thomas Muir, then to the spot at Crosshill, Bishopbriggs, where the gallows had been built. Guns were placed at the site in case of trouble. Militia and police accompanied the procession.

The men were comforted by Roman Catholic priests who rode with them in a cart. The magistrates rode in carriages and the hangman, the old and tottery John Murdoch, in another cart. The crowd were silent as the bolt was shot. The bodies hung for a few hours, then were taken down and returned to the jail for burial.

James Robertson

James Robertson was a Glasgow policeman, aged thirty-three, who was having an affair with Catherine McClusky, a woman from the Gorbals. She was aged forty and was found dead on a piece of waste ground on 28th July by a taxi driver. She appeared to have been run over. A hit-and-run attack was suspected but lack of clues puzzled the police.

It was deduced that she had been hit with a blunt instrument before being run over several times. Investigations revealed that the police constable had been driving a stolen car and had left his post. His story of having accidentally run over her body by chance was revealed as a pack of lies. A blood-stained cosh was found at his apartment. He was hanged on 16th December in Barlinnie, the only Scottish policeman hanged for murder.

Margaret Tindal or Shuttleworth

Margaret Tindal, previously a nursery maid, obtained employment
with Sergeant Johnston who kept a tavern in Montrose. There she
met and married Henry Shuttleworth, a marine from Birmingham.
In 1815, they returned to Montrose where they ran a shop selling
spirits; Mrs Shuttleworth doing her best to drink the profits. In a
letter to a friend, Henry let it be known that he often feared for his
life because of his wife's violent drinking bouts and that he was
considering returning to England alone.

On the morning of 28th April, 1821, Henry Shuttleworth's dead
body was found covered in blood. His skull was fractured and his
scalp had an open wound. Mrs Shuttleworth alerted her neighbour
that her husband had fallen down the stairs. The maid, Catherine
McLeod, gave evidence that her mistress threw pokers and tongs
at her husband when she was drunk. They often quarrelled and
Mrs Shuttleworth regularly broke the window with her fist.

Dr Crabb, Henry Shuttleworth's physician, when questioned
in court, said that such injuries could only have been caused by a
blow to the head and not by a fall. However, no blood was found
on the poker. There was no sign of forced entry and nothing
appeared to have been stolen.

The Perth Court found Margaret Shuttleworth guilty of
murder, and she was taken to the prison to be fed on bread and
water. She was then transferred to Forfar jail in a gig. Although
she was warned not to disclose who she was, she announced at
the first place they stopped that she was 'the wifie that had killed
her man'. She had a breakfast of three basins of tea, buttered toast
and two eggs. When she arrived at the jail she was presented with
the customary shilling.

She still had in her possession a gold watch which she traded
for strong drink. She had supporters on the outside who felt that
she was innocent and that all the evidence was circumstantial.

The hangman came from Aberdeen, for a fee of £10, and he
charged an extra £2 because there was a delay. There were around
4000 people gathered, including children. Mrs Shuttleworth arrived
at the scaffold, which was erected in front of the jail, on 20th
September, 1821, and was hanged, still protesting her innocence. 'I
loved my husband as I loved my life' were her last words.

Her body was taken to Dundee and across the Firth of Tay by
ferry, then on across the Firth of Forth to Newhaven where it was
conveyed to the dissecting rooms of Dr Munro and a receipt
received from the janitor.

Sharp Instruments

Knives and body-piercing instruments have always been easily obtainable and not difficult to conceal about a person. Many whose trade involves precise cutting have been tempted to exercise their skills on humans.

The Butcher

John Buchanan was a butcher in Glasgow and a rogue who enjoyed dog fights. In 1818, some of his associates had been charged with theft and the Crown had a young witness, Anne Duff. Buchanan went to her lodgings in the Bridgegate and left her for dead after attacking her with his butcher's knife. He then joined his friends at a tavern and boasted about 'sorting her out'. He even entertained them with songs, as was his wont. The girl, however, was still alive and managed to drag herself to the office of the Procurator Fiscal in the jail at Glasgow Green and named Buchanan as her attacker. She died on the 21st October, 1818.

Buchanan was incarcerated in the Tolbooth from then until April 1819 before he was tried. The fleshers, as the butchers were called, had taken up a subscription and had secured Francis Jeffrey, who later became Lord Advocate in 1832, as the defender. Buchanan's friends had also attempted to tamper with the landlady of the girl, a Mrs Miles, to prevent her giving evidence. The prisoner was taken to Edinburgh for trial at the High Court on 7th June, 1819, but the trial was delayed and John Buchanan was granted bail on a bond of £60.

> He went dancing and whistling about in the markets as if nothing in the least degree injurious to him had occurred. In fact he became perfectly callous and hardened in crimes of a lesser nature; but his neck, though he did not think it, was still in danger.
>
> *Old Reminiscences of Glasgow and the West of Scotland*, Vol 2, Peter Mackenzie, 1890

Anne Duff's fiancé complained about the continued delay and a date was set for trial at Glasgow on 27th September, 1819. Buchanan's friends advised him to slip bail and disappear but he had arranged betting on a cockfight at Dumbarton and went there instead. His execution took place on Wednesday 17th November, 1919, more than a year after the murder.

Thomas Young, the hangman, was a neighbour of the prisoner. Under Scottish law, should the executioner be unable to perform the deed, it befell the youngest bailie, who by this time was in a sweat, to pull the bolt.

Buchanan's eyes were bandaged.
'Tammas? Is that you?' Buchanan asked.
'Aye, it's me.'
'Are you ready?'
'Quite ready.'
Buchanan then flung the handkerchief to indicate his readiness. Thomas Young drew the bolt. The body was given for dissection.

Cash paid 16 officers attending the Execution	£3.4.0
4 officers sitting up with prisoner the night previous	12.0
4 officers on the scaffold	1.4.0
Thomas Young, executioner's fee	1.1.0
Cartage of corpse to College in terms of sentence	5.0
	£ 6.16.0

City Chamberlain's Accounts, Glasgow,
19th November, 1819

James Mackcoull

James, or Jem, Mackcoull was a habitual criminal very fond of picking pockets all over the United Kingdom. He came to Edinburgh, docking at Leith in 1805, and found lodgings in Edinburgh's Canongate, where he told everyone that he was a Hamburg merchant.

In the course of his occupation, William Begbie, porter of the Leith branch of the British Linen Bank, carried banknotes to and from the head office in Tweeddale Court. In the late afternoon of 13th November, 1806, a little girl was sent to the well there for water. She tripped at the foot of the stairs and screamed as she found the body of a man with a knife sticking out of its back. The body was identified as that of William Begbie and there was no trace of the £4000 which he had been carrying.

Mr Denovan, an early detective and former Bow Street runner, was then Superintendent of Leith Police. He knew of Mackcoull and became suspicious of him when two men strolling in Belle Vue Gardens, a favourite haunt of Mackcoull, found a packet embedded in a wall; the notes of higher value totalled £3000, which tallied with those stolen from the British Linen Bank. After the notes were discovered, Mackcoull disappeared from Edinburgh and was believed to be in Dublin.

In July 1811, two confederates of Mackcoull, French and Huffey White, used duplicate keys to rob, with Mackcoull, the Paisley Union Bank in Glasgow of £20,000. They set out for London with the spoils. Huffey White was seized in London and some of the money was recovered. In his possession were several items useful to a burglar, papers belonging to Mackcoull and a box of skeleton keys. Mackcoull returned to Glasgow, but the bank failed to prosecute within sixty days and he was released. He then set up in Glasgow as a broker under the name of James Martin. He even used stolen money, some of which was traced in 1813 after he was recognised by Denovan. However, he could not be tried twice for the same offence and he was again free.

Eventually a charge was brought against him. He was tried at the High Court of Justiciary but the verdict was 'not proven'. He died in 1820 of natural causes. Denovan discovered that a Bow Street runner, Sayer, was involved with Mrs Mackcoull and between them they had received a large share of Mackcoull's profits. This explained why Sayer refused to come north to testify against him.

Many years later Mr Denovan met a sailor who had been in Edinburgh on the night of William Begbie's murder. The sailor had seen both Begbie with his parcel and Mackcoull, the latter shadowing the former. He gave a description of the man who ran from the close at Tweeddale Court that night and it fitted Mackcoull. He had boarded ship the next day and did not know of the later events or that he had seen a murderer close-up.

James Mackean

Every week Mr Buchanan took money from the Glasgow bank to his factory at Lanark to pay out wages. James Mackean, a shoemaker, used this knowledge to stage a robbery. He struck up a friendship and invited Buchanan to spend an evening at his house. As was the custom of the time, Mackean opened his Bible to begin evening worship, then moved behind Buchanan who was writing something down, clapped a hand over Buchanan's eyes and, with a stroke, drew an open razor across his throat, almost severing his head from his body.

At Mackean's trial on 12th December, 1796, even though the evidence pointed to a planned attack, the razor having been attached securely to an iron bolt to give it strength, this church elder maintained that he had had a sudden divine passion which incited him to do the deed. He was executed on 25th January, 1797.

Jessie McLachlan

Sandyford was a middle-class area of Glasgow's west end. Here, in a mansionhouse in 1862, John Fleming senior, aged eighty-two, lived with his son and his family. They left their house at Dunoon on the Clyde coast, leaving him with their thirty-five-year-old servant, Jessie MacPherson, whom he admired. On John junior's return, he found Jessie dead in her basement room, her head having been chopped off with a meat cleaver. A chest had been forced open and items strewn on the floor.

The police decided that the murder had taken place in another room and the body dragged to her room. A blood-stained footprint was found on the passage floor. At first John Fleming the elder was suspected of the murder. However, some of the items turned up at a pawnbroker's, having been pledged by a Jessie McLachlan under a false name. The footprint in the passage also turned out to be hers. She was then arrested.

Her alibi was that she was a friend of the dead woman and visited her at Sandyford Place where she had seen Jessie MacPherson drinking with Mr Fleming senior. On the night in question they had run out of whisky and she had agreed to go out and buy some but could not find a shop open. On her return she found her friend, half-naked in her room, blood pouring from wounds which were the result of Fleming beating her with a cleaver. Mr Fleming had sworn her to secrecy and had asked her to pawn the goods since he needed the money.

He had also threatened to involve her in the murder if she refused to make it look like a robbery. Her friend had told her that 'the auld deevil' wouldn't leave her alone. Despite this, and the fact that Mr Fleming senior had been previously reported to the Kirk Session for irregularities, he was set free. She was sentenced to death but then reprieved and was imprisoned at Perth. The Flemings were forced to leave the area as public opinion was against them.

Peter McLean

Thomas Maxwell was a miner at a Bathgate pit who was unfortunate to be drunk when he met up with Peter McLean, his wife and their lodger, Mr Mansefield. All were of a different religious persuasion. Harsh words were passed and stones thrown before Peter McLean pulled out a knife and stabbed Maxwell to death.

At the trial for murder, the verdict on Mrs McLean was 'not proven' although the knife was found in her possession, whilst Mansfield received a sentence of two years' imprisonment for assault. Peter McLean, however, was sentenced to hang at Linlithgow on 2nd February, 1857. William Calcraft, the London hangman, was sent for and the scaffold was borrowed from Edinburgh. The day of execution was like a holiday in the town, with a large crowd ready to enjoy the sight. He has the honour of being the last man hanged in West Lothian.

Jealousy

Robert Balfour

Robert Balfour, Master of Burley, was infatuated with Miss Robertson, his sister's governess. His parents dismissed her and sent him on a tour of France and Italy to 'clear his mind' but before he departed he swore that should she marry anyone else, he would kill them on his return. Miss Robertson became Mrs Stenhouse and went to live at Inverkeithing.

  Balfour returned in 1707 and on hearing the news, headed for Inverkeithing and shot her husband dead. He was arrested and imprisoned in Edinburgh Tolbooth but managed to escape. He was caught, tried and sentenced to death. Being of noble blood he demanded to be beheaded by the Maiden.

> It is in the form of a painter's easel, and about ten feet high; at four feet from the bottom is a cross bar on which the felon lays his head, which is kept down by another placed above. In the inner edges of the frame are grooves; in these is placed a sharp axe, with a vast weight of lead, supported at the very summit with a peg. To that peg is fastened a cord, which the executioner cutting, the axe falls and does the affair effectually without suffering the unhappy criminal to undergo a repetition of strokes, as has been the case in the common method. I must add that if the sufferer is condemned for stealing a horse or cow, the string is tied to the beast, which on being whipped, pulls out the peg, and becomes the executioner.
>
> *Tour of Scotland*, Pennant, 1769

Edward Johnstone

A fit of jealousy over the attentions paid to his partner by another man infuriated Edward Johnstone, a miner from Fife, so much that he murdered her when drunk. The jury recommended mercy but he was hanged within the walls of Perth Prison on 19th August, 1908 and the black flag was raised.

William Pirrie

A jealous husband, William Pirrie, came home from work on 18th October, 1837, in a vile temper because he had heard that a man had paid attention to his wife. He pushed the children out of the house and after locking the door he hacked their mother to death. He was sentenced to be hanged at Paisley. John Scott, the Edinburgh hangman, was borrowed for the occasion.

Miscarriage of Justice

In 1908, Miss Marion Gilchrist was eighty-two and lived in a tenement flat in the west end of Glasgow. She had recently altered her will to leave the bulk of her money to a Margaret Ferguson, who had been her servant, although some said that she was her illegitimate daughter. She had a maid, Helen Lambie, aged twenty-one, who went out on 21st December for an evening paper.

While she was out, Mr Adams, who lived in the flat below, heard a thump. When Helen returned, he was going upstairs to investigate. They arrived at the door together and were astonished on entering Miss Gilchrist's flat to be pushed aside by a man who ran down the stairs. They found her in the dining room lying on her back and covered with the blood-stained hearthrug. She had been battered but was still breathing. A doctor was called but she had died by the time he arrived. The doctor believed that she had been battered with the back legs of the dining chair though the police did not agree. Although she owned a lot of good jewellery, only one piece was missing, a crescent-shaped diamond brooch.

Circumstantial evidence linked a local dentist named Oscar Slater (also known under the name of Anderson) with the murder. With his lady friend he set out for New York via Liverpool. He had recently purchased a hammer for breaking coal and pawned a diamond horse-shoe brooch before he left. Later it was discovered that the pawn had taken place three weeks before the murder.

The police set out to extradite Slater who, having heard about the accusations, was on his way back to Scotland. He was arrested on arrival, picked out at an identity parade and found himself on trial at the High Court of Justiciary in Edinburgh and sentenced to be hanged. A reprieve was granted on 6th May, 1909, the day appointed for his execution. Instead he was sentenced to penal servitude for life.

All along, some members of the police force suspected that a relative of Miss Gilchrist, not Slater, was guilty. They were, however, blaming the wrong relative, although the one they suspected had been involved in the plot. It was revealed that the Procurator Fiscal for Lanarkshire was a close friend of the brother of one of the relatives. Several witnesses, such as Mr Adams, the first to examine the body, were not called. There were suggestions of a deliberate set-up of Oscar Slater and a cover-up of the truth.

The Charteris family, Miss Gilchrist's closest relatives, were also covering up for someone – a man named Wingate Birrell. Like Margaret Ferguson, Birrell was thought to be Miss Gilchrist's illegitimate child. This would have given him the perfect motive as it was thought that the intention of the intruder had been to obtain the altered will.

Wingate Birrell is supposed to have died in London, of tuberculosis, in 1909. Since hospital records are sealed for one hundred years, his case notes cannot be examined until 2009. It has also been suggested that his death certificate was a fabrication and that he in fact emigrated, in 1909, to New Zealand under a false name

Oscar Slater was released in November 1927 but his conviction was not quashed until 1928. Two anonymous letters, sent to the Secretary of State for Scotland in 1909, only became publicly available in 1988; it was the second of these which brought about his reprieve. Officially, the murderer of Miss Marion Gilchrist is still person or persons unknown.

Pleas of Insanity

Insanity seemed a good excuse to many men when driven to murder their wife. Some of those who made such a plea were unlucky as it did not save their skin. Thomas Fergusson murdered his wife, in 1881, then pled insanity. Lord Deas recommended a plea of culpable homicide but the jury found him guilty of murder and he was hanged. In 1902, Patrick Leggett of Glasgow boasted that he would kill his estranged wife and would not hang. He stabbed her then jumped into the River Clyde at Whiteinch but was pulled out to face charges. He pled insanity but he was hanged at Duke Street Prison on 10th November, 1902. Two years later an ice-cream merchant was sentence to be hanged at Ayr after murdering his wife and family, but his sentence was reprieved on the grounds of 'extreme provocation'.

Shooting

John Merrett

Bertha Merrett died in Edinburgh on 1st April, 1926. A few weeks earlier she had been shot. It was discovered that for some time her son, John, had been forging her signature and spending her money unwisely. The case was found 'not proven' but he was imprisoned for forgery and served twelve months. It was, however, as a confidence trickster that he succeeded abroad and, under the assumed name of Ronald Chesney, duped many people into parting with their money.

He posed in many guises but mainly assumed the identity of a swaggering ex-naval officer. During his twenty-seven years in exile he committed several murders as and when the need arose. He returned to the United Kingdom in 1954 and sought out his wife who was living in London. He proceeded to drown her in her bath then battered his mother-in-law to death. Afterwards he fled to Germany and took his own life by shooting himself. His arms were dismembered by the German authorities and sent to England for forensic analysis. They are exhibited in the Black Museum at Scotland Yard.

Alfred John Monson

In 1898, a self-styled gentleman, Alfred Monson, managed to con people into lending him money and set himself up as Laird of Ardlamont, Tighnabruaich. In his wife's name, he took out insurance on Cecil Hamborough, a friend of the family and perhaps her lover. Monson and Hamborough were out shooting when there was an accident and Cecil Hamborough was shot dead. Monson was charged but a verdict of not proven was given. He later served five years' penal servitude.

William Smith

A young farmer, William McDonald, set out for St Fergus on the afternoon of Saturday 19th November, 1853, after saying to his mother that he was going to meet his friend Dr William Smith. He did not return home, so the next morning his brother walked to St Fergus to look for him. He found William's body in a ditch near Dr Smith's home. William had a bullet wound on his cheek and a pistol lay nearby. Robert ran to get help but the doctor was not at home. Smith implied that it was a case of suicide and when William's mother asked him if they had met the previous evening he denied that any arrangement had been made. The Procurator Fiscal was not satisfied and he called in medical assistance. These doctors told a different story and William Smith was arrested and charged with murder. He had for reasons unknown taken out two insurance policies on the life of William McDonald. The verdict of the court was 'not proven' but the insurance companies suspected fraud and refused to pay out.

Stranglers

Philip Stanfield

An aristocratic rogue and mercenary, Philip Stanfield was constantly in trouble and relied on the goodwill of his father to bail him out on numerous occasions from one continental jail after another –

Antwerp, Orleans, Brussels. Condemned to die at Treves in Prussia, he narrowly escaped the gallows and continued with his wild life, eventually returning to England to commit another crime and be imprisoned at Southwark.

Upon his release, his father welcomed him home to Newmills, East Lothian, where he married, but the villainy went on. His father's patience was exhausted and he told Philip that he was going to disinherit him in favour of his younger son, John, whereupon Philip threatened to cut his father's throat. On several occasions, and to many people, Sir James Stanfield made remarks that his family, and his son in particular, were plotting against him.

On 27th November, 1687, Sir James went to bed as usual at ten o'clock but was annoyed because Philip had refused to join in family worship or to take supper with him. Three servants, a man Thompson, his wife and another woman, were later supposed to have helped Philip remove his father's body after he had strangled him in bed. Sir James was reported missing next morning and a witness, John Topping, stated that he had seen a man watching a body swirling in a pool of the River Tyne. Estate workers were summoned and the body placed in an outhouse.

Philip stated that he had heard his father go wandering at night and had followed him but lost track of him. He feared, as did his mother, that Sir James was becoming demented and that he had committed suicide. A minister of the church who was staying at Newmills before preaching at the parish church the next day reported that he had heard a commotion during the night. However, the Lord Advocate, Sir John Dalrympyle, was suspicious and ordered the body, which had been buried at night, to be exhumed. A procession, carrying torches, attended at the graveside as the coffin was opened. The body was taken into the church and surgeons carried out a post-mortem.

By design, Philip was asked to help replace the body in its coffin. On touching his father's neck, blood spurted out and Philip was accused of the murder under an old supernatural belief used for centuries and known as 'ordeal by touch'. This belief was that if a corpse was touched by its murderer it would bleed.

At his trial in January 1688, the Prosecutor, 'Bluidy' George Mackenzie, said 'I'm to believe that after he strangled himself and broke his own neck, then he drown'd himself!' when asked by the defence to give a verdict of suicide.

Philip was charged with four crimes: treason, having drunk confusion to King James II, cursing his father and murder by strangling. He was disfigured by having his tongue cut out and burned and his right hand cut off before being hanged in chains at

Edinburgh's Gallowlea in front of a vast crowd on 24th February, 1688. Later, his hand was nailed to the east gate at Haddington.

In 1797, Sir Walter Scott doubted that anyone in 1688 could still believe in the truth of 'Ordeal by Touch', but when it is considered that witches and warlocks were then still being persecuted it is less surprising. The whole of Philip's life had a demoniacal feel to it. He prayed to the devil to take his father and cursed his father often. When a student, he is supposed to have thrown a stone at a great-grandson of John Knox when he was preaching a sermon. The minister stopped and predicted, 'There'll be more present at your death than are hearing me preach this day.'

Galloway

A young girl 'not the full shilling' was strangled in Galloway in the eighteenth century to save her lover's face. Since he was an upright man and found himself in an awkward position, he saw murder as the only way out. The sheriff, whose nickname was 'Leather-head', decided to turn detective after a footprint was found on the clay floor of the cottage in which the deed was done. The minister was asked to announce from the pulpit the day and time of the funeral and invited all the parish 'to show your detestation of such an enormous crime and to prove your innocence'. There was a great turnout at the church. The sheriff ordered the doors to be locked and the soles of the shoes of the men were examined to find the shoes which matched the footprint with a peculiar patch upon it. The murderer was caught and convicted.

Uxorocide

This is the term used for the killing of a wife by a husband.

John Kello

John Kello, a native of Linlithgow, was a minister in East Lothian. In 1570, he made some good investments and bought a piece of land in the parish of Spott. He had delusions of grandeur and felt that he had married beneath his station in life. He was stuck with a wife without a dowry and three children when he could have had the hand of the daughter of the laird. The idea that he might be better off as a widower came to him. He spread rumours that his wife felt depressed and then tried to poison her as she cared for him during a bout of illness.

'Lassie I'll no be wantin' ye
Ye'd best be restin' noo,
The Lord's restored my health tae me
I yet hae wark tae do,'
When her back is turned he takes the drug
And pours it in the stew.
Are Ye Sleepin' Mr. Kello?, Francis Merrilees, 1947

The ruse did not work so he decided to hang her before taking the morning service. He invited two parishioners to come home with him to the manse so that they would discover that 'poor Margaret' had committed suicide. Torn by his conscience at what he had done he eventually gave himself up.

The Tolbooth's down by Holyrood,
A muckle crowd is there
To hear the Minister of Spott
Offer his final prayer.
Are Ye Sleepin' Mr. Kello?, Francis Merrilees, 1947

He was tried at Edinburgh, found guilty by his own confession, and hanged in October 1570.

PIRACY AND PRIVATEERING

Pirates were those who acted without authority, who captured ships by force and who often murdered their victims. However, piracy was not considered a crime by those who took part. Many sea captains became involved in it by chance and several Scots were pirates. Privateering, on the other hand, was the official harrassment of an enemy's ships by a government's naval vessels. Prize money was then claimed from the appropriate government for carrying out this deed. There was often, in reality, little difference between the methods adopted and many lost their lives in the name of greed.

The Government was often weak and the king relied on hiring the ships of merchants for his fighting naval force. The burghs were asked to supply men for the Royal Navy as and when required, and were occasionally taxed to support naval warfare. It was not a permanent service of any great force.

Urquhart Castle on Loch Ness was given by King Robert the Bruce to Randolph, Earl of Moray. The earl was plagued by robbers so he appointed sheriffs to apprehend them. If the robbers were not caught, the sheriff had to pay the victim out of his earnings. The castle also had a fleet of ships to protect boats passing along the loch from pirates. Randolph charged a fee for this service and boat owners paid up. The pirates, realising that they would have little success, abandoned the area so some of the protectors became 'pirates' to ensure that their income remained in profit.

In the thirteenth century, Thomas Charteris killed an opponent in a duel. He escaped to France and took to being a pirate. He became known as the Red Reaver and, in 1302, was taken prisoner by William Wallace who had him pardoned. Later, he was knighted and Sir Thomas gave stalwart service to William Wallace. He retired to Lochmaben where he eventually died.

William Douglas was an illegitimate son of Archibald the Grim who, in 1387, led an expedition to the coast of Ireland to avenge raids by Irish pirates on Galloway. He burned down the town and castle of Carlingford, seized the ships in the harbour, loaded fifteen with plunder and raided the Isle of Man before returning to the safety of Loch Ryan.

Scottish ships, especially from those ports on the eastern seaboard, were harried both by the English and French ships. Complaints of attacks were regular in the fifteenth and sixteenth centuries. The parish church of Port Seton, near Tranent, was, in 1544, destroyed by English pirates who took away the bells, organ and everything which was moveable and put them on board their ships. Not content, they fired the building before sailing away. Long before this time, however, pirates from Norway had landed at Luffness to pillage the area but some of them did not leave and instead settled there. Jarron, a Norwegian name, still existed there many centuries later.

A rock known as Frenchmen's Rock stands in the bay of Borgue. By tradition, it is considered to mark the spot where French pirates landed and carried off the silver plate from the old parish church of Senwick. In the Kirk Session Records of Wigton from the early eighteenth century an entry is recorded: 'To two men who had been taken by the pirates - 8/-'. The firths of Forth and Tay were haunts of pirates. If they were caught, they were hanged. Towns often employed a sea captain to chase the pirates and, on occasions, the townspeople were so angry at the harrassment that local men joined forces, received a commisssion from the king, and went after the pirate ships themselves.

In 1491, an English ship had been terrorising the merchant ships which traded with Holland, Belgium and Scandinavia. Their cargoes were valuable hides, wool and salt herring. The merchants often sailed with their ships and they complained to King James IV about these attacks by the English. The king appointed Sir Andrew Wood of Largo to fit out his ships with adequate men, food and weapons. the *Yellow Caravel* and the *Flower* set sail and met up with the pirate ships of the English off Dunbar.

There were five English ships, all well equipped, but the Scots won the fight and brought the crews to Leith as prisoners. King Henry VII of England was furious at the action of Sir Andrew Wood and offered a reward of £1000 for his capture, alive or dead.

Stephen Bull took up the challenge and sailed north to await Sir Andrew's return from Flanders. To pass the time, he harrassed Scots fishing boats off the Fife coast. When Stephen Bull heard that Wood's ships had been sighted, he ordered ten casks of wine to be opened and shared with his skippers. When the ships met, battle commenced and the people lined the shores to watch. The wind drove them towards Inchcape and the Firth of Tay. The Scots forced the English ships towards Dundee and took prisoners who were later hanged.

At a meeting of the commissioners of the Convention of Royal Burghs held at Dundee in July 1587, a motion was passed that they should all contribute to fitting out a ship for the suppression of piracy on the east coast and, if necessary, also in the west. Although there were fewer cases off the west coast, the *Convention Records* for 1583 reported that, in August of that year, clans of robbers and broken men from Kintyre, Coll and Islay attacked burgesses of Renfrew while they were aboard a Renfrew merchant ship. They are described as approaching in a birlinn and a great boat. They boarded and wounded several of the occupants of the Renfrew ship and seized the contents.

James Melville, minister, writes about an attack at Anstruther, in 1587, where the English pirates killed a local captain. A commission was purchased, a fly-boat rigged out and many of his parishioners set sail to right this wrong:

> They, meeting with their admiral, a great ship of St Andrews, weel riggit out by the burghs, being fine of sail, went before her all the way, and made every ship with whom they foregathered with, of whatsomever nation, to strike and do homage to the king of Scotland, shawing them for what cause they were riggit forth, and inquiring of knaves and pirates.
> *Domestic Annals of Scotland*, Vol 1, *From the Reformation to the Revolution*, Robert Chambers, 1874

Off the coast of Suffolk, they met up with the English merchant ship that had harried them, and took prisoners and forced the ship back to Anstruther where:

> twa were hangit on our pier-end, the rest at St Andrews; with nae hurt at all to any of our folks, wha ever since have been free from English pirates.
> *Domestic Annals of Scotland*, Vol 1, *From the Reformation to the Revolution*, Robert Chambers, 1874

If anyone came to Scotland from a town where known pirates belonged, they were seized and imprisoned, even although they had done no harm, until the authorities of that town had made good any damage done and punished those responsible.

In 1609, Perking and Randell, aboard the *Iron Prize*, were the scourge of the Firth of Forth, the North Sea and Orkney. The Privy Council sent three vessels out from Leith to search for and attack them. Two government officers were killed but twenty-seven men, including the two captains, were captured and hanged on the pier at Leith. Three of the pirate crew escaped the gibbet by turning informer. They told the court that the ship had had a minister with them who said prayers and held a service twice a day. Although he had jumped ship at Orkney, he was taken prisoner at Dundee.

Piracy continued to flourish and, the following year, several crews were seized, tortured and hanged, or else they were set ashore in deserted areas such as Long Island, Ireland or on the more remote Western Isles of Scotland.

Court of Admiralty

The Court of Admiralty tried those accused of piracy. John Davidson was hanged, in irons on Leith sands, in 1551, 'to be consumed piecemeal by the elements'. In 1555, Hilbert Stalfrude and the crew of the *Kait of Lynne*, an English ship, were convicted for reiving and spoiling a hulk lying at Leith Harbour.

In 1612, Peter Lowe, an English pirate, was captured by Neil Macleod of Lewis and sent for trial in Edinburgh; he was hanged at Leith. In Galloway, in 1652, Sir James Montgomery of Portpatrick was a victim of pirates and the epitaph on his tombstone reads:

Sir James by pirates shot and therfore dead
By them i' the sea was solemnly buried.

In 1668, John Ramsay of Dundee and other men from Perth, Elie and South Queensferry were arrested and sent to Leith to be tried for this offence. Ramsay and two of his crew were hanged on Leith sands for 'piracy and murder committed on the high seas'.

While he was drunk, William Potts of the Dreadnaught plundered the White Swan of Copenhagen of four bags of dollars. Although the jury recommended mercy, he was still hanged.

In 1882, the High Court of Admiralty was abolished.

Hostages

James Brioch, a skipper from Dundee, was travelling to Norway when he was seized on by a French privateer who boarded his ship, stole £1000 and made holes in his vessel. He were persuaded to let him go on condition that he promised to pay a ransom of 600 guelders at Dunkirk on a specified day. They took his son with them as a hostage. The ship limped home, Brioch had lost everything; the money being saved towards a larger ship, his cargo and his son. The Privy Council ordered that a voluntary collection should be made in Edinburgh, Leith, Borrowstouness, Queensferry, and the towns of Fife and Angus to raise the ransom money and save the boy from being sent to the galleys.

In 1522, a young trader from Whithorn, Duncan McGowan, was released after his family paid a heavy ransom to pirates who plagued the Irish Sea.

In 1689, the crew of a ship from Grangepans were taken to Rochefort and put into prison. They were half-starved and expected any day to be sent to the galleys as slaves.

Captain Robert Graham of Dawsholm was captured by a pirate ship in the 1750s, off Algiers, and for years was treated as a slave before returning to Dawsholm and marrying Miss Mary Hill of Garbraid who gave her name to the burgh of Maryhill, Glasgow.

Pirates

The Bass Rock Pirates

Four Jacobite rebels, in 1691, locked the garrison out of the fort on the Bass Rock where they were being held prisoner. More joined them and they lived by attacking and capturing fishing boats which they later gave back to their owners on payment of money. The Government, alarmed, sent naval ships to capture them but the fort was well guarded and the rebels held out. They were joined by French privateers. All attempts by Government troops to move them were unsuccessful and the 'pirates' had many supporters amongst the ordinary people, who helped them with supplies. To frighten them off the Bass, the brother of one pirate was hanged on a makeshift gallows that was built opposite the rock so that the rebels could watch the proceedings. Undeterred, they made demands for free pardons and safe passage to France for them and the Frenchmen on the rock. This was finally agreed and they left the Bass in April 1694, having held out for three years.

Captain Glass

Captain Glass was born at Dundee and was the son of John Glass, the Scottish minister who founded the dissenting sect, the Glassites. He qualified as a surgeon, then went to sea to serve as doctor on a ship bound for Guinea. On his release from his post, he had saved a considerable sum of money and had bought trading rights in Senegal. Later, he sold up and moved to the Canary Islands where his wife and daughter were to meet him. The Portuguese arrested him as a spy and he communicated with the English consul by writing on a biscuit with a piece of charcoal. His release was achieved and the family set out to return home.

It became known to some of the crew that their passengers were carrying large sums of money. An Irish boatswain named Peter

McKinlie, the cook, George Gidley, Peter St Quentin and a Dutchman, Andrew Zekerman, planned to kill them and steal the money. Three times they made an attempt but failed each time. Then, one night they succeeded in seizing Captain Cockeran; Gidley felled him with a crowbar to the head and killed him.

Captan Glass grabbed a sword and tried to fight off the others, aided by some of the crew, but two of them were murdered and thrown overboard. His wife and daughter begged for mercy but were also killed and thrown into the sea. They scuppered the ship, leaving two young sailor boys aboard to drown and, off the coast of Ireland, the pirates took to the longboat which they filled with booty.

On arrival at Ross, the pirates buried 250 boxes of dollars in the sand. They hired horses and rode to Dublin where they spent a great deal of money. In the meantime, the wreck was driven ashore, the bodies remaining on board were discovered and the connection with the men who had gone to Dublin established. They were arrested, tried, and hanged in chains on the outskirts of Dublin.

Captain Gow

John Gow was second mate aboard the *George Galley* when, in 1729, she sailed for Vera Cruz. Complaints were made by the crew that there were not sufficient provisions on board and there was discontent. The crew broke into the cabins of the chief mate, cargo and supercargo while they were asleep and murdered them. The captain was chased on deck and killed, then his body was thrown overboard.

John Gow, who had conspired with them, took command and decided that they should hoist the black flag. The ship was renamed *The Revenge* and a course was set for the Spanish-Portuguese coast. They had thirty-eight men, not all happy at the turn of events, and twenty-two guns. The first ship plundered was from Newfoundland laden with codfish for Cadiz; the next, a Scottish ship with pickled herrings. This was not the cargo they sought. They refitted in Portugal but were detected so they decided to head for the Orkney Islands since Captain Gow, although born in Caithness, went to school in Orkney.

They took shelter in a small bay and ran the ship ashore, where they hoped to repair her. Some of the crew escaped by taking the longboat and made their way to Edinburgh, where they informed the authorities of what had taken place. Captain Gow was not alarmed and made plans to steal from the houses of the gentry.

Ten armed men, under the boatswain, attacked the home of the high sheriff, Mr Honeyman, in whose absence the servants opened the door and were tied up. One pirate stood sentry while the others ransacked the house. The sheriff's wife and daughter were at home. Mrs Honeyman grabbed a bag of gold and escaped, and her daughter threw family papers out of the window, then jumped out after them and escaped uninjured. The pirates took linen and silver items and forced the family pipers to play and to march in front of them as they carried their booty back to the ship.

John Gow had gone to school with a Mr James Fea who lived on the island of Eday, and he sent to him requesting a boat for which he offered £1000. Mr Fea pretended that his boat had sunk and entertained the five pirates sent to visit him in a nearby alehouse. Six of his men were hidden behind a hedge near his house. He persuaded the boatswain to leave the inn and accompany him on a supposed errand; the boatswain was captured. Fea and his men then returned to the alehouse where they seized the others. All the boats on the beach had been hauled out of the water so that the pirates could not use them. Captain Gow attempted to put the ship out to sea, but failed, and he and the remaining crew were arrested.

The pirates and their captain were taken to London for trial by the High Court of Admiralty. Gow refused to give up his sword or to plead. An eyewitness account states:

> John Gow would not plead, for which he was brought to the bar, and the judge ordered that his thumbs should be squeezed by two men, with a whip cord till it did break; and then it should be doubled, till it did break again; and then laid threefold, and that the executioners should pull with all their strength; which sentence Gow endured with a great deal of boldness.

He was sentenced to be pressed to death, on 27th May, 1725, the punishment for those who did not co-operate. At the sight of the heavy weights which were to be put upon him in the press-yard at Newgate jail, he relented and pled not guilty. Gow was tried, found guilty and hanged in chains with his first mate, Williams, and six of his crew at Execution Dock, Wapping, on 11th August, 1729.

After his body was taken down, his erstwhile fiancée asked to see his corpse so that she might touch his hand to formally renounce her troth. According to superstitious belief, without going through this ceremony, she could not have escaped a visit from his ghost should she give her word to another man.

Captain Green

An English vessel, the *Worcester*, was driven by storms into the Firth of Forth in March 1704. The captain and his crew were seized

and accused of conducting piracy off the coast of Malabar, Africa.
A black slave aboard described how, the previous year off the
Coromandel coast, the *Worcester* had captured a ship with an
English-speaking crew, had thrown the crew into the sea and sold
the vessel to a native trader. Captain Green and fifteen others were
convicted of piracy. They were condemned to be hanged on the
sands at Leith. Queen Anne intervened and the execution was
postponed for a week, but the Privy Council feared the wrath of
the mob if they showed any mercy. On 11th April, 1704, Edinburgh
was thronged with people when the news that Captain Green and
two other men were to hang.

> The prisoners were brought with the Town-guards
> accompanied with a vast mob. They went through all the
> Canongate and out at Water-port to Leith. There was a
> battalion of foot-guards, and also some horse-guards, drawn
> up at some distance from the place of execution. There was
> the greatest confluence of people there that I ever saw in my
> life, for they cared not how far they were off, so be it they
> saw. Green was first execute, then Simson, and last of all
> Mather. They, every one of them, when the rope was about
> their necks, denied they were guilty of that for which they
> were to die.
>
> *Domestic Annals of Scotland,* Vol 2, *From the Revolution
> to the Rebellion 1745,* Robert Chambers, 1874

Captain William Kidd

Born in Greenock, William Kidd ran away to sea as a young boy.
He was asked by the Earl of Bellamont, Governor of New England,
'to take sharp measures with pirates and sea-robbers'. A private
company was set up and £6000 raised to refit his ship, the
Adventure, and he was to receive a fifth of the profits. In 1698, he
seized the *Queddah Merchant* which was commanded by an
Englishman with Dutch officers who were not pirates and who
were simply delivering a cargo.

Kidd scuttled the *Adventure* and appropriated the *Queddah
Merchant.* This was an act of piracy. He was, at first, helped by a
Mr Button who sold him a sloop. Kidd sailed it to Long Island,
but on arrival, discovered that Button had already arrived on the
Queddah Merchant and had reported him to the authorities, who
arrested him.

He was brought to London and tried at the Old Bailey. He
protested till the end that he was only doing what he had been
ordered to do. He was hanged at Execution Dock on 23rd May,

1701. At the first attempt the rope broke and he fell to he ground
alive, but the noose was speedily put on again and he was finished
off.

It was believed that his treasure was hidden somewhere in
Hispaniola, but it was never found. Robert Louis Stevenson based
Treasure Island on this legend.

Privateers

While there are many reports about the brave Scottish ships which
repelled privateers of other nations, it was not unknown for these
same ships to take part in plunder for prize-money themselves.
John Brown of Leith, Robert Brown of Burntisland, and David
Dowie and Robert Duff of South Queensferry were accused, in
1636, of slaying under trust three Spaniards, appropriating their
goods and merchandise and throwing them overboard, 'beeing in
the middle of the sea and faar frae lande'. They seized a ship sailing
from London to La Rochelle, boarded her and attacked the officers
and crew whom they put in chains and confined in the hold, which
was twenty feet deep and overrun with rats. The officers and crew
were eventually sold as slaves and the privateers received a levy on
their return to Leith.

Two assurance companies and the Merchants of London
presented a two-handed silver cup to Captain John Lockhart, of
HMS *Tartar*, 'for his gallant service in protecting the trade of the
Nation and taking many French privateers in the years 1756-1757'.
In addition, Lockhart received a silver salver and a model of the
original twenty-four gun brig, *Tartar*, in which his ancestor, Admiral
John Ross Lockhart, sailed, for freeing the Channel of the same.
He was also presented with a gold cup from the Society of Merchant
Venturers of the City of Bristol for the important services rendered
to the trade of that city by ably protecting the merchantmen from
the distressing harrassment of privateers.

In 1760, the British Merchants in Lisbon made a presentation
of a silver salver to Archibald Kennedy, the commander of HMS
Flamborough, a man o' war with twenty guns and 160 men, for his
'singular vigilence and bravery in protecting their trade and
annoying the enemy, and protecting their vessels from privateers
around the coasts of Portugal'.

In 1775, Glasgow Town Council saw the war with the American
colonies as injurious to its trade and offered a bounty of £2 to every
able-bodied seaman who came forward to join His Majesty George
II's navy. Edinburgh also made this offer.

Glasgow, Port Glasgow and Greenock were threatened by
privateers; French, Spanish and American ships harrassed them.

Glasgow bought twelve cannon from Carron Ironworks and sent them to Greenock to set up the defence of the River Clyde, and a guardship was stationed at the tail of the bank. These towns fitted out vessels, which they manned and set out to plunder in return. At Greenock, on a Communion Sunday in 1777, a drum was beaten through the town, to the amazement of the people at the breaking of the Sabbath, to announce the capture of, and the taking of booty from, the French.

John Paul Jones

John Paul was born in 1747 in a cottage on the estate of Arbigland on the shores of the Solway Firth, where his father was a gardener. Because his father had no friends in the British Navy who could introduce John Paul into its ranks, the boy went across to Whitehaven when he was thirteen to join a merchant ship, and became an apprentice for seven years.

On completion of his apprenticeship, he found employment in vesssels involved in the West Indian slave trade, which he hated, and by chance gained a free passage home, in 1768, on a vessel from Kirkcudbright.

He became master of a ship called *John*, of Liverpool, which traded in the West Indies. The rum trade suited him and he transferred to a larger ship, the *Betsy*, in 1772. Some of his crew threatened a mutiny in 1773, and a Tobagonian was killed by John Paul, who defended himself with a sword. The man was a local hero in Tobago and Paul had to flee to America. He also changed his name, adding the surname Jones.

The incident which first branded him a pirate, in 1778, was the theft of the Countess of Selkirk's silver from St Mary's Isle, Kirkcudbright. Paul's men removed the silver because the Earl of Selkirk, whom they wished to take prisoner, was not at home. John Paul later returned the silver to the countess with an apology, having paid for it out of his own money.

It was also in 1778 that he harried the ships off the west coast of Scotland. Off the Flannan Isles he captured the *Union*, a ship bound for Quebec with uniforms for the British Army in Canada, and had it taken to Bergen.

In February 1778, he had aboard his ship 133 English prisoners of war whom he hoped to trade against American prisoners held in English jails. An under-the-carpet deal was done and, in 1779, John Paul sailed for America with one hundred American naval prisoners aboard. Over 1000 American sailors were imprisoned in England and such an exchange was not legalised until 1780.

John Paul was feted by the Americans and given the command of a task force. Their mission was to attack Liverpool, with the assistance of the French Navy. The plan was abandoned, but John Paul became a captain.

During the American War of Independence, he had command of a forty-gun ship which was spotted off the East Lothian coast in September 1779. He captured an outward-bound coal ship, the *Friendship*, off Kirkcaldy and held its master hostage to act as a pilot, quizzing him as to the strength of the defences at Leith.

Then he took as a prisoner the master of Sir John Anstruther's yacht, the *Royal Charlotte*, who had hailed Jones's ship, the *Bonhomme Richard*, as it entered the Firth of Forth, believing it to be British.

Great consternation seized the towns of Leith and Edinburgh. The minister of Kirkcaldy did a King Canute by taking a chair down to the shore and offering up a prayer to God to save the 'Lang Toon':

> Noo deer Lord, dinna ye think it a shame for ye to send this vile piret to rob our folk o' Kirkcaldy; for ye ken they're puir enow already, and hae naething tae spair.

His prayers were answered and the wind changed, blowing the enemy ships away. It was after this incident that a fort was built at Leith, in 1780, and a defensive band of volunteers put in place. Jones had planned to land at Leith and demand a ransom of £200,000 or he would burn down the town.

> Pray, tell us good neighbours, whence all this affray?
> (Quoth Trim), all this packing and posting away,
> With cartloads of luggage, aunts sisters and wives
> All driving as if t'was a race for their lives?
> Has d'Orvilliers's vast navy invaded our coast?
> Is Amherst cut off at Coxheath with the host?
> Cox-coxcombed! Yield the road, or I'll break all your bones,
> The pi-pirate, trai-traitor comes, damn him, Paul Jones!...
>
> All was then hurly-burly from Leith to Dunbar,
> With trenches, pallisadoes, and long guns to shoot far;
> Out marched the brisk sailors to man the platoons,
> All sweat, dust, and foaming, in march'd the dragoons,
> In dread of Paul Jones and his horse-stealing loons.
>
> *Fife Coast Garland, 1779*

This and another popular song was written about him:

Chorus
You have heard o' Paul Jones?
Have you not? Have you not?

And you've heard o' Paul Jones?
Have you not?
A rogue and a vagabond;
Is he not? Is he not? **chorus**
He came to Selkirk Ha'
Did he not? Did he not? **chorus**
And stole the rings and jewels a'
Did he not? Did he not? **chorus**

Traditional

After the War of Independence was over, America disbanded its navy. John Paul Jones has always been described as the 'Father of the American Navy'. In 1785, he was offered and accepted the rank of Rear Admiral in the Russian Navy and became known as Kontradmiral Pavel Ivanovich Jones.

POACHING

Poaching was a tradition in Scotland. Throughout the centuries, Scots believed that it was their inherent right to take game and fish, the bounty of nature. Salmon, trout, deer, rabbits and hares were always considered by country folk as legitimate prey and the game laws in Scotland were never as severe as those south of the border. Men were free to hunt outside protected hunting areas in Scotland until 1621.

Lord James Douglas foraged for delicacies for Mary, Queen of Scots and her four Maries, as her attendants Mary Beaton, Mary Seaton, Mary Carmichael and Mary Livingstone were known, near Blair Atholl in the sixteenth century:

> quhile he venesoon thaim brocht; and with his hands quhile he wrocht gynnes [snares] to tak geddis [pike] and salmonys, trowtis, elys, and als menonys [minnows].
>
> *Highways and Byways in the Central Highlands,*
> Seton Gordon, 1948

There were restraints placed on all killing of game at certain times:

> If there be any that slay red-fish in forbidden time or their fry in milldams or if there be any slayers of deer, by stalking within other lords' parks; if any steal hawks or hounds; if there be any breakers of orchards or dovecots or gardens or destroyers of rabbit-warrens they will be brought to tryall.
>
> Justice-Aire, Jedburgh, 1510

> Item upone the 29 of Marche to ane post that came out of Edinburgh with lettir to discharge the slaying of vennisoun and wyldefowlls and brot the generall missive fra the Burrowis. 9/-
>
> *Dumbarton Common Good Account,* 1616

These were warnings to poachers to obey the law or suffer the consequences.

The criminal records of Dumfries, in 1508, state that John Gordon of Crags was fined for poaching salmon on the River Urr and William Lennox the Younger of Cally, for poaching on the River Fleet. In 1793, Sir Walter Scott's first case in a criminal court was at Jedburgh, in 1793, where he defended a well-known poacher and sheep-stealer and won. 'You're a lucky scoundrel,' he told his client as the verdict was pronounced. The poacher thanked Scott and said, 'I'm just o' your mind and I'll send you a maukin [hare] the morn.'

Blood Sport Clearances

In addition to the creation of more grazing land, much of the countryside that was forcibly depopulated during the Highland Clearances was used for blood sports. When the price of wool fell in the nineteenth century, owing to imports from Australia, landowners let heather and bracken spread across the Highlands and found a lucrative alternative letting out their estates for hunting, shooting and fishing. From Inverness to Kirkcudbright, estates developed moorland and trees were planted to produce deer forests and their inhabitants were 'encouraged' to emigrate. From six forests preserved for deer in 1811 the number had grown to forty by 1842.

The deer were allowed to eat the corn on which the crofters depended for a living and no compensation was given to them. At Bernera near Glenelg, in 1887, over 1000 crofters banded together to drive the deer into the sea. Two hundred deer were drowned and massive resistance was given to the authorities. The ringleaders were taken to Edinburgh for trial and were declared not guilty by the jury. They were triumphant and were carried shoulder-high as the people thronged the High Street shouting, 'Down with the tyrants!'

There has always been a battle over the interests of the landowners and the common man and for many years poachers, like smugglers, prided themselves on their ingenuity. They were always scrupulous about sticking to their own code of law. They rarely poached in the closed season and disliked anyone who broke their code. Poaching provided food for the unemployed as there was no parish poor relief available to them and without foraging for food, their families would starve.

Commercial Poachers

Poaching was not always conducted solely by the simple poacher out to feed his family or to enjoy the challenge of outwitting the gamekeepers. There were, even in the nineteenth century, commercial poachers who were out for a big catch to sell on the open market. In the Borders, some poachers had the audacity to take their ill-gotten gains to the station and send them by rail to Manchester.

In modern times, poaching has become big business and there is nothing romantic about it. Despite the Poaching Prevention Act 1900, when fines of £6 per day or thirty days' imprisonment were the punishment, gangs continued to operate, making a quick kill in more ways than one. They had a ready market in hotels both in the United Kingdom and abroad for venison and salmon. They used high-powered rifles, dynamite and illegal nets and ran rings round gamekeepers.

Fishing

R. R. McIan, the nineteenth century artist, romanticised poaching in his paintings of Highlanders with titles like 'Sport for a darksome night'. Salmon-spearing could bring parties of around thirty men to a hopeful spot where, by the light of bracken torches, they used a leister – a three-pronged long-handled fork – to catch their prey.

'Leistering', or burning the water, was the name given to night fishing. A pole with a metal frame was erected in the bow of the boat. A cruizie, a vessel for holding oil, was attached to it and tarry rags, peat or bracken were set alight to attract the fish to the surface. The men stood in the boat holding a fork, which they then used to spear the fish. It was considered a sport by the participants, but this view was not taken by the gamekeepers, who saw poachers as a threat to their livelihood.

Sir Walter Scott, in company with his friends Mr Skene and John, Lord Somerville, took part in this sport, in 1805, spearing salmon by day in the sunlight and continuing in the evening by torchlight.

> The amusement of burning the water, as it is called, was not without some hazard; for the large salmon generally lie in the pools, the depths of which it is not easy to estimate with precision by torchlight, so that not unfrequently, when the sportsman makes a determined thrust at a fish apparently within reach, his eye has grossly deceived him, and instead of the point of the weapon encountering the prey, he finds himself launched with corresponding vehemence heels over head into the pool, both spear and salmon gone, the torch thrown out...quenched in the stream, while the boat has...receded some distance.
>
> *The Life of Scott*, J. G. Lockhart, 1893

Leisterers also rode on horseback at low tide along the shoreline of a saltwater river and speared flounders. On the Solway, they waded into the water and trampled for them with bare feet. If they were caught by the laird's ghillie or gamekeeper they were usually sent to prison.

Gamekeepers

They were often a law unto themselves and were more stringent than their masters in protecting what they saw as their rights. They believed that they fought 'a just war on the lower classes' and saw poachers as a threat to their livelihood. In the sixteenth and seventeenth centuries, poachers could have their hands cut off by gamekeepers without question.

Gamekeepers were not against using mantraps to catch poachers. These included pits sunk into the ground and covered with leaves with ferocious metal spikes inserted in them. They also used traps akin to gin traps used to catch animals; these had vicious springed jaws which would clamp shut on the poacher's leg, causing great damage and making it impossible for him to break free.

A flintlock spring gun was also used. Attached firmly to the ground by a trip wire, the barrel was activated when it was moved, releasing a charge of shot that left nasty wounds. Sometimes innocent people became entangled in these traps. Eventually, in the early nineteenth century, they were officially banned, although some keepers still used them.

In 1835, a gamekeeper who murdered a poacher was sentenced to nine months' imprisonment. In contrast, Henry Mullen and Martin Scott were executed within the walls of Duke Street prison by William Marwood, hangman, in May 1873, for the murder at Port Glasgow of two gamekeepers, Fyffe and McCaughtrie, on 3rd February, 1873.

Game birds

Game birds were also protected. Acts passed, in 1474 and 1579, dealt harshly with anyone who killed doves from doo-cots. Those found killing a deer from a royal forest risked having their hands cut off on the spot. Prior to 1812, when game laws again began to be enforced, game could usually be obtained above or below the counter from poulterers' shops.

In the 1800s a farmer's son was accused of shooting game in the woods on a moonlit night. He was identified by the keeper who saw him return home. He protested his innocence and said that he was elsewhere on the night in question. The jury rebutted his alibi and sentenced him to three months in prison. On his release he emigrated to South Africa. A few weeks later the real poacher was found, a man called Hammond, who was arrested for a theft. Knowing that since another man had been tried and convicted for the crime he would be immune, he confessed to the poaching incident. Although he received a pardon, the farmer's son remained in Cape Town as he could not face the disgrace of having blackened the family name.

At Gartloch Asylum, Lanarkshire, a rabbit-catcher was appointed in 1900 since the grounds were over-run with them and, as the newspaper stated, even the 'poachers were not catching enough'.

Poachers of Note

There were many well-known poachers. For instance, Donald Caird was a well-known poacher in the Borders.

> Donald Caird can win a maukin
> Kens the wiles o' dun-deer staukin'
>
> *Memoirs*, James Hogg, 1874

Heather Jock

John Ferguson of Dunblane was known as Heather Jock. He was transported to Botany Bay in 1812 for cattle stealing but returned and began his old tricks all over again. He was a poacher as well as a visitor to the illicit stills hidden in the hills around his native haunt. Jock was hunting deer on Slumaback Hill around Cambushinnie when John Drummond, the gamekeeper for Mr Stirling of Kippendavie, challenged him. Jock fired point-blank at the keeper. The bullet hit the turf a few yards in front of the keeper. Heather Jock was tried at Stirling in a Circuit Court of Justiciary in April 1812:

> 'You, the said John Ferguson, commonly called Heather Jock, ought to be punished with pains of law, to deter others from committing the like crimes in all time coming' . . . Accused having confessed his guilt, the libel was restricted to an arbitrary punishment; he was thereupon sentenced to transportation for life.
>
> *Vagabond Songs and Ballads*, edited by Robert Ford, 1904

A popular ballad was sung about him in the area for many years:

> . . . Nane wi' Jock could draw a tricker;
> Mang the muirfowl he was siccar;
> He watched the wild ducks at the springs,
> And hanged the hares on hempen strings.

Blass'd the burns and speared the fish;
Jock had many a dainty dish;
The best o' muirfowl and blackcock
Graced the board o' Heather Jock.

Keepers catched him on the muir;
Kickit up an unco stour;
Charged him to lay doun his gun,
Or his nose should delve the grun.
Jock slipped doun ahint a hurst,
Cried, 'Ye swabs, I'll empty't first!'
They saw his fingers at the lock,
And left the field to Heather Jock.

Aften fuddling at the stills;
Sleepin' sound amang the hills;
Blazin' heath and cracklin' whins,
Choked his breath and brunt his shins;
Up he gat in terror vast,
Thocht was Doomsday come at last;
Glowerin' dazed thro' fire and smoke,
'I'm in hell!' cried Heather Jock.

Vagabond Songs and Ballads, edited by Robert Ford, 1904

Alexander Millar

Alexander was a fit young man who was adept at dodging the gamekeepers around the Falkirk area. He had nearly been taken at Dunipace but had escaped by sliding down the rope of the bell tower, jumping through a glassed window, swimming a river and scrambling over a wall. However, he was eventually apprehended and tried. Alexander Millar was hanged at Stirling in April 1837.

The crowd was large, many of them hoping for an exciting attempt at an escape, but the jailors took no chances. They kept him tied up constantly and he was attached to the hangman by a rope which was wrapped around the leather strap pinioning his arms. The hangman wore a black wig and was disguised so that he would not be identified.

The Soutar of Selkirk

Sir Thomas Dick Lauder, when a boy, in about 1815, went with a soutar from Selkirk, whom he chanced to meet, to a long pool on the River Ale above Midlem Bridge.

> We came to a very gravelly-bottomed pool, of an equal depth all over from three to four feet. Here the soutar seated himself;

and shortening both our rods, and fitting them with three
hooks tied back to back . . . waded right into the middle of
the pool . . . 'There's a good one there,' said the soutar,
pointing to one three yards from him; and throwing the hooks
over him [the trout], he jerked him up, and in less than six
seconds he was safe in his creel.

Highways and Byways in the Border, Andrew Lang, 1913

Salmon, in autumn, were in good supply in Scottish rivers. The
water-bailiff could not be everywhere and poachers were active
with their cleeks.

> The pooches o' their moleskin breeks
> Contained unlawfu' things like cleeks,
> For folk that fish to fill their wame
> Are no fastidious at the game.
>
> *Poems*, J. Buchan, 1817

In the *New Statistical Account of Scotland, 1840*, many ministers
report of their parishes 'the only crime is that of poaching'. One
poacher, when cornered by the bailiffs, plunged into the swollen
river calling out, 'Here's death and glory for Jockie.' He did not
survive.

POISON

Scotland can boast many poisoners of both sexes, but this method of murder seems to have had a particular appeal to women. There were several poisonous substances used, including natural poisons found in plants and berries growing wild in the countryside; hemlock, poppy, deadly nightshade and monkshood were popular.

It was easy to obtain poison from a dispensary since many substances, including arsenic and prussic acid, had common uses. Artists used them and household cleaning materials contained many poisons. Laudanum was used as a stimulant by the working classes. There was no poison register kept and, therefore, no signature required for purchase until the late nineteenth century. Forensic science was still in its infancy, and it was rare for a doctor, or even a judge, to insist on examining the organs of a corpse. There was little knowledge of pathology.

Although tests could be carried out to detect poison in the human system, many were inconclusive. Several tests had to be made to be certain of the presence of arsenic, opium and strychnine broke down naturally after a short time. Sometimes the doctor carrying out the forensic test for either had to taste the contents of the stomach for a bitter flavour before signing their report that poison was the cause of death 'on soul and conscience', the traditional oath used in Scottish courts.

The crime was given the nickname of 'tipping the doctor'. It was always a premeditated crime and often took place over a long period of time. The illness would become established by tiny amounts which were increased until death resulted.

One of the earliest Scottish cases recorded was that of the widow of Lord Glamis, Lady Jane Douglas, who had remarried. In 1535, she was accused by William Lyon, a relative of Lord Glamis, of conspiring with her second husband and others to poison King James V and harm him by sorcery. The charge was treason. It was a false claim brought about because she had rejected Lyon's advances.

At one point the judges felt that more time should be allowed for further inquiry but Lyon persuaded Lord Otterburn, the King's

Advocate, to press ahead and Lady Jane, her husband and the family priest were tortured on the rack until they confessed. This instrument of torture does not receive many mentions in Scotland but it was occasionally used. It consisted of the prisoner being spreadeagled by the hands and feet and tied to a contraption which, by means of a handle, could then be stretched, causing great pain. She was then taken to be burned at the stake on Castle Hill. Chains bound her to it and oily rags and tar barrels piled around it ensured that she was well roasted.

In 1567, the First Earl and Countess of Sutherland were murdered, poisoned by her Aunt Isobel whose own son later drank from the same cup and died at Dunrobin Castle. She committed suicide on the day she was to be executed in Edinburgh.

It was believed, but never proved, that Simon Fraser, Lord Lovat, a notable rogue, disposed of his enemies in the eighteenth century by inviting them to dinner, when they were poisoned by his cook who took great pride in his art.

Mrs Jaffray, a Carluke woman who kept lodgers, poisoned two of them in 1838 with arsenic she had acquired to poison rats. She refused to confess to their murder and held her head high, swaggering out in a Rob Roy tartan shawl to take her place on the scaffold. Such was the horror at her attitude that women refused to be seen wearing these shawls, killing the retail trade for this garment.

Kirsty Cochrane was a young widow who set out for a new life in America in 1843, having lost her husband, John Gilmour, a Renfrewshire farmer, after only five months of marriage. Her father had insisted she marry him, although she was in love with someone else. Suspicions were aroused when a servant, Mary Paterson, mentioned that she had been sent to Paisley by Mrs Gilmour to buy rat poison. His body was exhumed and a post-mortem organised which showed that he had died of arsenic poisoning. Attempts were made to trace the widow; she was arrested in New York by a superintendent of Renfrew Police Department. The jury found the charge not proven.

Arsenic was easily obtained and was the choice of James Burnett, who had found a replacement for his invalid wife and was anxious to marry her, perhaps from necessity. His wife died and was duly buried, but he wasted no time in having the banns called at his local church. This aroused suspicion and the police ordered the body to be exhumed, at which point traces of arsenic were found. He was hanged at Aberdeen, in 1849, before a crowd of 12,000 people.

In 1858, John Thomson was convicted of poisoning Agnes

Montgomerie, to whom he had served beer adulterated with the addition of prussic acid. He was discovered after he had visited old friends where he had produced a bottle of whisky which both said made them feel ill afterwards. Suspicions were aroused and Agnes's body was exhumed from its resting place at Eaglesham. Thomson was hung at Paisley in front of a large crowd.

Passion

In 1749, Mary Blandy, a well-provided-for young lady of twenty-six, whose father could find no-one good enough as a suitor for his daughter, fell passionately in love with a handsome recruiting officer, Captain William Cranstoun. He was on military duty in London and was related to the Scots nobility. He was also, although he refrained from telling her, a married man with a family in Scotland.

Mary Blandy in irons.

Her father heard about his background, which Cranstoun stoutly denied, and banished him from the house but her mother, who was very ill, pleaded for the captain, who had made a deep impression upon her, to be permitted to visit her. She referred to him as 'my loving son' and kept him at her bedside until she died in September 1749.

It was made known that Cranstoun had 'seen' her death because he had second sight. It was also broadcast that he had predicted that her father would follow her mother to the grave. The young couple had concocted a plan to poison her father. Cranstoun went home to Scotland and dispatched some herbal powder to Mary. Mary began to put a little into her father's tea, but he thought it tasted bitter and left it. A servant who swallowed some became sick for three weeks.

Mary was then sent some Scotch pebbles with a little bag containing white arsenic powder, supposedly to clean them. At Cranstoun's instigation she doubled the dose. Her father became very ill and she confessed to him what she had done, blaming Cranstoun and begging his forgiveness. 'I bless thee, and hope that God will bless thee and amend thy life,' he said to her before he died and, to a neighbour, 'What will not a woman do for love?'

Several servants and neighbours were suspicious and built up evidence against the couple. Cranstoun fled to France, then later to Flanders, where he died eight months later of natural causes. Mary Blandy was arrested and executed at Oxford, in April 1752, her arms and hands tied with black ribbons.

Catherine Nairn lived in Glen Isla in 1765 and had several suitors, two of whom decided to fight a duel with swords over who was to win her hand in marriage. A local shepherd passing near the spot saw them fighting and was astonished when the taller of the two, who was being forced backwards and was about to fall, suddenly found his opponent at his feet. The shepherd saw Catherine creep up behind the loser and plunge a knife into his back. The taller man remonstrated with her but refused to finish the wounded man off by running him through with his sword. At this, Catherine, in a fury, threw herself upon the man and tried to strangle him with her bare hands.

On another occasion, another of her lovers was found at the foot of a cliff with his neck broken. When she agreed to marry Thomas Ogilvie, an older man not in good health, there was great astonishment. The marriage seemed to be working until the groom's younger brother, a lieutenant in the Indian Army, appeared on the scene. From then on, he and Catherine took little care to hide their affection for each other. Eventually, Thomas banished him from their home. His brother visited a surgeon in Brechin and bought arsenic and laudanum, giving it to a mutual friend to deliver to young Mrs Ogilvie. Her mother-in-law was suspicious and questioned the messenger, who told her of his errand.

Next morning, Catherine insisted on taking a bowl of tea to her husband's room. A maid going up to the beef-stand to bring meat down to cook for dinner saw Catherine go into an adjacent room and, watching her, saw her stirring the tea but could not swear that she put anything into it. Thomas Ogilvie developed horrendous pains and was sick. His wife refused to send for the doctor. By the time one was summoned he was dead.

Poisoning was suspected and, although there was no proof, Catherine and the lieutenant were tried for conspiring together to murder Thomas Ogilvie. Lieutenant Ogilvie was sentenced to death but as Catherine was pregnant her sentence was deferred. A bill survived which showed that her refreshment consisted of ale, double rum, white wine and tea twice a day. Her daughter was born in Edinburgh Tolbooth, 7th March, 1766. A week later, Catherine abandoned her baby and escaped dressed as an officer, wearing a tunic and a hat with a cockade. A reward was offered for her capture, but she escaped to France where it was believed she disposed of several lovers by her favourite means.

Margaret Masson was pregnant by a lover, John Skinner, when she poisoned her husband by dosing him with arsenic. The High Court of Justiciary passed a sentence making Skinner a fugitive because he escaped from justice, but Margaret Masson, after the birth of her daughter, was hanged at Edinburgh in January 1807.

A farmer from Newmills, Keith, George Thom committed parricide when he attempted to poison his in-laws by putting white arsenic in their salt cellar. He claimed that he bought the arsenic to kill rats which plagued him on the farm. He also insisted that frogs had polluted their drinking water, causing them to feel ill. His wife's brother, William Mitchell, died and the others suffered pains. Both George and Jean were arrested, but she was released. He was hanged at Aberdeen in November 1821, and his body became the subject of an experiment with a galvanic battery which caused his hand to open and close.

Mary Smith was a farmer's wife who set out to poison one of her maids because the girl was pregnant. The father of the baby was her son and, being a staunch Presbyterian, she could not face the shame if the word should get out. Instead she planned at first to force the maid to abort the baby by giving her herbal potions. However, at some point, possibly because these had not worked, she changed her mind and substituted arsenic.

At her trial, in February 1827, one of the jury suffered an epileptic fit and the trial was adjourned. The Lord Advocate, Sir William Rae, insisted that she should still be hanged. However, at her re-trial a week later the jury brought in a verdict of not proven.

Jealousy was also a strong motive for murder. Margaret Wishart had a younger sister who was blind and who had gained the affection of the lodger, a young man who was working in Arbroath. The sister took ill and died and his suspicions were aroused. Margaret was sentenced at Perth and hanged at Forfar in June 1827.

Robbery

John Stuart and his wife Catherine Wright were travelling on the *Toward Castle*, a Royal Mail Packet, which sailed from Inveraray to Glasgow. They boarded it on 15th December, 1828, at Tarbert, Loch Fyne, along with Mrs McPhail and her granddaughter. Mrs McPhail was upset because the customs officers had taken away the two kegs of whisky which she was taking to Glasgow; Catherine Wright sympathised with her, giving her a drink of beer. Mrs McPhail spat it out because it tasted bitter. Unable to persuade her to take another drop, Wright and Stuart turned their attention to another passenger, Robert Lamont, travelling with his cousin. He drank several beers and fell down drunk. The couple then robbed him of his wallet.

Lamont's cousin summoned the captain on finding his relative slumped across a table with his wallet missing. On arrival at the Broomielaw, Glasgow, a surgeon was brought on board. He pumped Robert Lamont's stomach and the result smelled strongly of laudanum. The victim died early that morning.

The Stuarts were arrested and were discovered to have a large sum of money in their possession, as well as a bottle smelling of laudanum. They were charged with murder. John Stuart said that they used laudanum to 'tip the doctor', meaning to put Lamont to sleep, but hadn't meant to kill him.

The trial commenced on 14th July, 1829 at the High Court in Edinburgh. Stuart confessed to seven deaths by poisoning and there may have been more. They were sentenced to death. On the appointed morning, Catherine is reputed to have smoked her pipe four times and John Stuart to have taken two pinches of snuff. They were executed at the same spot where William Burke met his end, in front of a crowd of around 10,000 people. Their bodies were given to the anatomists for research. Ballads were circulated for sale at a penny each.

Well-known Poisoners

Eugene Marie Chantrelle

Eugene Marie Chantrelle was a teacher at Newington Academy, Edinburgh, where he met fifteen-year-old Elizabeth Dyer who was one of his pupils. He became involved in a scandalous affair with her. Her parents insisted on a shotgun wedding when they discovered that she was pregnant, and this took place in August 1868. Their son was born in October of that year. They were married for ten years and had four sons, but Chantrelle was bored and craved excitement.

He mistreated his young wife by bullying her, beating her and threatening that he would shoot her dead. Her parents were aware of the circumstances, but were of the 'you've made your bed now you'll lie in it' school of thought and could not face the social disgrace that a divorce would bring to the family. Elizabeth wrote to her mother:

> He went out about nine o'clock and I waited till ten for him. I might have been sleeping for an hour or more when I was awakened by several severe blows. I got one on the side of my head which left me stupid. When I came to myself I could not move my face, and this morning I find my jawbone is out of its place, my mouth inside is skinned and festering, and my face all swollen.

There were reports that he locked her out of the house at night attired only in her night clothes. He was drinking heavily, was in debt and had taken out life insurance for his wife. On 2nd January, 1878, Elizabeth died and was buried in her wedding gown at Grange Cemetery. Her body was later exhumed and traces of opium were found. Chantrelle was arrested for her murder.

After his trial, which took four days, the crowds waited outside for the verdict. It was 'guilty'. He was executed in Edinburgh at Calton Jail. Later, it was revealed that he had ravaged a young woman when she had come for an interview for the post of housekeeper and that she had borne him a son in 1867.

Mary Hamilton

Mary Hamilton was a forger as well as a poisoner. She obtained money by falsifying her sister-in-law's signature and drawing £20 from a Strathaven bank. Instead of confessing and asking for forgiveness, she compounded the felony by poisoning her sister-in-law with arsenic. She was tried at Glasgow and hanged there in front of the High Court, where the gallows was erected 'facing the monument' on Glasgow Green, in January 1850. She was very nervous and begged the hangman, John Murdoch, who was then eighty-two years of age, to be gentle and not to let it hurt.

Catherine Humphrey

Catherine Humphrey's husband was a spirit merchant. After thirty-three years of marriage and his constant intoxication, she finally broke and forced sulphuric acid down his throat while he slept. The Edinburgh hangman, John Scott, having been sent for, she was hanged in Aberdeen in 1837, the last woman to be hanged there.

Look thro' this prison's iron bars,
Look thro' this dismal grate,
And see how sin and drynkin brings
So myserable a state.

Traditional

Dr Pritchard

In Glasgow, in 1865, a general practitioner named Dr Edward Pritchard was accused of the murder by poison of his wife and her mother. He had been married for fifteen years and had five children. Minnie Pritchard took ill and her mother, Mrs Taylor, came to help to nurse her. Her mother died suddenly, followed three weeks later by Minnie. He wrote gastric fever and apoplexy as causes of death on the death certificate, which was later declared laughable in court. A post-mortem was carried out on Mrs Pritchard and traces of antimony and aconite poison were found. Her mother's body was exhumed and showed the same results.

It became known that Dr Pritchard had had an affair with one of his servants, a seventeen-year-old, whom he had told, 'If my wife dies I will marry you.' The family doctor had been suspicious but had not voiced his fears that slow poisoning was causing Minnie's trouble. A chemist had noted that Dr Pritchard regularly bought 'tartar emetic' – antimony. Dr Pritchard also had life insurances on both women. Although the prosecution tried to place the blame on Mary McLeod, the servant girl, Pritchard was sentenced to death and taken to Duke Street Prison in Glasgow to await execution.

His execution took place during the Glasgow Fair holiday. This gave the authorities a problem as the crowds were bigger than usual; around 100,000 were present. He confessed his guilt from the scaffold before being hanged by William Calcraft, the London hangman, imported specially for the occasion.

It was later suggested that a fire in 1863 at his previous home, in which a young maid was burned to death, had been arson by the doctor to hide the fact that she was pregnant by him. His wife knew of this and his other affairs and held this knowledge over him as a threat. It was also rumoured that, in 1857, while practising in East Yorkshire, he had poisoned patients, including Betty Chandler, an elderly lady. On hearing of her death, he had quickly removed all trace of the medicine with which he had treated her.

Madeleine Smith

One of the most celebrated cases of poisoning was that of the twenty-year-old eldest daughter of a Glasgow architect, Madeleine

Smith, who became besotted with a man from Jersey, Pierre Emile L'Angelier, whom she had met in 1855. He used to visit her at the window of the basement of the Smiths' flat in Blythswood Square, Glasgow. The gap beneath the window sill and the wall was where they hid love letters to each other, hers on perfumed paper.

When her parents found out about her clandestine meetings they were horrified and persuaded her into an engagement with a Mr Minnock. Madeleine begged L'Angelier to return her love letters and her portrait, but he refused. At that time it was unthinkable that any respectable girl would have had a secret affair before marriage and, if this came out, it would have ruined her chances of a good marriage.

He wrote her a letter asking her to see him again and she agreed. She served him with a cup of chocolate, after which he was found on the floor of his room in great pain. Later, in February 1857, he was living at Stirling but had visited Glasgow after he received a letter from Madeleine. On returning to his lodgings that evening he was taken ill and died.

When challenged about a letter found in L'Angelier's pocket, Madeleine denied all knowledge of it and ran away to board a steamer to go to the Smiths' holiday home at Rhu. Her family found her and brought her home to Blythswood Square. It was discovered at a post-mortem that L'Angelier had died from arsenic poisoning. Madeleine Smith was known to buy arsenic which she used to enhance her complexion.

There was no proof that she had met L'Angelier on the night that he died or that she possessed arsenic at that time. Madeleine Smith had great charm and was very attractive and she conducted herself well in court. The sympathy of the jury and the judge was with her and L'Angelier's behaviour was seen to be caddish. They brought in a verdict of not proven and she fled to America where she later married and was known as Lena Sheey. She died there in 1928. Subsequently, it was discovered that L'Angelier took medication regularly which contained arsenic and that he had suicidal tendencies, so it may not have been Madeleine who administered the fatal dose.

It has recently been suggested that as L'Angelier was a regular visitor to the spa at Bridge of Allen, it is possible that, as the water there had a high arsenic content, it was that which contributed to his death.

PRESS GANGED

Recruitment sergeants needed to procure a number of men to serve in the king's navy and army. If there were no willing volunteers to 'take the king's shilling', as the bounty was called, the officers plied the young men with drink and told them tales of their adventures to encourage them to join up. If all else failed, they hit the boys over the head to knock them out and when they woke up they were fully-fledged servicemen. If they tried to escape they were punished. This action was called being 'pressed'.

The Privy Council sent hundreds convicted as vagrants to fight for the King of Denmark or Gustavus Adolphus, in 1650, and other prisoners followed. In 1682, a riot took place in Edinburgh at the attempt of soldiers to carry away two young men imprisoned for theft. As the prisoners were marched along the road to Leith under guard to be taken aboard a ship, a woman called out to them 'Pressed'. They nodded and another woman threw the pottery she was selling at a guard. Other people started to throw stones and other missiles. Major Keith ordered his men to fire on the mob and seven men and two women were killed. Twenty-five others were injured. One of the women killed was pregnant; she was cut open and the baby was saved. It was immediately baptised. Three people were arrested and tried, but they were found not guilty.

Captain John Burnet of Barns, in 1691, was recruiting for a regiment in Holland. George Miller, a fatherless boy, was coerced into accepting a bounty of fourteen shillings, Scots. Almost immediately he regretted his action and asked to be released. Two witnesses declared to the Privy Council that he 'had taken on willingly', whereupon the captain had him arrested, dragged to the Tolbooth in Edinburgh and imprisoned.

In the same year, Sergeant Douglas, of Douglas of Kelhead's Company, used unorthodox methods. He seized a servant of a Haddington merchant who was going to Edinburgh for his master to deliver papers to a solicitor. The man was warmly wrapped in a cloak which was thrust over his head and he was bundled aboard a ship at Leith that was bound for Flanders. On another occasion, Captain Douglas seized William Murdoch, a married man, who

'The ruffianly crew were armed with bludgeons and truncheons.'

pleaded that he had never agreed to accept the bounty, that his wife and children were waiting for him and that without his support they would be penniless. His wife petitioned for his release but the magistrates refused to uphold her cause.

James Waugh, the town piper of Musselburgh, agreed to play his pipes to lead a recruiting parade. He marched at the head of the troop then found himself carried aboard as a sailor. The recruiting officers insisted that he had accepted their bounty but he said that he had thought that it was a fee for playing his pipes. The magistrates of Musselburgh, upset at the idea of losing their piper, upheld his case and he was released.

The Privy Council, in 1692, agreed to a petition from a regimental officer to obtain the services of Archibald Baird, an Irish refugee imprisoned at Paisley. The verdict in the young man's trial was 'not proven' but, nonetheless, the Sheriff thought that he would be excellent material for Flanders and he was pressed into service.

Because the ships to transport the recruits, voluntary and pressed, to Flanders were not ready, several hundred of them spent the year of 1692 housed in jails in Fife and Lothian. They only had a blanket to lie on. Soldiers kept guard to ensure that none of them escaped.

Many full-time soldiers, disillusioned with their harsh treatment, deserted from the army. John McLachlan, a Glasgow schoolteacher, was tried in 1694 accused of encouraging soldiers to defect. He warned them that they would be sent to Flanders, forged passes of leave, provided them with civilian clothes and helped them run away. He was sentenced to be whipped through Edinburgh and then deported to the plantations of America. This was later changed from whipping to standing at the pillory with a paper on his brow stating:

> John McLachlan, a schoolmaster at Glasgow, appointed to be set on the pillory at Edinburgh and Glasgow, and sent to the plantations, for seducing and debauching soldiers to run away from their colours, and desert their majesties service.
> *Domestic Annals of Scotland*, Vol 2, *From the Revolution to the Rebellion 1745*, Robert Chambers, 1874

James Hamilton, keeper of the Canongate Tolbooth, petitioned the Privy Council in 1696 for 2/- Scots per night 'for his great trouble in keeping such unruly prisoners in order' and also 'being liable to the payment of ten dollars for every man that shall make his escape'.

In 1697, he again petitioned them as 'the prisoners became so tumultuous and rebellious that they combined together and assassinated the petitioner's servants, and wounded them and took keys from them, and destroyed the bread, ale and brandy that was in the cellar of the value of eight pounds sterling'.

As late as 1738, the practice was still in force and one hundred men recruited in Scotland for service in the Dutch Republic mutinied because some had been foiled in escaping. The four ringleaders were taken to the lowest dungeons. Angered even more, they seized the turnkey and an officer, put them in irons and locked them up, demanding the release of their comrades. The authorities starved them into surrender and two days later they hung out a white flag. There were no recriminations and a truce was declared.

Fairs, held in most towns two or three times every year throughout Scotland, were favourite places for recruiting officers. The young men would spend their money on whisky and ale and would be delighted to sign up and receive a bounty.

Recruitin' parties, wi' their drums,
Frae every ither county
Are makin' gowks gie up their looms
An' tak the listen bounty. –
Oh, hon! oh, hon! the wee drap drink
Has drown'd the thocht o' sorrow,
Their gilded graith, an' yellow clink,
Will darker seem tomorrow
Than on this day.

Humours of Glasgow Fair, Gabriel Neil, 1825

S. R. Crocket, the novelist, introduces the idea of being pressed as a favourite punishment for those caught for smuggling.

'Scatter!' she commanded, clapping her hands. 'Off with you lads! Take to the hills. The press-gang is landing at this moment at the Abbey Burnfoot to cart you off. Eben McClure is with them. He has heard of your cargo-running and he wants to send you all to the wars.'

The Moss Troopers, S. R. Crocket, 1812

During the American War of Independence, in 1796, gipsies were classed as vagrants. They were apprehended throughout Scotland and forced into the army or navy and sent to America. Gipsies, when pressed, were so determined to avoid serving that they would cut off a finger or thumb with a hatchet or razor. Mothers were known to have mutilated their sons in infancy to prevent them ever being called to serve in the army or navy. On the other hand, a few gipsies did join up voluntarily as musicians in the navy. On occasions, when they unavoidably took the King's shilling, they would then go on French leave (known as AWOL) as soon as possible.

My bonny lass, I work in brass,
A Tinkler is my station:
I've travelled round all Christian ground,
In this my occupation.
I've ta'en the gold, an' been enroll'd
In many a noble squadron:
But vain they search'd when off I marched
To go and clout the cauldron.

The Jolly Beggars, Robert Burns, 1785

PRISON

Frae a' the bridewell cages an' blackholes,
And officers canes, wi' their halbert poles,
And frae the nine-tail'd cat that opposes our souls,
Gude Lord deliver us.

Traditional

Prisons were originally not for the confinement after trial but for use as holding areas for those awaiting trial. Some forgotten prisoners waited for years for their case to come to trial.

> On taking office [as Lord Advocate in 1676] [Sir George] Mackenzie found the jails full of wretches whom [Sir John] Nisbet had left in chains, because he had not been bribed to prosecute them nor bribed to release them. The new Lord Advocate made up his mind to empty the prisons, and did so without a thought for the hardships he inflicted. In one case two men had been confined for six years without trial. The only evidence he produced was that of the Court of Session; but the jury convicted them and they were hanged.

The Lord Advocates of Scotland, Vol 1,
George W. T. Omond, 1883

The original evidence against these men had been forged and they had been trying to prove their innocence for many years.

Depriving people of their liberty as the answer to punish those who fell foul of the law became popular in the eighteenth century. Before this many different places were adapted for the purpose of detaining prisoners and it was the nineteenth century before fully-staffed, secure, State prisons became the norm. Dungeons, pits, vaults, arches, islands and almost any other convenient space were used.

Squalor carceris, literally 'dirty prison', was the name given to the punishment of imprisonment under Scots law. Prisons tended to be dark, smelly places. The prisoners were kept 'in irons', that is, a manacle on either the wrist or leg, which was attached by a chain to rings on the wall or floor. The blacksmith soldered them on and, upon release, cut them off. This was called being 'put to the gad'.

A bar of iron, about the thickness of a man's arm above the elbow, crossed the apartment horizontally at the height of about six inches from the floor; and its extremities were strongly built into the wall at each end. Hatterick's ankles were secured within shackles, which were connected by a chain at the distance of about four feet, with a large iron ring, which travelled along the bar we have described . . . With his feet thus secured the keeper removed the handcuffs . . . A pallet bed was placed close to the iron bar, so that the prisoner might lie down at pleasure, still fastened to the iron bar . . .

Guy Mannering, Walter Scott, 1815

Scott's description was based on Kirkcudbright jail. There was no segregation of the sexes and prisons were often insecure places, since the jailors did not live in. The prisoners had wooden boards to sleep on.

Through time, irons were removed but there was no attempt at providing prisoners with any occupational work and they rotted away in idleness. There were few jails with courtyards where the prisoners could have exercise. Prisoners wore their own clothes and were not given proper facilities for washing them.

In the twelfth century, King Malcolm the Maiden gave feudal barons the power of *fossa* and *furca* – pit and gallows. Barons' prisons were damp, uncomfortable places. Some were literally pits dug out of the ground at a depth too deep for a man to climb out. The ground would be water-logged and, if the prisoner was lucky, a boulder or stone could raise him above the water level. It was pitch dark and covered with an iron grille. The prisoner might be in chains, usually an iron ball attached to the ankles.

Many people were incarcerated in dungeons. These were usually situated in the bowels of tower-houses and castles and were foul, damp and dark. A dungeon in the old bridge over the River Ness served as a prison for that area. The prisoners were made to stand in water up to their waists. If the water level fell then rats appeared to torment them.

The Bottle Dungeon at St Andrews was so called because of its shape – being twenty-seven feet wide at the bottom, seven feet at the top, and thirty feet deep with smooth sides. Simon Fraser, Lord Lovat, had two servants who married each other without his consent. In the days of barons' law it was necessary to obtain permission from the laird to marry. He forced them into his dungeon, which had once been a well, and left them there for three weeks saying, 'You shall have enough of each other by then.'

The dungeons of Blackness Castle, situated on a promontory jutting into the North Sea near Linlithgow, housed prisoners from the middle ages onwards. It acted as a State prison, housing many notable names including Cardinal Beaton in 1543, the Earl of Morton in 1584 and many Covenanters in the 'killing times' of the seventeenth century. One dungeon was named the 'Black Pit' which jutted out into the firth and into which the water came at high tide. Lord Ochiltree was imprisoned for twenty years in the castle because he accused the Duke of Hamilton of treason. It became the central ammunition depot for Scotland between 1870 and 1874 as it was no longer needed as a prison.

Near Stonehaven, another castle, Dunottar, where legend has it the crown jewels of Scotland were hidden, was also used as a State prison. Into its vaults, Covenanters were crammed and, in 1685, 200 were assembled 'like a flock of bullocks'. They were starved and badly treated. They were charged with 'recusancy', refusing to submit to the authority of the king. Eventually, George Scott of Pitlochie was given a present of them as slaves for his plantation.

> The Privy Council of Scotland ... made a general arrest of more than a hundred persons in the southern and western provinces, supposed from their religious principles to be inimical to Government, together with many women and children. These captives were driven northwards like a flock of bullocks, but with less precaution to provide for their wants, and finally penned up in a subterranean dungeon in the Castle of Dunottar, having a window opening to the front of a precipice which overhangs the German Ocean...The guards made them pay for every indulgence, even that of water.
>
> *Introduction* to *Old Mortality*, Walter Scott, 1829

Islands were popular for use as prisons because they were considered secure. In 1671, King Charles II ordered his Government to buy the Bass Rock, opposite Tantallon Castle at the mouth of the Firth of Forth, from the Provost of Edinburgh and set it up as a prison. It became a fortress with cannons, soldiers and cells which were dug out of the rock. It housed many Covenanters, including Alexander Peden and Adam Blackadder.

Escape

Prisons, especially thieves' holes and early tolbooths, were insecure and prisoners often escaped. At Edinburgh, in 1600, Robert Auchmuchty had killed James Wauchope on St Leonard's Hill and was imprisoned in the Tolbooth. He told the jailor that he needed a curtain as he had sore eyes which were affected by light. He then treated the window with aquafortis which ate through the iron bars. His apprentice was to wave a handkerchief when the Town Guard were clear, allowing him to escape. Unfortunately for him, one of the guard noticed this and the attempt was foiled. He was duly beheaded at the Cross ten days later.

In 1683, Dumfries jail was ill-conducted, according to Sir Patrick Maxwell. In a complaint to the Privy Council, he claimed that having paid £200 of his own money to bring the notorious robber, Ludovic Irving, back from Ireland to be housed at Dumfries, the magistrates put him into an insecure room from which he escaped. Sir Patrick demanded his expenses be reimbursed and that the jailor should be punished.

The Tolbooth at Helensburgh had a barred window within easy reach of the street and friends used to pass food and drink through it. On occasion, the prisoners were given a key to go out and lock themselves in again on their return!

The day before the original date for the execution of Peter Young, a gipsy, he seized the jailor and forced him to lie on his back on the ground while he released every prisoner. After several escapes from Aberdeen Tolbooth, the authorities decided that Peter Young should be secured with an iron chain. He was a very strong man and, amongst other things, had been a blacksmith. He managed to break the bolts and sauntered out of the door. When he was eventually caught he was immediately taken to be hanged.

Many prisons, especially tolbooths, seem to have had jailors easily duped into letting visitors in, whereupon they would bring clothes for the prisoner, possibly female garments or those of a minister, who would then pass out unchallenged.

General State Prisons

The new prison at Perth was to serve as the General Prison for Scotland. Built in 1812 on the South Inch and covering eighteen acres, it held 7000. It was originally intended to house the French prisoners of war captured during the Napoleonic War, plus a guard of 300 soldiers.

In 1842, it was first used as a general prison and housed 535 prisoners, the number rising to 884 in 1881. It had a governor, depute, turnkeys, teachers, scripture readers, chaplain, a medical officer and his staff.

A new building was opened, in 1859, based on a system for treating juvenile delinquents at Parkhurst Prison, London. This later closed and it was then used to house criminal lunatics, epileptics and imbeciles who previously were incarcerated in the

old Fench quarters. There the windows were barred and four shared
a cell. Baths were only permitted once a month and many lunatics
were kept permanently in irons. Prisoners could be kept there
awaiting transfer to the hulks and transportation.

> August 1852. On the opening of the prison this morning, a
> nineteen year old man, a transportation prisoner, was found
> dead in his bed; he had been falling off for some time, but had
> no specific complaint.
>
> *Governor's Journal*, Perth Prison, 1651–55

In Aberdeen the prison accommodation was unsuitable and, in 1891,
Craiginches, built of granite, was opened. It was built to house
prisoners from the north and north-east and could accommodate
about eighty male and female prisoners.

The State Prison of Barlinnie was built at Riddrie Knowes
between 1880 and 1886. The name means 'the height by the pool'.
It was designed with four large halls of four storeys, all connected
by a corridor on the ground floor and each having cells for 200
prisoners. In 1891, it was already overcrowded and prisoners were
still being sent to Perth. It became famous for its 1970s experiment
as a Special Unit for hardened murderers.

Opened in 1888, Peterhead Prison caused a sensation as the
prisoners were taken out to quarry for stone.

> They were dressed in rough white sacking with broad arrows,
> and wore smart caps and shoes . . . The convicts quarried stone
> for the harbour travelling daily by train to and from a quarry
> some miles away, guarded by warders armed with rifles.
> Cutlass and scabbard were worn by every warder at Peterhead
> from its opening until 1939. Rifles were carried until 1959
> when all weapons were discontinued and batons substituted.
>
> *Prisons and Punishment in Scotland*, Joy Cameron, 1983

Insanity

Lady Grange was considered mad by her husband, James Erskine.
Her behaviour got on his nerves, so during the night in January
1732, he hurried her from her lodgings in Edinburgh . He first
took her to the island of Hespir then, after two years, to St Kilda,
where she remained for another seven. She was rescued by her
friends, in 1740, who had presumed her to be dead. They then
threatened her husband with prosecution but he was never charged.

Those unfortunate enough to be certified as 'mentally deranged'
did not receive treatment but instead were often kept imprisoned
in dungeons or garrets for years. Sometimes they were fed through

a hole in the wall because they were regarded as dangerous. The Lunatic (Scotland) Act was passed in 1857 and a General Board of Commissioners in Lunacy for Scotland was established in Edinburgh for the proper treatment of lunatics. However, those convicted as criminal lunatics were still sent to the county prison or the general prison at Perth. Those who caused trouble were put into strait jackets and some were chained to their beds.

The Dangerous and Criminal Lunatics (Scotland) Bill of 1861 and the Lunacy (Scotland) Amendment Act 1866 recommended retention in the general prison for all lunatics, the term to include 'every prisoner of unsound mind and every person being an idiot'. This caused overcrowding.

A farm at Carstairs in Lanarkshire was chosen as the site for the State penitentiary in 1930. A Criminal Lunatic Asylum and State Institution for Defectives was built but, before it opened for use, it was converted to a military hospital. It was 1948 before it reverted to its intended function; by then the inmates were to be called State mental patients, not lunatics. Criminals sent there as 'category one' could only be released with the consent of the Secretary of State for Scotland, a situation that still exists. It was not a prison and the staff were nurses, not warders.

Linlithgow seems to have been a model prison:

> Each cell is heated with a stove and lighted with gas, regularly cleaned and as well ventilated as the situation of the prison will admit. Each prisoner when brought in is washed and clothed in a prison dress. The diet is excellent. Dinner, oxhead broth, four ounce barley, four ounce bread and a portion of vegetables, each alternate day, pease brose, fish and potatoes. Supper is the same as breakfast. Provision is made for the religious instruction of prisoners. In addition to the services of a chaplain, each cell is provided with a Testament. Mr Alison, the governor, instructs the male prisoners who cannot read or write, and his wife, the female prisoners.
>
> *Parish of Linlithgow, Second Statistical Account of Scotland*, Rev. Andrew Bell, 1843

Jailors

Jailors were paid by their prisoners. They were allowed to charge for food and drink. They were deeply aggrieved if their prisoners were poor or vagrants because there was no money to be made.

Gavin Naismith was appointed the first jailor of Glasgow's new Tolbooth in 1627 at an annual salary of £2 4s 6d sterling. He had to supply coals for council meetings, receive fees from prisoners, a fee for booking them in and out, and 2/- for every twenty-four hours they were in jail. Meat, drink, fire and bedding could be provided by the prisoner or his friends without any payment to the jailor. Out-of-townsmen were to be charged 4d per day. In 1660, Charles McLean was paid by the treasurer for his trouble in having only'thiefs and lounes' as prisoners.

The night before Matthew Clydesdale was to be executed in 1818, the jailor at Glasgow gave him a bottle of ale instead of bread and water. He duly ironed the condemned man and left him. In the morning it was discovered that Clydesdale had broken the bottle and used it to lacerate himself in an attempt to commit suicide to avoid being anatomised. They had to patch him up to keep him alive so that he would die on the scaffold as ordered.

Tolbooths

Tolbooths existed in most towns. Originally, they were booths at the site of the fair or market area and were used, when the courts were officially set up, as the place where those who had broken the Peace of the Fair were held until punishment was declared. Later, they developed into fairly insecure prisons, especially for those who could not pay their fines.

The Edinburgh Tolbooth building may have been the home of the medieval Scottish Parliament and courthouse of the Court of Session. On the ground floor there were shops as well as the thieves' hole and a room which at one time was the guardhouse of the Town Guard. The upstairs rooms, where felons were chained to a bar on the floor, also had in its centre an iron cage where dangerous or violent prisoners were held. It was the scene of many historic events, but was demolished in 1817.

A stone on the causeway and a plaque marks the spot where the Heart of Midlothian once stood. Its replacement was Calton Jail, Edinburgh, built between 1791 and 1796 and designed by Robert Adam. Calton Hill was as spectacularly castellated as the historic Tolbooth in the old town and was the site of many burnings of felons. It was replaced by Saughton Prison in 1888.

In Glasgow, the original Tolbooth was very old and was replaced in 1626 by 'a sumptuous, regulated, uniform fabric, large and lofty, most industriously carved'. That one lasted until 1814 when, apart from the tower which is still standing, it was demolished. The town then used two prisons: the North Prison, Duke Street, built in 1798 and extended in 1824, and the South Prison at Glasgow Green built in 1814 but, from 1862, taking only criminal court prisoners.

At Dumbarton, in 1820, the Tolbooth was a room over the Town Council Hall. It was large and roomy. The beds were on the floor and were stowed away during the day. There was a huge fireplace at the west end and the prisoners were divided into messes and took turns at cooking. A dinner might be broth, followed by beef and potatoes, and there was plenty for all. The prisoners were mainly smugglers who had broken the excise laws and could not pay their fines.

There were protests from the tax-payers about the cost of keeping people in prison. Over a year it amounted to a tidy sum:

Expenses of Prosecution carried in the name
of the Authority by the Lord Advocate £13,775.00

Sum required by the Sheriffs of Scotland to
settle accounts for the Prosecution £49,000.00

Expenditure under the Prison Boards of the
Several Counties of Scotland £43,366.00

Proportion effeiring [sic] to Scotland for convicts
sent to Millbank Prison, London £3,932.00

total £110,073.00

Expenditure for Criminal Prosecutions,
Maintenance of Criminals etc., for Scotland, 1846

RIOTS

'Riot' was a word used to describe any form of action when people turned on the authorities. Some were large gatherings, while others were fairly small assemblies, but they were always treated with a display of force from the authorities, who felt threatened by such behaviour.

Black Friday

In 1919, unemployment was increasing and the demand for a forty-hour week was growing when a Forty-hours Strike Committee was formed in the Clyde area and a strike and demonstration was arranged. It was to be held at George Square in Glasgow on 19th January, 1919. Huge crowds gathered to hear the speakers. A deputation was invited into the City Chambers and the crowd waited for the result. A scuffle broke out. The crowd was dense, and as the police tried to get through, a tramcar was prevented from passing. The demonstrators were hemmed in by the police on one hand and traffic on the other. Fifty-three people were injured and the Riot Act was read. The speakers, among them David Kirkwood, William Gallacher and Emmanuel Shinwell, Chairman of the Committee, were arrested and the military took control of the city.

The Blue Blanket

When there were no official lawkeepers within the town of Edinburgh, the mob took it into their own hands to gather and oppose any legislation or action that displeased them. In 1482, angered by the restraint of King James III in the castle, they made such a tumult that he was released. In gratitude, he granted the use of the Blue Blanket, a banner or flag which was looked after by the Convenor of the Trades and which was used as a rallying sign for all gatherings from then on.

May Games

After the Reformation, all things papist or pagan were to be repressed. The May Games were held every year to celebrate the summer. Archery contests, races and challenges on horseback were all part of the fun. A Robin Hood, Little John and an Abbot of Unreason were chosen. An Act of Parliament was proclaimed against the games in 1555, but the people ignored it. George Durie was chosen as Robin Hood, in 1561, and on Sunday 12th May he and many others arrived in Edinburgh and occupied the Castle Hill as they had done for generations. They were armed in case of trouble and, when the magistrates tried to stop them, they resisted. James Gillon, a shoemaker's servant, was unfortunate enough to be arrested and, as an example, he was tried and sentenced to be hanged.

> When the time of the poor man's hanging approachit, and that the [hangman] was coming to the gibbet with the ladder, upon which the said cordiner should have been hangit, the craftsmen's childer and servants past to armour; and first they housit Alexander Guthrie and the provost and bailies in the said Alexander's writing booth and syne came down again to the Cross, and dang down the gibbet, and brake it in pieces, and thereafter passed to the Tolbooth, whilk was then steekit [shut]; and when they could not apprehend the keys they brought fore-hammers and dang up the same Tolbooth door...and brought forth the same condemnit cordiner.
>
> *Domestic Annals of Scotland*, Vol 1, *From the Reformation to the Revolution,* Robert Chambers, 1874

Gillon was brought down the Netherbow and the magistrates regained the Tolbooth. They began shooting at the craftsmen. Stones were thrown and for five hours rioting ensued. Eventually, the Constable of the Castle came down and acted as arbitrator, breaking them up. No further charges were to be brought on either side.

Highland Clearances

The clan chiefs and lairds, after the Jacobite Rebellion in 1745, no longer saw their tenants as assets. They were not required to fight since most private armies had been abolished by law. Sheep provided a better income than the rents of crofters, so the owners drove the people from many areas of the Highlands, forcing them to emigrate or occupy only certain planned townships, such as those provided by the Duke of Sutherland at Helmsdale in 1792.

The ministers of the Church preached that it was the will of God and had to be accepted. Many emigrated or moved away without great protest. The law of the land supported the landowners.

The people were afraid of transportation to Australia if they resisted and, geographically, it was difficult to make a concerted effort to resist. A Crofters' Commission was set up in 1882 which led to the Crofters' Act and ended the absolute right of a landlord to treat his tenants unfairly without compensation.

There were unnecessary acts of revenge by sheriff's officers if any resistance did take place. Notices were placed on church doors warning that if anyone offered shelter to relatives, they in turn would be evicted. Cats were roasted in the flames as houses were burned down; sick people and invalids were occasionally left to burn as the thatch was fired. Anyone refusing to emigrate was sent to jail.

Ross-shire

In Ross-shire, however, there were serious riots, with the people attempting to drive the sheep out. The military were called in and arrests made. The crofters built up a cache of gunpowder and weapons to defend themselves. At Coigeach, in 1792, the women disarmed the police and the sheriff's officers, burned their summonses, threw away their batons and ducked them in a pool. The men of the township stood by, but did not join in. No one was arrested and they were left in peace.

On another occasion, in 1820, a sheriff dispensed with the Riot Act, ordered the soldiers to shoot, and a young girl was killed and many others injured. This so infuriated the crofters that they attacked the soldiers, smashed up the sheriff's coach and the militia fled. The glen was spared and the crofters continued to live there.

In 1843, at Greenyards, 200 women took a stand against Sheriff Taylor and the police, many of whom were drunk. The officers bludgeoned a women, causing the others to throw stones. The women fought well but were eventually overcome by the police force. Undeterred, the police continued to beat them to a pulp, break their arms, then handcuff them with coarse rope, push them onto carts and imprison them at Tain. It was said that 'scalps with long hair adhering to them' were picked up on the battleground next day.

Skye

The Battle of the Braes at Portree, in 1882, was the name given to an incident when the sheriff officer was forced by the people to burn their summonses, and his assistant had the contents of 'certain domestic utensils fully charged' poured over his head. This angered the authorities and a host of policemen were drafted in from as far as Glasgow because they felt that Highland troops would be too sympathetic. Twelve police were wounded. The ringleaders were taken prisoner and refused trial by jury. This further angered the mob and the masts of ships were used by the people in an attempt to break down the prison door to release their friends.

Home Rule Demonstration

Serious party riots broke out in Coatbridge, Lanarkshire, where a considerable amount of excitement and bad feeling had existed since the Orange demonstration on the 12th of July. Today a great demonstration of Home Rulers was held, in which not only the Irishmen of the district, but others from various parts of the country, took part. The procession, numbering about 3,000 persons, passed through the streets without obstruction until they reached the Sunnyside quarter, where a large body of Orangemen lying in wait attacked them with great violence. Many persons were injured by stones and otherwise, but the police succeeded in turning the procession into another street.

The Home Rulers held a meeting in Cowheath Park, and on their return to the town another fight of an even fiercer character took place, Commander McHardy, Captain Stewart and other members of the police force receiving serious injuries by stonethrowing. Rioting renewed next day (Sunday 19th August, 1883).

The Annals of Our Time from Feb. 24, 1871 to June 20, 1887,
Joseph Irving, 1889

Inverness Fair

It had always been the law that the Peace of the Fair must be upheld and in all places special courts were 'fenced' at fairtime to deal on the spot with any breach of the peace. In Inverness, a fair held for centuries at Marymas in August was the scene of a slaughter in 1665. It was sometimes referred to as 'Kebbuck Day' because the affray took place at the booths of the women who were selling cheese on the hill near the castle.

Finlay Dhu asked the price of a cheese and, on being told, let it roll down the hill – whether by accident or design was never discovered. It set off a chain of events which led to the killing of three men by the Town Guard who were called out to quell a riot between those who supported Finlay and those who supported the women, and probably those who just wanted a good old-fashioned fight. Swords were drawn, guns shot and many were wounded.

Levellers

Galloway was the leading area in agricultural improvement. Enclosure was going ahead apace as markets for farm produce opened up south of the border after the Treaty of Union in 1707. Not only were dry-stone walls built to make safe pasturage for cattle, but the common land was also fenced in by the landowners, to the distress of the ordinary people who lost their livelihood when fewer herds and other agricultural workers were needed. When they lost their employment they also were evicted from their tied cottages.

> Great depopulations have been made in the south, and multitudes of families turned out of their tacks and sent a-wandering. The lairds of Murdoch, Herron and others have turned much of their estates into grass. Some parishes, particularly that of Girtoun, are almost whole enclosed, and scarce six or seven families left.
>
> Letter, Robert Woodrow, May 1724

The people rebelled and large gatherings took place which the authorities referred to as riots. Basil Hamilton, a wealthy farmer, was on the side of the tenants and tried to warn the authorities that, unless help was forthcoming, trouble would ensue. He received no answer. At Kirkcudbright, in June 1724, declarations were made at market places where the Levellers read their manifesto, stating that they wished 'to abide in the land of their fathers'. Again, no action was taken by the Government. Men and boys set out at night to scatter the 'dykes', as the dry-stone walls were called. Each man carried a 'kent', a piece of wood from six to eight feet long. They placed these levers beneath a run of dyke and on the command 'Ow'r wi' it, boys!' tumbled the stones and gave a great shout.

> The lords and lairds they drive us out
> From maillings where we dwell;
> The poor man says, 'Where shall we go?'
> The rich says, 'Go to Hell!'
>
> Levellers Ballad, Traditional

The lairds were fighting a losing battle as hundreds of yards of wall were being collapsed nightly throughout Galloway. The militia were called in on several occasions. When sixteen prisoners were taken by soldiers at Balmaclellan, several women appeared and forced them to release the prisoners. More troops were called in. In one of the last stands, 200 prisoners were taken at Duchrae in the parish of Balmaghie. Many of the soldiers, including officers like Major McNeill and Major Du Carry, supported the Levellers and allowed many to escape as they were being marched to Kirkcudbright. Their leaders were tried, fined, put in prison and several were transported to the plantations of America. In May 1725, an agreement was made by the Earl of Stair to provide alternative employment in the woollen industry in Wigtown, Stranraer and Kirkcudbright. Many others emigrated, 'West awa' yonder', never to return.

Malt Tax

The cry of the Jacobites was 'No Union, no malt tax, no salt tax'. In 1713, the Malt Tax was extended to Scotland. The English landed gentry were annoyed that Scots did not have to pay the tax and demanded that Parliament enforce it in Scotland. It was opposed as a breach of the Treaty of Union but some MPs did support it. One of them, Daniel Campbell, Member of Parliament for Glasgow, voted for the extension and, in 1725, it was finally imposed on Scots.

Malt was a staple ingredient of ale, and yeast was needed for baking bread, so great exception was taken to the tax. Crowds gathered to hinder the excisemen who should have tried to collect it, but, forewarned, none attempted to do so. The magistrates of Glasgow were worried about the number of people out on the streets, so they summoned the militia and planned to house them in the guardhouse. The crowd, realising their intention, locked its doors and kept the key.

On 24th June, 1725, at ten-thirty at night, the crowd advanced on Mr Campbell's house, Shawfield Mansion, in Argyle Street and began knocking it down. When the militia arrived they were stoned. Captain Bushel ordered his men to open fire and two of the rioters were killed. Many others were wounded. The soldiers began to retreat to Dumbarton but were attacked by more people with stones along the way. They retaliated and seven others were killed.

The Lord Advocate, Duncan Forbes, wrote to London that he personally would go to Glasgow to rout the offenders. He sent spies to mix with the people and discover the names of the leaders. A court was set up on 9th July at Glasgow and the Lord Advocate examined witnesses. This resulted in nineteen men being put in prison. On 16th July, Captain Bushel received the prisoners, tied their hands with rope, and proceeded to march them with an escort of soldiers to Edinburgh.

The next day the magistrates of Glasgow were charged with gross neglect of duty and imprisoned in the Tolbooth. The Royal Scotch Dragoons were given the task of escorting them to Edinburgh. The two sets of prisoners were placed under guard in Edinburgh Castle and were later escorted through jeering crowds to Edinburgh Tolbooth.

On appearance at the Court of Justiciary, Lord Dundas, a former Lord Advocate, spoke for the magistrates who were given bail on 20th July and released. As they arrived six miles from Glasgow they were met by 200 citizens and conducted to the city where the bells were rung. All nineteen perpetrators of the riot were whipped through the streets of Glasgow by the hangman, after which some were set free, while others were transported to the plantations.

The matter was taken up by the brewers who continued in defiance, helped by Lord Dundas, but they were threatened with imprisonment and had to submit in the end and pay 3d per bushel of malt.

Bread Riot

Staple ingredients were in short supply in the 1840s. The crops had failed and many people were going hungry. Demand for the town councils to do something about it boiled over. People were angry when stone-breaking for roads was offered as the only means of averting unemployment. Soup kitchens were set up but more food was needed. Bread prices were high owing to the shortage of flour.

It was decided to hold a meeting on Glasgow Green and 3000 turned out to beg for more food. The representatives of the town council, realising that the situation was becoming dangerous, decided to open the city hall in the evening and give out food. On 6th March, 1848, there was a massive turnout on Glasgow Green, estimated at around 5000. They started marching through the streets shouting out 'Give us bread!'

The mob attacked and ransacked shops, looting and carrying off cheese, ham, oatmeal, potatoes and anything they could get their hands on. They also provided themselves with any item which could be used as a weapon, including guns and ammunition. Another armed mob appeared on the south side of the bridge and many more poured across to form an uncontrollable rabble.

The magistrates called for help from the militia and mounted dragoons arrived to quell the riot. Over fifty were arrested but the rioting continued into the next day. Stones were thrown at the police by rioters from the upstairs windows of buildings. There was shooting by the special constables and several men and a woman were killed, including a special constable.

Militia Ballot Act, 1792

The extension of the Militia Ballot Act to Scotland was unpopular. The Government needed to raise 6000 men. They were worried by events in France and that there would be a copycat revolution. As recruits were not readily signing up, it was decided that the registers of births held by the parish schoolmasters would provide names of single men aged nineteen to twenty-three, not already volunteers, to be balloted as candidates for the army.

However, it discriminated between the rich and poor by allowing someone to avoid or delay being called up if they could afford to pay officially for someone to stand in for them as a substitute. Young unemployed men were often willing to do this.

Riots broke out throughout Scotland. Men were arrested and were transported to Australia by Lord Braxfield. This was the signal for political reform and led, in 1797, to the establishment of the Society of United Scotsmen.

> These do certify that Thomas Young, weaver, who was balloted on the 5th day of April 1820 to serve in the Militia for the Parish of Louden in the County of Ayr hath produced David Orr as a Substitute to serve for him; and the said Substitute having been sworn in and enrolled accordingly, therefore the said Thomas Young is exempted from serving in the said Militia, until, by rotation it shall come to his turn
>
> *Pictorial History of Newmilns*,
> David Mair, compiler, 1988

Battle of Garscube

A mob of weavers at New Kilpatrick entered the schoolmaster's house and tore out pages from the register of baptisms so that their liability to be called up could not be proven. Another serious disturbance took place at New Kilpatrick, where rioters threatened to set fire to Garscube House, the home of the Lord President of the Court of Session, Ilay Campbell of Garscube. The volunteers were summoned and marched out from George Square, Glasgow, to Garscube Bridge. On arrival on a sunny July day they discovered that the rioters had dispersed, so they ransacked the hen-roosts, helped themselves to cheese and bannocks, and drank the public houses dry.

Tranent

At Tranent, on 29th August, 1797, a platoon of six men and a sergeant were sent to deal with a protesting crowd. They shouted 'No Militia' and a few stones were thrown. The Riot Act was read and the Cinque Ports Cavalry turned on men and women who were trying to present a petition to the ballot officers. The crowd were attacked indiscriminately. William Hunter, who was on a rooftop, was shot at and killed. George Elder and Joan Crookston were shot dead on the street and Isobel Rodger was also killed.

People walking along the road were shot at or speared. Men were left lying injured and dying. Peter Ness was hacked to death as he ran through a field of corn. Stephen Brotherstone was killed with a sabre. Eleven was the official number killed but, after the harvest, more bodies were found amongst the corn. Many others were wounded. No action was taken against the cavalry.

Tree of Liberty

At Galston, a Tree of Liberty was set up in defiance of the Militia Act and to show sympathy with the workers in France. The schoolmaster's house was invaded and the baptismal records removed.

Porteous Riot

Five smugglers, Andrew Wilson from Pathhead, Peter Galloway from Kinghorn, and George Robertson, William Hall and John Frier from Edinburgh, angered by their cargo being lifted by the excisemen, broke into the quarters of James Stark, customs officer at Kirkcaldy, and proceeded to recover goods to the value of those taken from them. They were caught and sentenced to death, then put into prison. However, on the Sunday before the execution they were taken from the Tolbooth to St Giles' Cathedral at which time Robertson, with Wilson's help, managed to escape. Hall and two others gained a reprieve and were sentenced to transportation for life.

John Porteous, the captain of Edinburgh's Town Guard and an unpopular man, was in charge of his men at the execution. He was angered at the action of the provost ,who had brought in a troop of soldiers in case any attempt was made to rescue Wilson. When the handcuffs would not fasten around Wilson's wrists, he forced them shut by brute strength, injuring Wilson and leaving him in agony. This upset the crowd, most of whom did not consider smuggling to be a crime and who were already sympathetic to Wilson.

Twenty minutes after Wilson was hanged, as the hangman began to cut him down, stones were thrown at Porteous and the Town Guard. Porteous retaliated by firing at the mob, and his men, who were armed with muskets, did likewise. Six people were killed and nine more were injured. Some were looking out of windows of the tall houses and there was such a crush that they could not move out of the line of fire. Porteous was arrested for murder and sentenced to death but was reprieved by Queen Anne. A letter was also sent to General Wade by Catherine Allardice stating that Porteous was innocent and that someone else had fired the first shot.

On 7th September, 1736, the eve of the day which would have been his execution, a group of men entered the city through the West Port at about nine o'clock. They beat a drum through the town to alert the people, then marched to the Tolbooth where Porteous was celebrating with friends. Stones were thrown at a group of magistrates who came out of a nearby tavern. They burned down the door of the Tolbooth; since it was strong it took a long time to burn, but eventually they dragged Porteous from his cell. The men broke into a chandler's and collected a rope, leaving a guinea to pay for it on his counter. When they reached a spot close to the Gallow's Stone they threw the rope over a dyer's pole and strung Porteous up until he was dead. Parliament attempted to levy fines on the citizens of Edinburgh, but did not succeed.

Prohibited Imports

Oatmeal was declared a prohibited import. On 1st February, 1770, the *Freemason* was prevented by customs officers from landing a load. On 13th February, a group of women, led by an old soldier and a piper, boarded the vessel in defiance of the tidesman and helped themselves to the meal. They, likewise, removed potatoes from a vessel bound for Greenock, and beans from one bound for Inveraray. They attacked the controller as he tried to reason with them, but, since the customs officers had no authority to arrest the women, they sent for the civil authorities to deal with them.

The Radical War

There was a great fear of revolution in 1820 when the authorities overreacted to rumours of uprisings by the 'army much talked of but never seen', as Lord Cockburn described the radical force which was believed to consist of weavers and other workers who were about to usurp the Government. Rewards were offered in the newspapers for information leading to those involved in conspiracy, using words like felons and traitors for those who were meant to be printing and distributing treasonable addresses.

Bluidy Batterie and Ryot

Politics resulted in numerous outbreaks of fisticuffs when feelings ran high. In many cases, the participants were magistrates, professional folk and landowners enraged at what they saw as chicanery. The desire to reform the old system of representation led to disaster, especially since it coincided with the French Revolution, which stirred up in the Scottish authorities the fear of a similar revolution. This meant that severe measures were taken to quell unrest and forbid meetings at which unrest could ferment.

Dumfries

The 'Corbies' were the merchants and capitalists, while the 'Pyets' were the tradesmen or artisans. A serious disagreement took place over the conduct of the election of the provost and councillors in 1759. The anger escalated into action, the Riot Act was read and twelve Pyets were tried at Edinburgh. The leader, a weaver, was transported for life and two others, a tailor and a shoemaker, for seven and fourteen years respectively. Others were fined and imprisoned. Two who failed to attend their trial were outlawed and their goods were confiscated.

Red Cap of Liberty

The red cap of liberty was worn by the French Revolutionaries. Demonstrations demanding electoral reform were held throughout central Scotland on 23rd October, 1819, at which weavers and miners paraded to meetings. Flags, which were then banned by the Government, were carried by many groups, while others, keeping to the letter of the law, waved giant thistles. Thousands of workers responded and listened to speakers who supported political reform.

> The females of Galston presented a cap of liberty and a flag to the committee in the name of two hundred and seventy female reformers and gave a paper to the chairman expressive of their sentiments.
>
> Private Diary, John Wallace, 1832

The Riot Act

The Riot Act was passed in 1714 to deal with the growing number of protests by the common people. They gathered in the streets or at market crosses to make their feelings known to the authorites. They often disagreed with Acts of Parliament, with taxes being imposed, and also took a moral stand against actions such as anatomists interfering with graves. This latter type of protest often included taking the law into their own hands, damaging property and rough-handling the people involved. The desire to force political reform through Parliament became a serious issue resisted ferociously by the authorities.

The Act prohibited unlawful gatherings of twelve or more persons behaving 'riotously and tumultuously' to the disturbance of the public peace. If the gathering had not dispersed an hour after the Riot Act was read, they were adjudged to be felons and could be put to death without the benefit of clergy. It was to be read by a Justice of the Peace 'with a loud voice'. The civil magistrate could, without waiting an hour, command the use of immediate force to maim or kill if in his opinion an outrage was committed, even if fewer than twelve people were involved.

Turnpike Act

There was great exception taken at Duns, in 1792, to the passing of the Turnpike Act. The charges were considered a nonsense, and the fact that the tolls were to include a profit for the landowner who appointed the toll-keeper was a factor that incensed the mob. The people organised a party to go out and destroy the toll gates by burning them or throwing them in the river. A few men were arrested and punished. Some were imprisoned for four months, then transported abroad for seven years, while others were transported for life. The Act was repealed in 1878.

SABBATH OBSERVANCE

The Sabbath began at dusk on Saturday evening and lasted until dusk on Sunday when a hot meal could be eaten. 'To inquire gif the Christiane Sabbot be reverentlie observit' was the task set for the commissioners. The observance of the Sabbath was of the utmost importance to Presbyterians, and the elders were considered as 'watchmen ower Christis flok'. Breaking it was a 'vice and enormity'.

In the seventeenth and eighteenth centuries the Church of Scotland possessed considerable powers over evil-doers, and was not slow to exercise them. The man who failed to attend church, and to cause his household to do likewise, speedily found himself in conflict with a power before which he must bow. His fate served as a warning to the like-minded. Hence church-going was universal; but, in a good many cases hypocritical.

The Auld Kirk and Its Worthies,
Dean Ramsay, 1912

The Church, as well as acting on the Word of the Bible, made an attempt to woo the people away from their old ways. The Roman Catholic Church had grafted many rituals onto what were originally pagan celebrations because they could not change the habits of the people; they had even permitted sport on Sunday as long as the people attended church.

The Presbyterians knew that the people clung to old practices, such as visiting sacred wells, and the only way to break the habit was by threat and punishment. Fines were imposed for breaking the Sabbath. In Aberdeen, in 1562, the threat was issued that the 'benefit of the kirk' would be withdrawn from all who did not attend services. The complaint was made by the elders to the town council that people were:

gaming and playing, passing to taverns and ale-houses, using the trade of merchandise and handy labour in time of sermon on the week-day.

Aberdeen Kirk Session Records, 1602

The statute against Sunday markets was passed in 1577, under penalty of goods being forfeited. Seven people were fined for 'slaying of flesche and working on the Sondaye, contrar the statutis' and again, in 1580, the Privy Council passed an Act against:

> Disturbance of kirks in time of divine service, the holding of markets and labouring on Sunday, or playing and drinking in time of sermon, requiring householders to have Bibles and psalm books, the punishment of strong and idle beggars, and the relief of poor impotent persons.

In every town, two elders were appointed to go through the streets 'in time of sermon'. They had the power to search any house, noting down the names of anyone at home, and to watch the ferry boat and note the names of those going off and on. A couple could be fined 13/4d and a craftsman 6/8d. In Perth and Aberdeen, in 1582, the fine was 20/- according to the Act of Parliament.

In 1585, tavern keepers were fined for selling ale in time of sermon. In 1591, tavern keepers complained of the new devoutness being urged on the populace, for sobriety affected their trade. John Pitscottie of Luncarty was fined for playing football and made to sit on the stool of repentance, others were fined for playing golf. The secular courts were also under the influence of the General Assembly of the Church of Scotland.

Complaints were also made about Highland reapers wandering the streets on Sundays waiting to be hired at the Monday market. The Kirk Sessions had the support of the town councils on this matter and both passed sentence when required.

> At Glasgow, in 1600, the Session ordains the Deacons of the Crafts to cause search for absents from the Kirks of all the freemen, the one-half of the fine to go to the Kirk and the other to the Craft.
>
> *Glasgow and Its Clubs*, John Strang, 1864

At Lasswade, in 1696, the laird decreed that all his tenants, their wives, colliers, servants and children, must meet at the grieve's house and march with him to the parish church every Sunday. In 1617, an Act of Parliament was passed allowing a servant under fourteen years of age to be fined or whipped for not observing the Lord's Day. This tendency to permit nothing to be achieved on a Sunday bar worship led to a satirical song:

> There was a Cameronian cat
> A-seeking for its prey,
> Went ben the hooses, an' caught a moose
> Upon the Sabbath day.

The elders they were horrified,
An' they were vexed sair.
Sae straicht they took that wicked cat
Before the meenistair.

The meenistair was sairly grieved,
An' much displeased did say,
"O bad, perverted pussy cat
Tae break the Sabbath day.

The Sabbath's been, frae days o' yore,
An IN-STI-TU-TI-ON.
Sae straichtway tak' this wicked cat
Tae EX-E-CU-TI-ON."

Traditional

In the eighteenth century, town councils were ever ready to support the Kirk Sessions in combatting Sabbath desecrators, and often appointed persons called 'compurgators' to arrest those found strolling or idling when they should have been in church. In Edinburgh, barbers were fined if they trimmed hair or shaved a man on a Sunday, and no child was permitted to play in the street without the parents being warned and reported to the civil magistrates to be fined.

The minister of New Macher was taken before his presbytery, in 1735, for powdering his wig on a Sunday and, when the wife of a nobleman gave birth to a deformed child, it was considered as God's punishment because he went hunting on the Sabbath when he should have been in church.

Bailies and provosts could punish people for not attending church on Sunday and twice during the week for prayers. In Glasgow, a man was employed to search out swearers who were reported to the town council and fined.

It was even considered an offence for cattle to be grazed outside on the Sabbath. At Moray, no-one was to attempt to rescue fishermen, even if their boat was sinking, for they should not have put to sea, and children at St Andrews found playing out-of-doors were to be whipped. At Lasswade, in 1696, parents whose children were caught playing out-of-doors were told to belt them privately, but if a child should be reported three times it would be belted publicly on the coal-hill by its parents.

SMUGGLING

Smuggling was never thought of as a crime by the majority of Scottish people. The Lothians, Ross-shire, Angus, Fife, Ayrshire and Galloway were the main areas where contraband was brought ashore, and Leith was a common place for tobacco smuggling. 'Brandy for the parson, baccy for the clerk', is the opening line of a poem describing the 'trade'.

The English imposed many more taxes than the Scots and, after the Union of 1707, the Scottish people resented having to pay extra for importing goods or making ale, whisky and cloth. Duty was paid on printed linen and calico. Excise officers were constantly on-site at textile factories. They had to mark each bale with an official stamp. While they were eating and drinking, the stamp would be stolen and copied. The counterfeit stamp would then be used on bales which were smuggled out and sold without tax. This tax was repealed in 1831.

In 1725, when the malt tax was imposed, 'No Union! No Malt Tax! No Salt Tax!', was the cry. There were riots in many places, the Riot Act was read and the instigators were thrown into prison.

Taxes were needed to finance wars but were resented by the public. A taste was developing for foreign goods. This annoyed the Government, who tried to protect their own revenue and trade by the Navigation Acts and by placing prohibitive taxes on these goods, but this resulted in people finding ways and means of obtaining them which ensured that no tax was paid.

In 1744, in the burgh records of Glasgow the city magistrates agreed to the republishing of a pamphlet against smuggling because the non-payment of the duties levied upon malt and spirits cut the revenues of the city.

Hiding Places

Often the goods required to be hidden until they could be transported away. There were caves, cellars, brandy holes – hidden beneath floor boards – and bolt holes beneath kilns. Coffins with false bottoms were made to transport goods. Balcary Bay on the

Solway was a safe haven for many loads. The smugglers were so successful that they built Balcary House with their profits. Beneath the house they had cellars built which were connected by a secret passageway to the caves on the shore. The Brandy Cave in Portling Bay was another place where nature was in tow with the smugglers. It ran inland for some distance and was an ideal hideout.

Signals

The smugglers depended on the cargo arriving offshore at a time suitable for its offloading. The tide had to be right and the organisation had to be in place for the removal of the goods. Many sea captains were involved in the trade. They looked for signals along the coast to inform them if it was safe to heave-to. A white sheet might be innocently, or so it seemed, placed on a thatched roof to dry; the blacksmith, at night, would work his bellows so that the sparks would send a signal or a bonfire would be lit on a cliff top. News of a landing brought everyone to the shore where it was all-hands to bring the goods onto the beach and load up the ponies and horses, often as many as two hundred with panniers on their backs.

Solutions

In 1806, Acts against smuggling were passed in Parliament and William Pitt the Younger reduced tax on goods which were favourites for smugglers. This cut their profits and reduced the activity. A tougher line was also taken with regard to smugglers who were caught. Heavy fines were in force, plus seizure of any boats involved. Signalling from the shore could lead to imprisonment, if proven, and if men were caught smuggling or handling smuggled goods, they faced three years of penal servitude, including stone-breaking, or else they were impressed into the Royal Navy for five years. As late as 1855, however, a carpenter, Richard Mendham from Spittal, Berwick, was executed for concealment of goods in secret cellars, theft and smuggling.

The Train

The 'lingowomen', called this after the ropes which they carried, were those who travelled inland with the pony train to its destination. They were often armed with pistols, cutlasses or knives. Sometimes the smugglers were bold and landed cargoes during the day. At Port William, Stairhaven and Monreith as many as one hundred and fifty to two hundred ponies set out while the customs officers watched from a distance, unable to interfere as they needed the back-up of the militia to cope with such a number. Eventually, in 1788, a customs office and a military barracks were established at Port William in an attempt to curb the trade.

Commodities

Malt

The imposition of a malt tax led to a drop in the brewing of ale which was being replaced by spirits, brandy, rum and wine brought to Scotland from France, Holland and Spain and offloaded in coves and bays all around the rocky coastline, usually under cover of darkness. The American War of Independence required an increase in taxation and further duties were imposed in 1770, which accelerated the smuggling trade.

Salt

Salt was an essential supply as everyone used it to preserve meat for use during the winter. Pans on the seashore were used to remove the salt from salt water. Place-names such as Prestonpans, Saltcoats and Salterness, now Southerness, indicate where this trade existed.

Girnels, where the salt was stored, were under the scrutiny of customs officers as it was a taxable property.

Under an Act passed in the reign of King George III, salt sent to the Isle of Man was duty-free. This salt often found its way back to Galloway to be sold in Scotland. Many magistrates turned a blind eye to the trade and appreciated the anker of brandy which mysteriously arrived for their own use. Fish-curing companies often became involved in salt smuggling.

Spirits

Spirits could be bought in France for ten to fifteen shillings per cask. It was of very high proof and could be watered down so that a cask containing three gallons when bought, plus the addition of two gallons of water, could be sold for three or four guineas, thus giving a handsome profit.

Locations

East Coast

Montrose, on the east coast, was a haven for smugglers for over forty years. The tide-waiters, whose job it was to patrol the shores, despite being armed were still unable to stem the trade and goods were brought ashore and sold on throughout the United Kingdom as far as London. At Slains, in Buchan, in 1798, Philip Kerney was killed by a revenue officer as he was delivering a load.

At Cromarty, an enterprising smuggler imprisoned for the offence bribed the jailor to allow him out at night to supervise a 'drop', promising that he would return in good time for being wakened in the morning. On that occasion the smugglers told stories of ghosts haunting the caves to keep away anyone who was too curious.

At Dundee, in 1707, the merchants raised willing mobs to raid the customs house and take tobacco. Excise officers were attacked and some of them were wounded. The militia were called out.

The Isle of Man

'Isle of Three Legs' was the name given to the Isle of Man. It was inherited by the Duke of Atholl in 1736 and it became known as 'the duke's storehouse'. He received customs dues from these loads. The island had its own separate laws so goods prohibited from being imported legally into Scotland could be freely brought to the Isle of Man.

Scottish ships were not above sailing to Boston with a legal load then returning with New England rum via Barcelona, where they also took on board Spanish brandy. This was then deposited on the Isle of Man, to be transferred later into casks, specially made on the island, for distribution by smaller ships in the coves around the Scottish coast.

> And at the Ross, wi' yawcking Johnie Dowall,
> And Manksman gabbling frae the manor-hole;
> What noggins hae we drank o' smuggled rum,
> Just hot frae off the Isle o' Three Legs come
> The Parish o' Borgue, Hackston in The Scottish Gallovidian
> Encyclopedia, John Mactaggart, 1824

Tragedy

A smuggler from the Isle of Man, on the eve of his wedding, along with his future brother-in-law was bringing salt to land it at Port o' Warren where he had a ready market and would make enough money for the forthcoming celebrations. Unfortunately for them they sailed past the *Prince Ernest Augustus*, a revenue cutter commanded by Sir John Reid, which lay at anchor nearby. The scout was hailed by the cutter and told to 'lay to', but they did not understand the language and kept going, whereupon a cannon ball hit it and the bridegroom was killed. His companion ran the boat aground at Colvend and ran away. The corpse was thrown onto the beach and the scout was towed away to Kirkcudbright.

Some local folk buried the body. When the brother of the bride eventually made his way home, the family were distraught and the father insisted that they launch a ship and go to collect his son's body. They all, including the bride-to-be, set sail for the Solway but a storm came up and the ship sank with all on board. Sir John Reid was tried before the High Court of Justiciary in Edinburgh for the Manxman's murder, but was discharged.

Western Isles

The islands of Sanda and Rathlin were haunts of smugglers. The goods were landed from a lugger onto the islands and were hidden away. When enough were accumulated they were distributed to the mainland in what appeared to be fishing boats. They were taken as far as Ayrshire. Money was offered to informers, though few ever took it, preferring to keep their knowledge to themselves. In one successful seizure many casks of spirits and chests of tea were captured.

Smugglers

Several gentlemen made a fortune out of running goods. Kirkman Finlay of Killearn, the cotton king, was the most daring of the traders involved. He smuggled goods onto the continent after Napoleon had declared a blockade on British goods.

Whole communities earned more from the trade than from their legitimate business. The famous firm of Coutts and Company, Edinburgh, had a member who was a partner in a firm in Rotterdam and who supplied goods for smuggling to the north and east of Scotland.

The seizure of a vessel, and subsequent discovery that avoidance of excise duty was taking place, meant that the ship was usually burned or scuttled on the spot. Sometimes it would be sold and the revenue taken by the Crown. Local people often tried to salvage the cargo once the customs vessel had sailed away.

The most active era for the 'fairtraders', as the smugglers preferred to call themselves, was the mid-eighteenth century. The ships were well-equipped, often having twenty or more guns. Warning systems were in place, the routes throughout the country well-defined and plenty of ponies and horses were available to move cargoes to their destinations.

The owners of these luggers were very powerful men and made a fortune from smuggling. The revenue cutters, which gave chase when they suspected that a ship was involved in a 'drop', rarely mangaged to catch them as by the time that they left port, the smugglers' ships would be well out to sea.

Johnnie Girr

He was well known in Auchencairn as being 'a penny short of a shilling', but he was not so daft when he was smuggling. Crossing from the Isle of Man in his wherry with a cargo of spirits, he was sighted by a revenue cutter which gave chase. Johnnie tied his barrels to a rope and sank them, told his lad to hide under a tarpaulin, then sat quietly at the helm. The cutter fired and hailed him as they came alongside. Johnnie looked up as in amazement and said 'Gude guide us! If I had kenned it wis me that you were firing at, I wad hae been terrible fleyd [afraid].' The revenue men, seeing only a stupid old man aboard, sailed away leaving Johnnie to retrieve his cargo and deliver it to its destination.

Excisemen

Excise men, or 'gaugers' as they were known, were few and despised by the ordinary people, who often refused to cooperate with them. People placed obstructions in the way of customs officers when they attempted to investigate reports of illegal landings of salt, brandy, rum, lace, silk, tea and tobacco. These gaugers had large territories to cover so it was easy to lay a false trail and to lure them in the wrong direction. Many tales exist of the game of fooling the gauger.

Bauldy Corson

An ex-recruitment officer named Sergeant Bauldy Corson was appointed a tide-waiter on the Solway Firth. He disguised himself as a smuggler and, on hearing of a drop, would run into a house where a group of smugglers were gathering and shout, 'The hale o' the Corbies o' the custom-house are less than a mile frae the Burnfoot. Hide yer goods!' The smugglers would oblige and he would help them. Next day he would come back with his men and arrest them.

Ministers

Ministers of the Church turned a blind eye to the practice and elders became involved, despite the condemnation of the General Assembly of the Church of Scotland in 1719, 1736 and 1744. In Hall's *Travels in Scotland*, published in 1807, the author remarks that it is a shame that the clergy in Orkney and the Shetland Isles should so often wink at their churches being made depositories for smuggled goods, chiefly foreign spirits.

The contraband trade had become about as common an investment for men of capital as any other business. Merchants fitted out well-found vessels for smuggling; lairds and ministers not only connived at it, but put their money into the venture. Mr Carson, minister at Anwoth, was deprived of his living [livelihood] in 1767 because he was proved to be deeply implicated in the 'fair trade'.

A History of Dumfries and Galloway,
Sir Herbert Maxwell, 1896

There is some evidence, however, to suggest that he was framed by those of the smuggling fraternity because he would not cooperate with them. Kirk Session records reported the punishment of members of their congregations for running goods on a feast day, the crime being not so much the smuggling but the breaking of the holy day.

TREASON

After King James I was murdered at Perth, the conspirators were taken to Edinburgh and imprisoned in the castle dungeon. Before they were executed, in 1437, they were carted for three days down to the market cross where red-hot iron crowns were placed on their heads and their limbs gradually dislocated one after the other. They were disembowelled and quartered while still alive and, after death, parts of their bodies were displayed at strategic places across Scotland.

The Black Dinner

William, sixth Earl of Douglas, was fifteen when he succeeded his grandfather as Lord of Galloway. He and his younger brother David rode to Edinburgh Castle in November 1440 as guests of the boy king, James II, who was then ten years of age. The two regents, Sir Alexander Livingstone and Sir William Crichton, betrayed them and charged the Douglases with treason. A black bull's head was placed before them at dinner, a sign which denoted death. The young king was forced to preside at their trial when they were sentenced to execution and beheaded.

Impeachment

This is the term used for the act of accusing and prosecuting another of treason or violation of allegiance to the head of state. The King's Advocate, in April 1601, took the decision to prosecute Archibald Cornwall, a town's officer of Edinburgh. It was customary for household goods poinded for debt to be sold by auction in the street. A sale was to take place close to the public gibbet and, as part of his job, Cornwall was putting the goods on display. Amongst them there was a portrait of King James VI. Unthinkingly, he hammered a nail into the frame of the gibbet on which to hang the portrait. Some of the gathered crowd objected to its proximity to the gibbet and he immediately took it down.

He was reported to the King's Advocate, Lord Hamilton, who, although there was no precise statute under which this 'crime' could be tried, accused him of impeachment. He was tried, convicted and hanged with a paper stating his offence stuck to his forehead. After twenty-four hours he was cut down and the gibbet was burned.

Execution

The populace, having little else in the form of entertainment and not having modern sensibilities on such matters, enjoyed an execution and turned out in their hundreds. For most crimes, a ladder was placed against the beam of the gallows and the rope attached to the gibbet, an arm sticking out at right angles to the beam. The prisoner walked out, climbed up and stood waiting as the hangman adjusted the noose around the neck. The hangman then pushed the prisoner off the ladder and the weight triggered the noose and tightened the knot, which eventually strangled the victim.

For treason, a heading sword, which cost around £5, was used. The head was cut off and caught in a basket. It was then placed on a spike and displayed, usually at the tolbooth or at a gate or port, as the entrance to a walled town was called, as a warning to others.

Other parts of the prisoner's anatomy were also displayed for this purpose. The Marquis of Montrose was hanged in Edinburgh, in May 1650, on a gibbet which was thirty feet high, for his part in opposing the Solemn League and Covenant.

> The Marquis of Argyle appeared on the balcony to see him driven on the hangman's hurdle [a wattle sledge] to the prison from which he was two days after to walk to the gallows, and that Lord Lorn took post at a window near the scaffold, to see the body cut to pieces after death. The head being stuck on the Tolbooth of Edinburgh and the limbs sent for exhibition over the ports of Glasgow, Perth, Stirling and Aberdeen, Charles the second was compelled to behold those ghastly relics of the most loyal of his subjects, when, less than a month after, he progressed through the country.
>
> *Domestic Annals, From the Reformation*
> *to the Revolution*, Vol 2, Robert Chambers, 1874

The remains of Montrose were buried in a pit on the Burghmuir.

> They brought him to the Watergate,
> Hard bound with hempen span,
> As though they held a lion there,
> And not a fenceless man.
> They sat him high upon a cart—

The hangman rode below–
They drew his hands behind his back,
And bared his noble brow.
Then as a hound is slipped from leash,
They cheered the common throng.
And blew the note with yell and shout,
And bade him pass along.

> *The Execution of Montrose*, W. E. Aytoun, in *Domestic Annals*
> *of Scotland*, Vol 1, *From the Reformation to*
> *the Revolution*, Robert Chambers, 1814

After 1587, anyone making a claim of treason which was not proven was himself to be punished as a traitor. This was to stamp out malicious accusations by one family against another.

The Radicals

The last execution in Scotland for high treason was in 1820, after an armed radical rising by those who wanted to reform the voting rights. Around thirty men defied a troop of the Hussars at Bonnymuir. The leaders, Andrew Hardie and John Baird, and twenty others were tried at Stirling for high treason and sentenced to be hanged, their heads severed and their bodies drawn and quartered. The others were to be transported. The leaders were hanged on 8th September by a hangman who wore a black mask and a sack-cloth cloak for disguise. After they were dead, he cut off their heads, but the bodies were not quartered as advised and the crowd moved away.

John Knox

In 1563, during the absence of Mary, Queen of Scots, her household and some of the citizens of Edinburgh held mass at Holyrood Palace. They were invaded by townsmen who were Protestants, and accused of transgressing the law. Two of the invaders were arrested. John Knox wrote a letter to the Protestant leaders asking that they attend the trial to prevent any violence breaking out.

The queen was angry and accused Knox of treason. The Queen's Advocate, John Spens, himself a reformer, summoned Knox to the council chamber where the queen interrogated him. He was found not guilty.

> That nycht [there] was neither dansing nor fyddilling in the
> Courte; for Madame wes disappoyntit of hir purpois, quhilk
> wes to haif Johne Knox in hir will, be vote of hir Nobylattie.
> *The Lord Advocates of Scotland*, vol 1,
> George W. T. Omond, 1883

Robert Lesley

He made history by being convicted as a traitor, though already dead. In 1540, his body was exhumed and brought to the bar of the court in order that his lands and possessions could be declared forfeit. Doom was pronounced and his heirs deprived of their estate. This caused an uproar in high places and an Act amending the law was reluctantly passed by Parliament.

WITCHCRAFT

Throughout Europe, in the sixteenth and seventeenth centuries, and in Scotland as late as the eighteenth century, ordinary men and women were being pursued, tried and put to death for witchcraft. There were three main witchcraft panics in Scotland during which many men and women were tortured and put to death: 1590–1597, 1640–1644 and 1660–1663.

In 1479, Thomas Cochrane, a courtier at the Scottish Court, accused King James III's brother, John, Earl of Mar, of melting down a waxen image of the king with intent to harm him. He and his other brother, Alexander, were taken to prison in Edinburgh, where John was bled to death.

In 1488, the *Malleus Maleficarum* – The Hammer against Evildoers – was published in Germany. This was a guide to questions which should be asked to determine a witch, together with the appropriate answers expected. It was published to help judges stamp out the 'international conspiracy of witchcraft' which was then believed to exist. Should any judge question these guidelines and defend a witch, he could also be held guilty of witchcraft. Scotland was closer to the continent of Europe in legal matters than to England and so followed European methods of dealing with witches, which included torture and burning at the stake.

An Act was passed in 1563 stating that:

> Nae person take upon hand to use ony manner of witchcrafts, sorcery, or necromancy, nor give themselves furth to have ony sic craft or knowledge thereof, there-through abusing the people [and] nae person seek ony help, response or consultation at ony sic users or abusers of witchcrafts... under the pain of death.

A poem published in the nineteenth century attacks the gullibility of the people who suspected all old women of dabbling in witchcraft:

> But, Robin, your mither was auld and puir,
> And the seasons cauld and keen,
> The white snaw was on her hair,

The frost film ower her een . . .
O Robin, Robin, I kenna hoo
The lee was faither'd first,
But (whisper again, lest they ken, lest they ken!)
They thought the puir body accurst!
They thought that the spell had been wrought in Hell,
To kill and curse and blight;
They thought that she flew, when naebody knew,
To a Sabbath of fiends, ilk night.
Then ane whose corn had wither'd ae morn
And whose kye sicken'd doon,
Crept, scared and pale, wi' the leein' tale
To the meenisters, up the toon.
They bade her tell she had wrought the spell
That made the tempest blaw,
They strippet her bare as a naked bairn
They tried her wi' pincers and heated airn
Till she shriek'd and swooned awa'!
O, Robin, Robin . . . they doomed her to burn
Doon yonner upon the quay . . .
This night was the night . . . see the light! see the light!
How it burns by the side o' the sea.

Robert Buchanan, 1797

The trial of witches before James VI (from a drawing of the time).

The power and influence of witches, those with an evil eye and malign fairies were believed in by the majority of the population of Scotland. Those who may have had doubts usually hedged their bets and played safe by observing certain rites and customs which would ensure against the possibilites of upsetting such sinister entities.

Many of the women, and the few men, who were charged were suffering from delusions, were natural healers, or were bothersome to their neighbours who delighted at taking revenge by accusing them of witchcraft.

The Reformation's aim to obliterate things popish took a strange turn on the subject of witchcraft. Rather than pouring scorn on the idea, the Presbyterian Church took up the search for anyone suspected of dealing in the white, as well as the black, arts or of being in league with the devil.

The Old Testament stated a belief in witches, wizards, enchantments and effective curses. The Bible admonition, 'Thou shalt not suffer a witch to live' was taken literally. Kings, privy councillors, lawyers, judges and ministers of the Kirk sincerely believed in their existence and in pacts with the devil to harm the community.

These pacts involved the renouncement of a person's baptism and their being marked with a special devil's mark. The crime to be investigated was that of being a confessed witch in league with Satan. These intelligent and educated men gave credence to the idea that ordinary men and women could fly through the air on a cornstalk or put a curse on anyone who displeased them, making them wither away and die. In addition, they tortured those accused of these crimes until they confessed that they consorted with the devil, and believed that in doing so they were saving their soul.

It is worthy of remark in almost all cases of witchcraft the trial and the punishment following upon conviction, were as frequently for the public profession of the art, using sorcerie etc., and for abusing people with their devilish craft, as for the act of witchcraft itself.

Criminal Trials in Scotland, Vol 1, William Pitcairn, 1833

In Pitcairn's opinion, it was the blasphemy of the people believing in supernatural powers that inflamed the Presbyterians more than the acts themselves.

Church and State worked hand in hand in organising trials for witchcraft. Church law helped to frame the political agenda and keep those who might stray from the faith in place; self-interest caused the heritors to pursue those whom they wished removed for economic gain, often charging them with 'diablerie'.

The doctrines of Scottish Calvinism, hinging as they did on souls being in a state of grace, and the fear of the power of the Devil to deprive them of reaching this, could have convinced the ministry that they were saving, rather than punishing, those who confessed to making a pact with the Devil or to practising witchcraft.

In 1640, the General Assembly reminded ministers and elders

to be vigilant and to 'carefully take notice of charmers, witches, and all such abusers of the people, and to urge the Acts for Parliament to be execute against them'. In 1646, the Kirk Session of Auchterhouse initiated a fast day 'because of the scandal of witches and charmers in the district'.

> The Minister made report that the Presbytery having considered the affair relative to Janet Kennedy suspect of witchcraft, found many things in her carriage which were very unchristian, yet in regard it is very difficult to know what will amount to a legall probation of witchcraft. They resolved to consult his Majesties Advocate (as also the Committee of the Commission of this General Assembly, who are to be in their bounds sometime this summer) anent her and others in ye like circumstances. The [Kirk] session having considered the foresaid report, left that affair in the Presbytery's hands, and delayed [kept in prison] Elspet Goldie, till that be discussed.
>
> *Minnigaff Kirk Session Records*, 18th May, 1699

King James VI was fanatical in routing out witches and became obsessed with witch-hunts, accusing men and women of meeting with the Devil to plan acts of sorcery against him. This led to the persecution of the North Berwick witches for treason, and, in 1590, around seventy persons faced the charge of attempting to destroy the ship in which he was returning from Denmark by causing storms through the use of enchantment.

Ordinary people saw the practical proof of witchcraft everywhere. If something went wrong, a local witch would be blamed. There were people believed to have the evil eye, and those who could cast spells that would bring harm, cause storms, blight crops, cause illnesses in people and animals, and were even capable of changing themselves into hares and other creatures in order to go unnoticed.

In the late sixteenth century, the Justice Court had a mania for trying witches. The King's Advocate, who appeared for the prosecution, sanctioned torture. Ministers of the Church, privy councillors and the Lord Justice-Clerk were also present. King James VI often attended these occasions and was praised for his courage in witnessing these acts.

Acts of Parliament were passed, in 1649, imposing capital punishment on blasphemy, the worship of false gods and incest. Consultors of spirits, not mentioned in an Act of 1563, passed under Mary, Queen of Scots, that banned the practice of witchcraft, were now included.

During the lulls in persecutions, confessions of seeking out magic powers was punished by whipping and banishment from the district on pain of death, should the accused return.

Janet Scott ane little aged woman suspect of witchcraft is ordained by the magistrates to goe presently out of this Burgh and never be seen in it again.

Dumfries Burgh Records, May 13th, 1658

From 1662, torture was abolished as a means to extract confessions of practising witchcraft and no convictions were permitted unless there was strong evidence. However, in the reign of King William III, there was renewed zeal and more witches were put to death. As late as 1702, Margaret Myles was hanged at Edinburgh but, in Ross-shire, witches were set free at Fortrose with a rebuke.

In 1727, however, also in Ross-shire, three women were burned in barrels of pitch. One of them, burned at Dornoch, was so cold that she warmed herself at the fire before being put into the tar barrel. Her 'crime' was that she transformed her daughter into a pony and rode on her back to carry out her evil deeds. The proof was that her daughter was lame and also had twisted hands.

In 1736, the Act against witchcraft was finally abolished and the death penalty replaced by a year in prison. Practitioners of occult arts, who 'pretended to tell fortunes and discover stolen goods', were made to stand on the pillory weekly for three months.

As late as 1805, Jean Maxwell was tried at Kirkcudbright under this legislation, and during her prison sentence, was made to stand in the jougs for an hour once per quarter on a market day.

Church Courts

Presbytery and Kirk Session records across most of Scotland contain references to the examination and trials of parishioners for witchcraft. There were three types of evidence – circumstantial, voluntary confession and delation. The first accusations, 'delations', were made to the Kirk Session of the parish to which the witch belonged by one or more parishioners. These were often anonymously placed by fellow parishioners in a special box left for this purpose at the door of the church.

The man or woman was then 'compeared', that is, called to appear before the session, 'interrogat' (questioned), 'deponed' (heard the evidence given against them), and told of their punishment. Often a dossier was built up before drastic action was taken. One of the earliest recorded trials for witchcraft was in 1563, when Agnes Mullikane of Dunfermline was banished from her parish on pain of death should she attempt to return.

The Kirk Session often decided to forward the case to the Presbytery for action to be taken and, on many occasions, this led to a request from the Presbytery to the Privy Council and later to the Committee of Estates to set in motion an enquiry into such behaviour. Most trials took place within the sheriff courts of the town council, but some trials reached the High Court of Justiciary in Edinburgh.

Some judges refused to convict for witchcraft and voiced doubts as to the legality of the evidence against the accused. In 1597, these men were threatened with excommunication by the General Assembly of the Church of Scotland if they refused to sentence a witch to death. The magistrates were offered the property of the witches as a bribe. There are records of witches having been found not guilty by the Privy Council, but then being persecuted by the clergy in the hope of further evidence coming to light.

Disposal of Witches

There were many methods of disposing of a witch. The courts pronounced sentence on the accused, usually that they be 'wirreit', which meant strangled then burned or to be 'burnt quick' which meant being placed alive in barrel of tar that was set alight.

> Paid Mr Andrew Wilson, vicar of Peebles, £3 Scots, as part payment of 100 merks due by the Presbytery for burning witches.
> *Records of the Parish of Drummelzier*, 28th July, 1652

In 1588, Alison Pierson of St Andrews, who cured many people, including the Archbishop of St Andrews, with ointments and other herbal treatments, believed that she could speak to the fairies and was convicted and burnt at the stake.

Forres was once a town of great importance and on the Castle Hill stood the residence of the hereditary sheriffs of Moray.

> Forres, in the days of yore,
> A name 'mang Scotia's cities bore,
> And there her judges o'er and o'er
> Did Scotland's laws disperse.

After a visit there, in 1600, King James VI took ill at Scone. Word was sent to the governor of the castle that an enquiry should be made and, at midnight, some witches were discovered with a wax image of the king which they were slowly melting in front of a fire. They were dragged to the top of Cluny Hill and placed in empty barrels which were rolled down the hill. When they came to rest, they and their contents were set on fire. A stone was put up to mark the spot.

At Biggar, in December 1649, the Commission of Enquiry met with members of the Presbytery of Biggar and examined Janet Bowis, lately imprisoned at Peebles, regarding her confession and accusation against various others whom she had declared to be witches. Much to the dismay of the Presbytery, she broke down and said that she had made false accusations. However, their hearts fired with zeal, they set out to uncover every witch within the boundaries of the Presbytery of Biggar. As parish records show, by 1650, several women had been accused. In 1652, at Kirklawhill, Peeblesshire, a number of men and women were burned at the stake.

In Teviotdale, in 1650, a horse dropped dead suddenly and the local people immediately suspected that a witch had cast a spell on it and other animals. In order to break the spell, the owner of the dead horse cut out its heart and roasted it on a fire lit outdoors for that purpose. A greyhound appeared out of the wood and attempted to grab the heart from the fire. It was struck on the back by a spectator because he believed that it was a witch in disguise.

Another villager appeared on the scene to ask for help as his wife had suddenly suffered acute back pain and could not move. The gathered crowd concluded that this was because she had been the witch who had caused the horse's death. It was believed that she turned into the dog and when it was struck by the stick and fled, changed back into the form of the woman, the injury remaining. Most likely, it was a slipped disc or an attack of lumbago which she suffered, but the feelings of the crowd ran high.

The enraged villagers dragged the dark-haired, black-eyed woman from her cottage, insisted on her repeating the Lord's Prayer and, when she stumbled on some of the words, tied her hands and feet and threw her onto the fire where she burned to death. The reaction of her husband is not recorded.

Out of ten women accused of witchcraft at Dumfries in 1659, nine had to find £50 security for good behaviour and were then banished from the parish. Eight ministers were appointed by the Presbytery of Dumfries to attend the nine convicted women, speak with them and be present at their execution. The victims were taken by carts to the place on the sands where they were to be bound to stakes, strangled, then burned to ashes.

At Forfar, nine witches were burned at the stake between 1650 and 1662. They were led in chains to the Witches' Howe, a small hollow north of the town, where the stake at which they were to be burned was erected. They wore an iron bridle – a four-part collar with a chain and a prong which was placed in their mouth as a gag. This was recovered from the ashes afterwards and used again. There were complaints about so many witches being burned.

> But now belyke the Colles this happy yeare
> By burning witches are grown wondrous deare.
>
> William Lithgow, 1660

The following items refer to a commission granted on 8th June, 1624, for the trial, at Dumbarton, of Marion MacLintock, Marion Fallisdaill and Janet MacKinlay.

> Item gevin to John Sempill's boye for going to Burrowstouness and for extracting of a process lettir against the witches in Apryl, 1624. £3

> Item to John Sempill to ryd to Stirling to the chancellar and certaine Lords of the [Privy] Counsall thair for getting ane comissioun to put the witches to ane assyze the fourth of May, 1624. £20

> Item debursit upone the witches eftir thair apprehension in the Tolbooth as follows:

> First for aill and breid to Janet Boyd, witche, the 25 of August, 1628. 1s 4d

> Item for collis and pettis to the Tolbooth for hir at sundrie tymis and for Marion MacLintock with sum aill.11s 4d

> Item to Mr. Alexander Colvill at delyverie to him as Justice-Depute of the said Jonat Boydis confession in writ whairon the Commission was grantit, his disjoone with the majestrattes. £2.2s

> *Dumbarton Common Good Accounts, 1614–1660*, I. M. M.
> Macphail, 1972

Further information was gathered against them from a variety of people. Janet Boyd confessed that she had disowned her baptism, made a pact with the Devil, received his mark and had carnal dealings with him. She also admitted to charming, which made people ill. The executioner was sent for from Renfrewshire and items of expenditure are recorded for wine, watching the witches, rope to bind them to the stake and also to strangle them. David

Glen was the doomster and executioner who burned them at the stake.

There are many reports of old women being harassed as witches. Elspeth McEwan lived alone in Dumfriesshire. She was compeared by the Dalry Kirk Session, in 1696, for having a wooden pin with which she could draw off the milk from her neighbours' cattle, and she was also accused of affecting the laying power of their hens. For this she was sent to Kirkcudbright jail where, for two years, she waited to be tried. She was so badly treated that in March 1698 she pleaded with her captors to kill her.

A Commission, led by Sir John Maxwell, with the power to recommend burning to death, examined her along with another woman, Mary Millar, in June 1697. The Lords of His Majesty's Privy Council sentenced them to death in July 1698, Elspeth McEwan upon her own confession 'of a compact and correspondence with the devil, and charms and of accession to malefices'. She was burned in a tar barrel at Kirkcudbright in August of that year.

For peats to burn the witch	£5 Scots
For coals to burn the witch	16/-
For ropes to bind her as she was roastit	4/-
A tar barrel for to burn her	£5.4/-
For a cart to carry her	6/-
For a pint of ale for the executioner when she was burning	2/-
For the drummer	8/-
Drink money for the executioner	£5.5/-

The Account Book of the Burgh
Treasurer of Kirkcudbright, 1698

Maggie Osborne was an illegitimate daughter of the Lord of Fail, known as 'The Warlock'. The Presbytery of Ayr at last forced her to confess that she was a witch by making her dance on a red-hot iron plate. She was condemned to death, in 1698, by burning at the stake. Legend says that even as the flames consumed her, she started to rise above them and waft away as if by magic. The Town Officer hooked her petticoats with his halberd and forced her back into the fire.

In 1704, Lillias Adie was accused of witchcraft at Torryburn, and admitted meeting the Devil behind a stook in the field and having danced with him. On this 'confession' she was burned within the tide-mark. Her minister, the Reverend Logan, claimed to know a witch by looking her in the eye.

Bessie Carmichael lived near Biggar and was feared because of her 'grewsum' looks. She had the power of healing and a wide knowledge of natural cures. One day, she told a man that he would rue his decision not to help her to take grain to the mill: his horse kicked him and he died from the blow. This was seen as Bessie's revenge and the people demanded that she be burned as a witch. Luckily for her this incident took place in the late eighteenth century when the practice had more or less ceased.

In 1688, Sir George Maxwell, Lord of Pollok, who became known as the 'bewitched baronet', was seized with a severe illness and the cause was considered to be witchcraft. A young vagrant woman offered to name the offenders and proceeded to take revenge on many women who had despised her in the past. She placed clay figures in their houses which were used as evidence of their guilt. A Government Commission consisting of several Lords of Justiciary and local landowners was convened. They found the accused guilty and seven innocent women were strangled and burned.

Overcrowding of Jails

The accused was held in jail until a date for a trial was set. This led to overcrowding within the jails and to complaints from local authorities that the cost of maintenance was getting out of hand. In March 1650, the burgh of Lanark complained that the Marquis of Douglas had sent eleven women accused of witchcraft by Janet Couts, 'a confessing witch' in prison at Peebles, to the jail at Lanark. The burgh declined to maintain so many women awaiting trial. A decision was made that the parishes of Douglas, Peebles and Lanark had in turn to produce twelve men every twenty-four hours to guard them, and the minister of that parish had to try 'by prayer and exhortation' to make them confess.

> One Marion Purdie, dwelling at the West Port of Edinburgh, once a milk-wife, and now a beggar, was apprehended and imprisoned as a witch. She was accused of laying diseases and frenzies upon her neighbours. The king's advocate was now giving little heed to such cases, and so poor Marion 'dies of cold and poverty in prison about Christmas'.
>
> *Domestic Annals of Scotland*, Vol 2, *From the Revolution to the Restoration*, Robert Chambers, 1874

> On the 12th March 1698, the Magistrates granted an allowance to the jailor for keeping warlocks and witches imprisoned in the Tolbooth by order of the Commission of Justiciary.
>
> *Annals of Glasgow*, Vol 1, James Cleland, 1816

Prickers

All those accused of witchcraft were searched for the Devil's Mark. Any brown patch of skin or blemish of any kind would be considered as evidence of guilt. As many of those accused were elderly, they would naturally have liver spots and small warts. Men were employed as prickers. They would pierce such marks with a long pin. If the accused did not scream or the spot did not bleed they were considered to be guilty. Sometimes these men would travel miles to carry out the examination.

In 1590, Geillis Duncan, maidservant to David Seaton, the baron's depute-bailie at Tranent, was examined for the Devil's Mark. It was discovered on her throat and, after having her fingers squeezed by the 'pilniewinkles', another name for the thumbscrews, in panic she confessed, naming as fellow witches a midwife, the daughter of a late Lord of Session and the wife of a notable citizen. All were hanged at Edinburgh on the strength of her accusations.

John Fian or Cunningham, a schoolmaster at Prestonpans, confessed to what now appears to be ludicrous accusations.

> Passing to Tranent on horseback, and ane man with him, [he] by his devilish craft, raisit up four candles upon the horse's twa lugs [ears], and anither ane upon the staff whilk the man had in his hand, and gave sic licht gin it been daylicht, like as the same candles returnit with the said man at his hamecoming, and causit him fall dead at the entry within his house.
> *Dumbarton Common Goods Accounts, 1614–1660,*
> edited by Fergus Roberts and I. M. M. Macphail, 1972

On his being searched, no mark was found, but he was put in prison from which he escaped. On being re-arrested, he was tortured by having needles driven into his fingers beneath his nails which were then torn off by pincers. His legs were crushed by the boot until 'the blood and marrow spouted forth'. He was sentenced to death and hanged, his goods being forfeited to the Crown.

> Item to Alexander Boigs in Innerkip for his paines for tryall of the marks of these givin up for witchcraft.
> £13.6.8d [£1.36]

> Item for my awin chairges in going to bring the said Alexander
> £6.13.4d

> Item givin to Andro Davie for rowing Johne McWilliam
> the warlock   8/-

John Hay, from Tain, aged sixty in 1661, was denounced as a wizard and was searched by John Dick who shaved his head in case any mark was hidden beneath his hair. He pierced Hay's flesh several times with a needle. Hay was accused and taken to Edinburgh and locked in the Tolbooth. He raised a petition as to his innocence and was one of the few who were released.

John Kincaid was one of the most famous witch prickers. These men seem to have had knowledge of parts of the body which do not feel pain. It was on this fact that the accused was condemned. Some of those accused complained about the torture which they suffered at the hands of men like Kincaid and, eventually, many of the prickers were themselves tried and imprisoned for fraud.

Torture

Forcing a woman to admit to being a witch and encouraging her to name her associates was the stated aim of the accusers. She was nearly always put into prison where her head was shaved and she might be stripped naked and left alone in the dark. The woman was often tortured to make her confess, and she was shown no mercy.

> Item payet to Walter Campbell for ane paire of sheirs for taking the hair aff Margaret Corruith, Jonet Davidsoune, who was in the Tolbuith for the cryme of witchcraft.
>
> *Dumbarton Common Goods Account, 1657–58*, edited by Fergus Roberts and I. M. M. Macphail, 1972

The King, James VI, and his Advocate looked on as an iron frame was fixed around the leg of a man or woman and the leg thrust into a furnace until the iron grew hot and burned the flesh. The advocate would ask questions while this was happening, in the hope of extracting a confession. The victim's head had a rope tied around it drawn so tight that their eyes bulged. Needles were pushed under their nails or the nails pulled off with pincers. All these tortures might be applied to the same person until they confessed.

Branks

A special witch's bridle was placed over the accused's head. Instead of one tongue piece, it had four prongs which were forced into the cheeks, on the palate and against the tongue. She was chained to an iron ring in a prison cell and starved of food and drink.

Pressing to Death

The use of weights to squeeze the life out of those convicted was also used for witches. In Orkney, in 1597, Alison Balfour was put in hot leg irons for forty-eight hours and forced to watch her husband being stretched by the 'lang irons' with a fifty-stone weight, and her eldest son being whipped fifty-seven times. Her daughter, aged seven, had her fingers crushed by thumbscrews to force Agnes to confess.

In 1618, Lord Eglinton of Ardrossan ordered Margaret Barclay to have bar after bar of iron continually added, pressing down onto her legs until she confessed. She was then, along with a fellow accused, 'wirriet' – strangled and burned.

At Pittenweem, in 1704, an old woman, Janet Cornfoot, was accused of causing harm to a fisherman, Alexander McGregor. He was determined to have her put to death, but she was simply banished from the parish, which displeased him. The parish minister of the place in which she sought refuge forced her to return to Pittenween accompanied by two men.

An angry mob seized her, dragged her by the heels through the streets, tied her to a rope strung between the harbour wall and a vessel at sea and, as she swung back and forth, pelted her with stones. Brought ashore, the mob beat her with sticks, then some of them found an old door with which they covered her body and they stood on it until their weight crushed her to death. She was denied a Christian burial. The ringleaders were investigated by the Privy Council but not punished.

Sleep Deprivation

Wakers were men who worked in shifts to keep the witch awake by applying lighted candles to the soles of her feet, between her toes and even in her mouth. Sometimes, she was strung up by her thumbs. A hair shirt steeped in vinegar was used to strip her skin from her body.

In Dunfermline, every citizen had to take their turn as a 'waker of witches'. One woman complained to the Privy Council that she had been kept awake for twenty days, naked but for a sackcloth. Thomas Palpla of Kirkwall spent eleven days and nights being tortured with the thumbscrew and the boot.

> He being naiket in the meane tyme and skairgeit [whipped] with tows [ropes] in sic sort that thay left nather flesch nor hyde upon him.
> *Ancient Criminal Trials in Scotland, from 1488 to 1624,*
> Robert Pitcairn, 1833

Beatie Laing of Pittenweem was accused of being a witch in 1704. She was supposed to have cursed a young lad of sixteen, Patrick Morton, son of the blacksmith, because he refused to give her some nails. He began to waste away and to have fits. She was forced to confess, but her friends organised her escape from prison and took her home. She was again taken and thrown into the 'Thieves' Hole' and was tortured by pricking and being deprived of sleep for five days and five nights. She was then placed in a deeper dungeon with no light; no-one was to speak to her and there she lay for five months before being released and banished. She returned home, in 1705, after applying to the Privy Council for protection. They ordered that the magistrates of Pittenweem were to defend her from violence from other citizens.

Swimming a Witch

The idea of swimming a woman to determine her guilt or innocence of the crime of practising witchcraft was often used. She was forced into deep water; if she sank she was innocent, the only satisfaction being that her family rejoiced that she had been cleared of suspicion. If she floated, this indicated that she was guilty and she was then dragged from the water and tied to a stake to be burned alive.

Many places had specific pools or water-holes which were used for this purpose. At Jedburgh, a coven of witches, which included the local schoolmaster's wife, was accused of drowning the local schoolmaster in 1787. They were put to trial in the pool, a spot beneath the Townfoot Bridge used for such activities and, as all floated, they were burned. At Aberdeen, it was The Pottie in the harbour, in Edinburgh, the Nor' Loch, where not only witches, but those convicted and sentenced at private courts held at night were immediately dispatched of in its grim waters. At Elgin, the Order Pot, perhaps a corruption for 'ordeal' pot, was the place where witches and Lossiemouth sheep stealers were drowned. Gaun's Pool at Keith was where 'old women, who were found guilty of familiarities with the Devil were drowned'.

At Dumbarton in 1624 they were tied to the incoming tide-mark:

> Item to William Makkie, merchand, for furneishing ane hundereth naylis to the wattirmark and certane towis [rope] to bind the witches specialle Jonet McKinlay and for the candill for the Tolbuith. £1.0.4d Scots [10p]
>
> *Dumbarton Common Goods Account, 1657–58*, edited by Fergus Roberts and I. M. M. Macphail, 1972

Whipping

A woman convicted of witchcraft was often publicly whipped before being banished. In 1709, Janet Harestanes of Kirkbean was 'scourged through Dumfries by the hand of the common hangman and branded on the cheek by a hot iron'.

Warlocks

There were a number of men throughout the period of the witchcraft trials who were accused and burned at the stake. Thomas McKean McAllan McKendrick, in 1590, helped Lady Foulis of Ross-shire dispose of her step-son, Hector, by means of making an image of butter into which shots were fired in an attempt to cause him harm. McKendrick was later accused and burned at the stake.

In 1633, John Colquhoun of Luss was tried in his absence for sorcery, witchcraft, necromancy, incest and adultery. His goods were 'put to the horn with three severall blasts of ane horn as use is'. They were forfeited to the Crown.

Major Thomas Weir was a captain of the Edinburgh Town Guard. He never went anywhere without a tall black staff. He was a devout man, unmarried, who lived quietly with his sister Grizel. He became ill and hallucinated, confessing to diabolical crimes. He was put in prison awaiting trial for this confession. He kept saying, 'Torment me no more – I am tormented enough already'. He was sentenced, in April 1670, to be strangled and burned at Gallowlea, between Edinburgh and Leith. His 'magic' stick was burned with him and his sister was also sentenced to be hanged in the Grassmarket. At her trial she declared that their mother was a witch. She had inherited from her a peculiar horseshoe mark on her forehead. Both were probably suffering from delusions or dementia.

Nicol Neville was burned at St Andrews in 1569 and Thomas Paton of Kirkcudbright was found to have the Devil's Mark in 1650. George and Lachlan Rattray were accused at Inverness of mischievous charming, witchcraft and malefice, sorcery and necromancy in July 1706. The Lords of the Privy Council found it inconvenient to go to Inverness and gave them over to trial by 'bailies and other gentlemen' residing there. They were duly executed on the last Wednesday of September 1706.

In the same year, Alexander Deuart, a gardener at Maxwelltoon, was charged with having brought back stolen goods by charm or enchantment, a quantity of herbs along with some mutterings and gestures 'as makes him commonly a charmer that he is sought by persons from divers corners of the country to the great scandal of religion'.

John Robeson lived in Lenzie and was consulted about perpetrators of crimes. John Braid had lost some of his clothes and John Robeson was invited to turn the 'riddle' or sieve to find the culprit. It was placed on a pair of tongs held by two fingers. The name of the suspected party was mentioned. If the riddle trembled or moved round then they were guilty. For this heinous sin, he had to make repentance at the pillar with Kate Hopkin who also tried the riddle.

In 1697, at Caerlaverock, John Fergusson acknowledged his scandalous behaviour in charming and turning the key. About the middle of January, two men returning from Dumfries entered the tavern of William Nairns at Bankend, Caerlaverock. They were John Fergusson of Woodbarns and William Richardson of Cummertreestown. Richardson discovered that a sack that was in his saddlebag in the courtyard was missing. He returned to the tavern to find the thief. John Fergusson said that he would discover who was responsible if the landlord would bring him two Bibles. He took a key from his pocket and put the end of it in one Bible with the bowl end sticking out. He began reading from the fiftieth psalm: 'When thou sawest a thief, then thou consentedst with him...' Each time the verses were read he then named one of the people present. On naming William McKinnell, the key turned around and fell from the Bible. This happened three times and was witnessed. He was charged with the theft and Fergusson was charged with charming.

GLOSSARY

A

ahint	behind

B

barley-banna	bannock
bauld	bold
baxter	baker
blue-gown	licensed beggar
blunderbus	gun
brunt	burned
buliments	uproar
by-bag	side bag

C

cairt	cart
cerements	dead clothes
cit	citizen
confluence	gathering
coroner	plea guardian
coulter	nose
cruizie	lamp

D

dub-scoupers	mud ladlers
dunt	big bit
durdens	uproar
durst	dare

E

Egyptian	gipsy
escheat	forfeit

F

fence	set up
fenceless	unarmed

flyte	argue
forfaultit	forfeited
fuddling	drinking

G

gauger	excise officer
gausy	swollen
gear	goods
gibbet	gallows
gill	measure
girnel	grainstore
gleuves	gloves
glower	glare
gowk	fool
graith	property
groat	coin

H

hadden	held
hagglements	uproar
hained	enclosed
halberd	pole
halberdier	carrier of a halberd
hauld	home
hempen span	hangman's rope
heryit	harried
hie	high
huliments	uproar
hurdens	uproar

I

ilka	every

K

kane	rent

L

land-loupers	vagabonds
lees	lies
lock	handful
lockman	hangman
loup	leap
lug	ear

M

Martinmas	November quarter day
maukin	hare
member	limb
mercat	market
muckle	big
multer	multure

O

out-in-towns man	stranger

P

paper	notice
poinded	impounded
pooches	pockets
powny	pony

R

rash bush	peaceful
raw	row
reft	stolen
riggit	rigged

S

sair	sore
saugh	willow
sautit	salted
sax	six
scurging	whipping
sic	such
siccar	safe/sure
siller	money
skelp	hit
skep	hive
Soudron	southerner
sough	sigh
soutar	shoemaker
spauld	split
splent	gush
stour	stramash

T

toddy	drink
tow	hemp

trikker	trigger
tron	weighbridge
truff	turf
twalpenny	twelve pennies

U

unco	very
utheris	other
utherways	otherwise

W

wame	stomach
wean	child

Y

ydle	idle